ADULT LEARNING IN THE 21ST CENTURY

ADULT LEARNING IN THE 21ST CENTURY

Editor

Dr. Digumarti Bhaskara Rao

M.Sc., M.A., M.A., M.Ed., Ph.D.,
Secretary
Academy of Communication Culture
Education Science and Service
Srinivas Nagar Colony
Guntur–522 006
Andhra Pradesh
India

DISCOVERY PUBLISHING HOUSE
NEW DELHI-110002

First Published – 2004

Reprinted – 2024

ISBN: 978-81-7141-797-1

Adult Learning in the 21st Century

Published by:

DISCOVERY PUBLISHING HOUSE

4383/4B, Ansari Road, Darya Ganj

New Delhi-110 002 (India)

Phone: +91-11-23279245; 23253475; 43596065

Mobile: +91 9811179893 / +91 9871656464

E-mail: discoverybooksindia@gmail.com

orderdphbooks@gmail.com

web: www.discoverypublishinggroup.com

Printed at:

Infinity Imaging Systems

Delhi

Dedicated

To My

Beloved Brother

Mr. Digumarthi Venkata Rao

Andukur, Guntur, A.P.

Foreword

The Fifth International Conference on Adult Education was held in July 1997, in Hamburg, organised by UNESCO and in particular the UNESCO Institute for Education, the agency's specialist centre on adult learning policy and research. Approximately 1500 delegates attended from all regions of the world, with representatives of 140 member states and some 400 NGOs. In addition to the work of the commissions and plenary which debated the official documents of the Conference *The Hamburg Declaration* and *The Agenda for the Future,* there were 33 workshops organised around the themes and sub-themes of the Conference.

A part of its CONFINTEA follow-up strategy, the UNESCO Institute for Education has produced a series of booklets based on the presentations made and discussions held during the Conference. The recordings of all the workshops were transcribed and synthesized over one year, edited, and then formatted and designed. A tremendous amount of work has gone into this process. Linda King, coordinator of the monitoring and information strategy for CONFINTEA, was responsible for overseeing the whole process. Madhu Singh, senior research specialist at UIE undertook the mammoth task of writing almost all the booklets based on an analysis of the sessions. She was helped in the later stages by Gonzalo Retamal, Uta Papen and Linda King. Christopher McIntosh was technical editor, Matthew Partridge designed the layout and Janna Lowrey was both transcriber and translator.

The present book with the content of the booklets is intended to draw out the central issues and concerns of each of the CONFINTEA workshops. It is the memory of an event that marked an important watershed in the field of adult learning. We hope that it will be of use both to those who were able to attend CONFINTEA V and those who were not.

Paul Bélanger

Secretary General of CONFINTEA

Preface

Adult learning throughout life is felt by everybody across the world and needed action is under implementation everywhere around the globe. Recognizing the very importance of adult education, the UNESCO organised the Fifth International Conference on Adult Education (CONFINTEA V) in Hamburg, Germany in July 1977. Scores of delegates from 140 member states of UNESCO enriched the Conference with their expertise and experiences. The result of this effort is the Hamburg Declaration and the Agenda for the Future.

This book is prepared by reproducing the material from the booklets produced by the UNESCO Institute for Education, Hamburg based on the presentations made and discussions held during the Conference, finding the material useful to everyone engaged in the field of adult learning.

I am thankful to the UNESCO Institute for Education for reproducing the material from its publications. I am also thankful to the contributors and particularly to Madhu Singh, Linda King, Gonzalo Retamal, Uta Papen, Matthew Partridge, Christopher McIntosh and Janna Lowrey for their efforts in preparing the booklets on various themes appeared in this book.

I am grateful to Prof. Paul Belanger, Secretary General of CONFINTEA V.

Dr. Digumarti Bhaskara Rao

"Sai Soudha"

D-43, S.V.N. Colony

Guntur–522 006

Andhra Pradesh

India

Contents

Part 1
Adult Learning and the Challenges of the 21st Century

1

Adult Learning, Democracy and Peace

Introduction

The workshop "Adult Learning, Democracy and Peace" at the Fifth International Conference on Adult Education (CONFINTEA) held in July 1997 in Hamburg had the important role of examining the relationship between adult learning, democracy, citizenship, gender, civil society. and a culture of peace. It discussed adult learning strategies that are required to meet democratic aspirations, foster a culture of peace, build identities, take into account the globalisation of economies, deal with ecological threats, cultivate active and informed citizenship, alleviate poverty and address gender issues.

The speakers expressed a variety of opinions on the issue of globalisation. Some speakers rejected globalisation as aggravating existing social tensions and inequalities, and as leading to increasing marginalisation, while others partially acknowledged that globalisation is offering fresh possibilities and opportunities. All participants underlined the need of new intercultural learning experiences that help in deepening the understanding of other cultures. The Universal Declaration of Human Rights states that violence can be the consequence of the suppression of democratic aspirations, just as it can be the result of intolerance. Thus democracy becomes essentially interlocked with friendship among all nations, racial or religious groups and with promoting understanding and acceptance of the other.

Substantive democracy and a culture of peace are not given; they need to be constructed. Any effort that emphasises initiative from below, as well as the capacity to recognise diversity, is part of the project of adult learning for democracy and peace.

The session on adult learning, democracy and peace was organised by the UNESCO Institute for Education Hamburg´, and the Association of World Education (AWE) Denmark. The first part, chaired by Owe Korsgaard, President AWE, highlighted the international context of adult education with regard to democracy. The second part, chaired by Jacob-Erle also from AWE, focused on the pedagogical challenges of promoting democracy and a culture of peace. It included a practical demonstration of the possibilities of using adult education to prevent conflicts. The panel for the first part included Edicio de la Torre from the Philippines, founding Chairperson of the Education for Life Foundation; Teresa Quiroz Martin, of Arcis University, Santiago, Chile; Shirley Walters, founder Director of the Centre for Adult and Continuing Education at the University of Western Cape, South Africa; Professor Dani W. Nabudere from Uganda, who held a professorship in. law at the University of Dar es Salaam, and is currently active in initiating the school project "learn as you work".

Globalisation, Democracy and Adult Learning

Globalisation is raising new issues for democracy and adult learning. Economic globalisation is leading to the marginalisation of large numbers of people. Many countries and facing major problems concerning human rights and equity. Even in countries that are experiencing high economic growth rates there are growing disparities between rich and poor. Governments are often left with little choice but to accept structural adjustment strategies proposed by external agencies.

When countries have to adjust their economies to compete effectively internationally this creates training opportunities for people to master new technologies. But it also creates social problems, dislocation and disruption of communities, often jeopardising effective participation in democratic political processes.

Drastic cuts is essential services such as health and education have led to social tensions and loss of political credibility for governments. Civil societies have become weaker and people are becoming increasingly demoralised. Culturally, more and more people and succumbing to the homogenising tendencies of the global market-place.

The 21st century must cope with the reality that globalisation—just as the history of the development of capitalism—creates centres and peripheries, as well as new contradictions within a new global competitive context. At the social level this can mean unemployment, poor conditions or work, as well as discrimination in access to benefits and services. Other dangers include the jeopardising of basic social rights, such as the right to education and health.

Adult learning is confronted with new social, political, economic and cultural issues that are linked of globalisation—a key concept in our understanding of the world today. Globalisation is also opening up new possibilities for world-wide information exchange and communication. Both the global risks and the new opportunities facing today's societies make the participation, creativity and competence of all citizens a necessity, a key to the prevention of intolerance and racism and the building of a democratic world.

Discussing Globalisation Implies:

- rethinking the asymmetrical relationship between technology, society and the economic life of countries;
- critically analysing the current globalisation trends at the local and global levels, in order to arrive at a better understanding of them;
- discussing the different views on the significance of globalisation;
- working on the central perspective of globalisation and re-assessing the neo-liberal model in order to understand its consequences;
- understanding that individuals have more than one identity;
- identifying the conflicts that are now being intensified through the processes of globalisation;

- developing a more holistic and strategic framework in responding to globalisation, using its strengths and opportunities, as well as recognising the inequalities in creates.

Designing Strategies to Reinforce Democracy and Peace

Forward-looking strategies relying on adult learning and required to promote democracy, equality and gender justice, and strengthen human rights from the local, the national and regional level to the global level, and to construct a culture of peace and of substantive democracy.

Peace and democracy require new adult learning policies to include the excluded and reach those who today are not being reached by regular channels of education, cannot participate and do not count as full citizens.

The expectation of continued expansion of economic markets in a global economy assumes that education is one of the driving forces behind the new path of economic development. However, this form of education tends to focus on quantifiable results such as levels of literacy and numeracy. Seldom does it deal with culture, democracy and other less measurable things.

It is a regrettable fact that education has been provided unequally, and those without economic resources are at a disadvantage when it comes to competing in a system of human capital formation provoked by economic globalisation. Perhaps more discouraging is the possibility that the benefits to be derived from the human resource explosion and "education for all" may not be realised.

New Strategies to Reinforce Civil Society, Democracy and Peace:

- making democratisation, culture, human rights, gender justice, diversity and peace essential components of any educational project;
- ensuring that adult learning contributes to the attainment of gender equality;
- including adult learning for democracy in the agenda of every proposal and action in gender relations;
- guaranteeing equal opportunities in education.

Understanding the Local, the National and the Global

One of the challenges for adults in the context of globalisation is to grasp the different meanings attached to the local, the national and the global, as well as to understand the tensions between them.

The local is to be understood as pertaining to an area with its own geography, history and culture. While it is important to keep in mind that nations have been products of both colonialism and resistance, larger national identities have emerged in opposition to the definitions given by the colonisers. The global impinges on the local in several ways-economically, politically and culturally. For example, economic globalisation may threaten traditional livelihoods. Global media also influences peoples' imagination. Though it can open new perspectives, it can also breed homogenisation in tastes and consumption.

The globalisation of the economy may open up possibilities for a global civil society and international solidarity, but it can also expose new divisions and rivalries.

Democracy

Democracy, understood as parliamentary democracy, guarantees citizens' rights to choose their governments, express their opinions and create associations. Adult learning is needed to inform citizens on their rights and responsibilities. But democracy also means the active participation of citizens at local, national and global levels. Democracy in this sense has been achieved through, collective action and is often the way for new social movements. Adult learning is both an outcome and a tool of democracy.

Adult Learning for Democracy Means:

- self-determination, participatory skills and informed citizenship;
- social commitment to build a society that favours more liberty, gender equality, solidarity and equity;
- opportunities for every citizen to exercise her or his rights to participate fully in the construction of a more just society, and to become involved in social decision-making and train his or her capacity to work with others.

Gender Justice

In all the UN conferences during the last 20 years on women's empowerment it has been stressed that women are central to the economy, politics and to social and cultural development. Substantive democracy cannot be achieved without practising gender democracy, an issue that cuts across the categories of class, colour, ability and geographical area. Nevertheless, the situation of women has not improved—has even in some cases worsened—in many countries.

Focusing on issues of gender justice is central to all aspects of adult learning. But the issue of gender needs to be dealt with more holistically than in the past. Overcoming gender inequalities through adult learning is only possible by an engagement of both men and women.

> **Gender Justice**
>
> - is a matter of human rights and a condition for social justice and should not be seen in isolation as a women's issue only;
> - involves society as a whole, central to effective democracy in the state, economy and in civil society, and reaches from the smallest family units to the largest economic and political structures;
> - cannot be viewed in isolation from the broad context of discrimination that women face.

From Cultural Confrontation to Intellectual Communication

The challenge of the 21st century, as far as adult learning is concerned, is to face these problems of globalisation and marginalisation by moving from cultural confrontation to intercultural communication, and to recognise cultural diversity as a positive human value.

Intercultural communication and understanding and lifelong processes, just as culture is ongoing and dynamic. They are particularly important at a time when many communities are striving to defend their local identities against the effects of globalisation and marginalisation. The aim of these local processes is to promote democracy by encouraging dialogue, solidarity and the reconstruction of lost identity.

Active Civil Society through Adult Learning

These social issues, and global risks facing today's societies are calling upon the participation, creativity and competence of all citizens. In short, adult learning needs to promote an active civil society.

Adult learning for an active civil society requires:

- the formation of a broad coalition of responsible, committed and active citizens;
- the building of new alternative global economic and cultural links by reorganising social relations and responsibilities from the local and the national to the global level;
- the creation of a new global order that involves actors who clearly identify with an commit themselves to the welfare of the community and the ecological system;
- the balancing of the tension between individual freedom and collective solidarity;
- enhancing solidarity and responsibility, feeling the passion as well as the pain of others;
- building the capacities of the weaker sections of society by fostering the strengths of their cultures and promoting their self-determination;
- recognising the multiple options of globalisation, rather than creating a polarity between permanent resistance and co-opted participation;
- helping people to determine their own dreams of development and fulfilment.

Adult Learning for Gender Democracy

In order to move towards gender justice, adult learning is crucial. But adult learning is itself highly gendered and can reinforce gender inequalities if not consciously checked by adult educators at all levels of provision.

Adult learning for gender democracy requires:

- legislation for adult education which has clear commitments to lifelong learning for women;
- a gender framework which takes into account structural, substantive and environmental issues in places of learning;
- including gender in specific contexts such as national qualification frameworks;
- providing financial support adapted to the life conditions of women;
- rethinking the conception, delivery and hidden curricula of learning programmes.

Pedagogical Challenges for Promoting Democracy and a Culture of Peace

The right of adults to learn will not be respected unless policies are adopted to that end. There is a need to create a methodology, and a pedagogical approach appropriate for adults, and to reinforce research in adult education. The big challenge for adult education is to build on the foundations that it has already laid in different regions, especially with respect to:

- learning conditions of the various social groups;
- concepts and androgogical approaches which deal with self-development and empowerment, with self-esteem, with constructing a stronger civil society and with the organisation of grassroots initiatives according to the needs of everyday life;
- support for participatory methods such as action research and evaluation.

Pedagogical Exercises dealing with Conflict Situations and Reconciliation

Adult learning has an important role to play in helping to solve conflicts between different countries and groups. Adult learning opportunities for all are a critical precondition for stable societies, and for the reduction of the probability of conflict. NGOs and UN agencies like UNHCR and UNICEF have extensive experience of this. The sharpest declines in school enrolments occur in low-income countries suffering from war or internal strife. In many parts of the world, sustained turmoil has led to large segments of entire generations being denied the opportunity to go to school.

Pedagogical initiatives need to promote an understanding of the dynamics of conflict situations and how conflicts arise and, in the absence of just negotiation, escalate to the level of war. When conflicts end, adult learning is also particularly relevant in bringing people to find ways of cooperation. Reconciliations are difficult and can often take a full generation or more to achieve.

Adult education in conflict situations has a double role. In the first place it implies a political agreement which defines and re-defines the relationships between the conflicting actors. In the second place it implies the development of curricular methodologies and approaches to a new situation. Mor specifically the task of adult educators is to:

help to recognise

- the strengths and the weaknesses within different countries;
- the areas of international cooperation;
- the interdependence between rich and poor nations;
- the political, economic and environmental aspects of conflicting issues;

involve adults in

- acquiring more informed images of the 'other';
- active learning;
- sharing skills and experiences in dealing with real life conflict issues from around the world;
- learning in groups;
- negotiating with persons from other groups.

explore possible means such as

- use of the object of conflict (e.g. water sharing) to raise issues which would directly concern families and local communities;
- use of the Internet;

- establishing peace committees;
- organising regional meetings focusing on issues around which conflicts and most likely to arise.

encourage

- the local community to participate in adult learning for conflict resolution;
- technical, cultural and research exchanges in the interest of reconciliation.

emphasise

- both internal and external relations;
- the connection and links between people around issues that they once valued and shared in common;
- the understanding of the 'other' party's problem.

A major part of androgogical techniques should deal with the construction or the modification of the representations of the other. The prejudices and the stereotypes require different methodologies from those of conventional learning.

The involvement of learners in real life situations encourages them to share a variety of skills, backgrounds and efforts.

Many analyses of present conflicts indicate that hatred and violence against the 'other' are ideologically often instigated by highly educated sections of the society, such as political leaders and intellectuals. In this regard, adult learning needs to be directed not only at adults who are vulnerable in conflict situations but particularly at those groups who create conflicts.

Post-conflict resolution brings about several other problems. Reconstructing histories becomes especially problematic in post-conflict situations, because after a conflict the participants views are coloured. The experience of conflict involves new and very fundamental changes in the way the parties perceive each other. Dealing with these new concepts of the 'other' is one of the most fundamental tasks of post-conflict adult learning.

2

Cultural Citizenship in the 21st Century:

Adult Learning and Indigenous Peoples

Introduction

The session on indigenous peoples and adult education at the Fifth International Conference on Adult Learning (CONFINTEA V), held in 1997 in Hamburg, was attended by an estimated 120 peoples, a third of whom were indigenous representatives. The first part of the session presented the international context and current status of adult education with regard to indigenous peoples. The second part focused on the views and perspectives of indigenous peoples' representatives. Rudolfo Stavenhagen, research professor at the Colegio de Mexico, a leading international expert on human rights in relation to indigenous peoples and members of the Delors Commission on Education for the twenty-first century, presented the keynote at the first session. In the second part of the session, chaired by Jack Beetson, President of the Federation of Independent Aboriginal Education Providers of Australia, the panel included representatives from some of the independent indigenous organisations from around the world: Nora Rameka was present for the Maori Adult Education Association; Carl Christian Olson from Greenland represented the Inuit Circumpolar Conference; Hilda Canari from Peru represented the Andean regional organisation CADEP; Rosalba Jimenez represented the Organización Nacional Indígena de Colombia; and Natalio Hernandez from Mexico, the Vice-Chair of the session, represented the Casa de los Escritores Indígenas.

Representatives of indigenous peoples came together in this workshop to compare the situations in their own countries with regard to human rights and cultural and social identity. There were calls to establish and international framework for indigenous people so that they are not isolated from the rest of society, and for the international community to recognise that indigenous peoples have special rights and possess a unique store of knowledge which the world needs and must value. There were also calls for the recognition of the minimum international standards applicable to indigenous peoples, laid down in a series of UN documents over the past few years.

Indigenous people in many parts of the world are still struggling for agreements with their governments to be implemented. An important task of the workshop was to present a global adult education programme for indigenous peoples.

The Current Situations of Indigenous Peoples

The 1989 ILO Convention 169 defines indigenous peoples as "peoples in independent countries who are regarded as indigenous on account of their descent from the populations which inhabited the country, or a geographical region to which the country belongs, at the time of conquest or colonisation or the establishment of present state boundaries and who, irrespective of their legal status, retain some or all of their own social, economic, cultural and political institutions" [Article 1 (b)].

The ILO Convention makes a distinction between indigenous and tribal peoples. Tribal communities are "peoples in independent countries whose social, cultural and economic conditions distinguish them from other sections of the national community and whose status is regulated wholly or partially by their own customs or traditions or by special laws or regulations" [Article 1(a)].

The distinction between indigenous and tribal peoples is fluid and remains a cultural or linguistic choice for the communities involved. This distinction tends to be blurred in Asia and Africa, while in the Americas, Australia and New Zealand there is a greater tendency to use the term indigenous peoples.

There are some 5000 different indigenous and tribal groups in the world, comprising in total almost 300 million people, living in around 70 countries. Together they account for 4 per cent of the world's population although in some countries they make up the majority, such as Bolivia. In India there are about 400 different indigenous and tribal groups making up a population of 90 million.

Indigenous peoples participate usually in non-industrial modes of production. Many struggle so survive under very poor circumstances compared to the general standards of the societies in which they live. Their health conditions are often deficient, and they generally have significantly lower chances than others in getting a high school education or a decent job. Within indigenous communities the gap between the educated and the illiterate is growing, and there is a marked discrepancy between male and female literacy, owing to the tendency among these communities to favour men over women when it comes to education. Research indicates that poverty and lack of access to basic services including health and education are closely linked to tribal identity.

Basic Changes in Thinking with Regard to Indigenous Peoples

In recent years, two basic tendencies in thinking with regard to indigenous peoples have emerged, which can be said to be crucial to adult education policy.

1. A change from government-directed and government-generated policies—towards a human rights approach in which indigenous peoples are no longer just the passive objects of governments' policies but are active participants in the struggle for recognition of their own human rights, and in the redefinition of their relationship with the rest of society.
2. A change in policy content, from a policy of assimilation to a concept of cultural citizenship.

Towards a Human Rights Approach: Three Sources of Human Rights for Indigenous Peoples

Three approaches to human rights for indigenous peoples are now being used in order to build up a special framework of indigenous rights within the UN system.

1. The concept of universal human rights.
2. The system of protection of minorities within existing states.
3. The right of peoples to self-determination.

1. A Universal Framework for Indigenous Peoples

Various UN agreements over the past few decades indicate a collective effort to build up a new structure of human rights within the international community, in which indigenous peoples have a special role to play. The Universal Declaration on Human Rights is one of the basic sources for the rights of indigenous peoples. The idea behind the Declaration is that all human beings, whatever their culture, race, colour, religion, national origin or gender, and inherently endowed with the same essential rights. This document represented a historic breakthrough.

2. Protection of Minorities in General

However, simply affirming equality before the law has not been sufficient to guarantee the enjoyment of full human rights. Consequently, there are two other developments in the context of international law which have relevance for adult education policy with regard to indigenous peoples. One is the system of protection of minorities and the other is the recognition of the right to self-determination.

The UN General Assembly has been active since 1992 in promoting the rights of persons belonging to ethnic, national, linguistic or religious minorities. Some would argue for the applicability of such an international system of legal rights to indigenous peoples as well.

However, over the past few years, representatives of indigenous peoples through the United Nations and their particular organisations have rejected the idea that indigenous peoples should be put into the same category as ethnic, linguistic or religious minorities. The basic reason is that indigenous peoples in some countries are not actually, minorities but demographic majorities. Moreover, the concept of indigenous peoples has come about as a result of colonisation and conquest, while that of the minority does not necessarily imply historical subordination. Furthermore, in contrast to many minorities, indigenous peoples share common ancestral territory that is ethnically delineated, and which is distinct from the general territory inhabited by the majority of the population.

3. Individual Human Rights and the Rights to Self-determination

Indigenous peoples as such claim the historical right to territory, right to their own government, to existence and survival as well as to land and resources even prior to the rights of states. In short, they claim the right to self-determination, which has become one of the principle human rights that the United Nations has recognised. This is the third source of human rights for indigenous peoples.

But states do not always see it that way. States, for reasons of their own, consider that the right to self-determination applies to states rather than to peoples, and there is a long history of debate as to which communities should enjoy this right.

Towards Collective Rights and Cultural Citizenship

Crucial to adult learning policy with regard to indigenous people is also the focus within the UN legal framework on the notion of collective rights in addition to individual human rights. The UN agreements over previous years clearly recognise the need for collective rights, such as the right to culture, as upheld by UNESCO. In the various conferences organised by UNESCO around this theme, as well as in several UNESCO documents, it has been emphasised that this right means not just the right to culture in general but the right to one's own culture—that is the culture which one identifies with and which is linked to a specific history and territory.

Closely associated with this notion of the right to culture is the idea of "cultural citizenship". It introduces the notion of collective rights to culture, and in some cases it implies the struggle for the reconstitution of indigenous cultures and communities which have been seriously eroded through conquest, colonisation and assimilation.

The development of democracy in the western world has been a process of progressive acquisition of individual citizenship rights. In the present context, however, indigenous rights are about the consolidation of collective rights of culturally distinct groups within a wider framework of the so-called nation states.

In the context of this new understanding of collective human rights, indigenous peoples are considered to be active subjects in the implementation of their own human rights. Human rights as we understand them today cannot be taken for granted. They must be demanded from governments and from other members of society. The protection of human rights involves making the broader society recognise them in law and in institutions as well as setting up political and social organisations to implement those rights.

The Four Pillars of Learning with Regard to Indigenous Peoples

Adult learning, conceived in the perspective of lifelong learning, is education that people pursue in many different places and environments—in the workplace, at home, in the community, or in non-formal settings. Education is seen not as a transient phase that prepares one for the rest of life, but as part and parcel of an individual's and a group's constant development and evolution throughout a life cycle. This involves an approach in which people use more and more educational opportunities in order to take more effective control of their lives through the acquisition of skills, from basic skills such as literacy and numeracy, to more complex ones such as data processing.

Yet, adult learning goes much beyond the acquisition of skills and learning abilities. Adult learning inculcates values and attitudes and patterns of behaviour that are relevant and appropriate to the culture of the learner. It also plays a vital role in the creation and consolidation of personal, collective and national identities. All of these aspects of adult learning are crucial for sustainable livelihoods and the development of viable societies.

In dealing with adult learning with regard to indigenous peoples it may be useful to reinterpret the four pillars of lifelong learning for the 21st century—as outlined by the UNESCO report of the Delors Commission—in terms of the human rights situation of indigenous peoples.

Learning to be	=	the right of self-identification and self-definition
Learning to know	=	the right to self-knowledge
Learning to do	=	the right to self-development
Learning to live together	=	the right to self-determination

Learning to be = the Right of Self-identification and Self definition

Many nation states have had problems coming to terms with the definition of the concept of indigenous people. Nevertheless, it is becoming increasingly clear that there can be no single definition of indigenous peoples, and indigenous populations should have the right to define themselves subjectively as belonging to a particular indigenous community. The UN Working Group on Indigenous Peoples, in consultation with the indigenous peoples of the world, has come to the conclusion that indigenous peoples and tribal communities have the right to self-definition, and the right to refer to themselves as indigenous or tribal.

As the situation stands today, indigenous peoples prefer to describe themselves using tribal or ethnic names, rather than using a blanket term such as "indigenous" (from the Latin *indigenus*), or "autocthonous" (from the Greek *autokhthon*). However, recently some indigenous peoples have come to recognise their identity as such and to see that they share similar situations and problems with other indigenous communities in terms of denial of human rights and the right to cultural identity.

The right to self-definition goes hand in hand with self-identification. It means the right of indigenous peoples' to their own interpretations of their history as well as the right to learn in their own languages.

An indigenous peoples move into the 21st century, adult learning is playing a crucial role in the interpretation of their own history. Young people are learning their own languages and culture. Indigenous organisations and adult education associations are active in helping indigenous peoples to go back to their culture and their languages, despite the homogenising tendencies of globalisation and economic development. There are calls for indigenous peoples around the world to take a greater control of their education systems including evaluation and monitoring of their own qualification frameworks.

There are programmes for women from indigenous communities to learn their language and history through arts and crafts. There are also programmes for urbanised indigenous persons now returning to rural areas. In some cases in involves a complete reversal or previous government programmes based on the integration of indigenous peoples into modern urbanised culture.

At present, the education system of many indigenous peoples is a hybrid between indigenous and formal western education. But the latter tends to foster imitation rather than promoting indigenous cultural values although many indigenous peoples are dynamic and flexible and open to formal education, they nevertheless feel the need to defend their own identity, as they consider it of special significance to their survival. Many consider it necessary to participate in the world community with regard to adult education. One attempt has been to promote cultural integration of indigenous adults in different parts of the world through cultural education. So, although adults are necessarily open to globalisation, there is a demand from the communities themselves to have a strong cultural element in their education.

Learning to Know = The Right of Self-knowledge

The international community must recognise that indigenous peoples not only have special rights but also possess special knowledge which the world needs and must value if it is to survive the next century.

This right to self-knowledge has been denied to them through the official education system generally and through the imposition of foreign values on their societies. Indigenous peoples have their own informal learning systems which are compatible with their livelihood systems. Adult learning is not a new concept for indigenous people but a part and parcel of their life and livelihood.

Therefore, when we talk about "indigenous education", this has to mean something different from "education for indigenous people". The latter is mostly conceived in terms of access and participation in the mainstream education system, which historically has been deeply divisive and exclusionist. Indigenous education which promotes indigenous languages, cultural and religious beliefs and legal systems is often dismissed as primitive and uncivilised, and generally receives inadequate funding.

Recently, however, indigenous education and training of indigenous peoples have been particularly stressed in the 1989 ILO Convention 196. Several articles emphasise the need for the peoples' participation in the design of a system appropriate to their needs, traditions and cultures. Sub-paragraph 3 of Article 27, for example, recommends that: "Governments shall recognise the right of these peoples to establish their own educational institutions and facilities, provided that such institutions meet minimum standards established by the competent authority in consultation with these peoples. Appropriate resources shall be provided for this purpose". Article 31 calls for measures to be taken to educate the members of the dominant society, to eliminate prejudice and to provide information on indigenous cultures.

Part IV the *Draft Declaration on the Rights of Indigenous Peoples* focuses exclusively on education and establishes the right of indigenous peoples to create and maintain their own educational systems and institutions while not being denied access to all levels and forms of education. The Draft Declaration is being ratified by the UN General Assembly.

There are however specific policies and strategies needed to ensure respect for indigenous knowledge, in a world increasingly interconnected and economically competitive. In programmes of indigenous education great care must be taken not to perpetuate educational racism in its more subtle forms. An understanding of the distinctive but complementary roles of indigenous and exogenous knowledge can help to build bridges towards a brighter future for humankind in the global society.

Learning to do = The Right to Self-Development

The third pillar of education, learning to do, translates for indigenous peoples as the right to self-development. It implies the idea of the right to develop one's own concepts about development. Very often, development projects or programmes of national bureaucracies as well as of international financial agencies impose their ideas of development on indigenous peoples.

Indigenous concepts of development are inextricably linked to culture, education, environment and self-determination. Sustainable development for indigenous peoples is possible only by protecting indigenous languages and culture.

Many indigenous communities practise a subsistence economy in contrast to a cash economy. This non-industrial mode of production is closely intertwined with cultural survival and education, including education for life skills. Indigenous peoples' rights to subsistence and to retention of their own value system should therefore be included in any discussion of sustainable development and self-development.

Accepting the basic relationship between learning and culture and promotion of the right to self-knowledge, those involved in education should seek to understand and see that indigenous learning is centrally associated with the transmission of the culture of indigenous peoples and to identify local strategies associated with these learning and transmission processes.

Learning to Live Together = The Right to Self-Determination

The right to self-determination implies the right to be able to reorganise the relationships between indigenous peoples and the wider society, but on terms defined unilaterally by the dominant society, but an terms defined in consultation with the indigenous peoples. In several societies a process of national cultural cooperation is underway. In Mexico for example this comprises three fundamental objectives:

1. A shared commitment to raising the living standards and broadening opportunities for indigenous peoples.
2. The acknowledgement of the interrelatedness of various elements of society and the interlocking history of both indigenous and nati)nal societies.
3. A mutual acceptance of the importance of working together and of respecting and appreciating differences.

In order to make the right of self-determination a reality, it is necessary to establish partnerships among equals rather than treating indigenous peoples as deserving beneficiaries of a one-way education system. In fact, the decade 1995-2004 has been proclaimed as the International Decade, of the World's Indigenous People (IYWIP) and the theme of this decade adopted by the UN General Assembly has been appropriately termed "towards a new partnership".

An indigenous people move to the next millennium, their aspirations to partake of the benefits of globalisation, without giving up their identity and dignity, must be respected. For this to happen there is need for a constructive dialogue between cultures.

Intercultural Education: Recommendations for Follow-up

Adult learning for and by indigenous peoples must be rooted in the *principles of intercultural education*. This calls for a review of contents, a development of a methodology, a promotion of dialogue between educator and learner, and an understanding of the socio-cultural contexts of adults.

On the *methodological level,* it may be necessary to develop new strategies of learning such as "intercultural dialogue" and "constructive confrontation between cultures". These strategies could be helpful in identifying distinctive types of logic, different visions of the world, and distinctive knowledge and forms of learning. This would enable adults to develop a critical attitude towards their own culture, and help in the selection of cultural contents.

At the *decision-making level,* indigenous peoples must participate at all levels of decision-making—educational, cultural, developmental and political—in order to create within broader societies an awareness of the principles of mutual respect and equality, as well as the right to be culturally different. Concrete proposals should be formulated to favour changes in the attitudes of adults towards culturally mixed populations. Many initiatives could be promoted that support precisely this kind of intercultural dialogue, through courses in indigenous languages, seminars, workshops, conferences and cultural programmes.

While indigenous languages and imparting basic educational competencies in the mother tongue is a key to promoting cultural identify and personal development, it is equally important to promote global languages of communication as well as the national or official languages, so that indigenous peoples have access to the opportunities offered by globalisation.

Conclusion

The task of adult learning is to raise the quality of life and the possibility for indigenous peoples in recognising this to the fullest, to develop reading and writing skills, promote the participation of indigenous populations in urban and national life, promote the training and specialisation of indigenous peoples in different sectors of work, as well as training them in the administration of enterprises and organisations, and in the development of technologies.

Yet adult learning is more than this; it should be about teaching the values and possibilities of multicultural citizenship as a new way of regulating the relationship between the indigenous peoples and the rest of society.

The Sum up the recommendations:

1. Basic educational competencies in indigenous languages, but also in the national and global languages of communication, should be a fundamental entitlement.
2. Bilingual intercultural education should be included in national adult learning systems.
3. In a civil society adult learning empowers all communities including indigenous communities as it enhances chances for participation in society and for economic survival.
4. Indigenous peoples should participate in the design of adult learning opportunities and materials. Their ways of learning form an intrinsic part of the programme offered. They should also be involved in monitoring and evaluation. This will help prevent ineffective on inappropriate programmes.
5. Curricula should address indigenous peoples' cultural heritage and history.
6. Case studies should be undertaken that deal with realities of indigenous peoples.

3

Minorities and Adult Learning:

Communication Among Majorities and Minorities

Introduction

"The way in which we treat minorities is the measure of civilisation of a society".

—Mahatma Gandhi

The workshop on minorities at the Fifth International Conference on Adult Education (CONFINTEA) held in July 1997 in Hamburg, had an important role in examining the issue of the importance of adult learning for advancing minority rights and inter-community relationships. The basic thrust of the workshop was that majority and minority communities should work together towards a common issue of justice and towards common respect, dignity and security. For the first time the right to socio-cultural identity and the right to be different were acknowledged as important rights in adult learning policy.

The attendance of over 40 different minority (and indigenous) communities contributed significantly to arriving at a consensus on minority issues, which was part of a process of sharing information and experience. The workshop focused on adult learning needs of minority communities as well as on the need for majority communities to be informed about these communities and their rights.

The exchange was also useful in finding new methodologies in adult learning and matching these to concrete cases and locations. Civic education, it was felt, must address broad questions of peace and mutual respect and reflect the minority community's needs, rather than serving to assimilate minorities into the norms and values of majority community. The potentially homogenising effect of national curricula needs to be avoided, and the role of minority knowledge and learning systems must be recognised. Adult learning must help minorities to practice their right to identify with their own traditions and livelihood systems, rather than inculcate imposed characteristics.

The thematic workshop was chaired by Saad Eddin Ibrahim, President of the Ibn Khaldoun Centre for Development Studies, Egypt. Panellists included Alan Phillips, Director of Minorities Rights Group UK; Mona Makram-Ebeid, President of Egypt's Association for the Advancement of Education and former Member of the Egyptian parliament; Smaranda Enache of Liga Pro Europa Romania; Teeka Bhattaria from Seacow, a non-governmental organisation working with indigenous minority groups in Nepal, and Ambassador Nowal K Rai, also from Nepal. The Minorities Rights Group UK played an important role in bringing people to this workshop.

The Situation of Minorities

Minorities have made great contributions throughout history, despite their marginalisation from economic and political life, and despite suffering social discrimination. Many have rich cultural traditions, and although many and known to have strong traditional health facilities, they often lack modern health facilities. Minorities are also known to have education systems based on livelihood systems in which social, cultural, economic and political elements are closely intertwined.

Although identifying minority groups can be difficult and, while it is almost impossible to find a universal agreement on a definition of minorities, the emerging consensus is: minority communities should be understood not only in terms of nationality, ethnicity, religion or language, but also in terms of political, economic and social marginalisation. There is also a growing understanding of the importance and acceptance of minority rights which include many social, cultural, economic, civil and political rights. A recent example is the 1992 UN Declaration on the Rights of Persons Belonging to National or Ethnic, Religious and Linguistic Minorities, Articles 4 (3) and 4 (4) relate to education rights and state:

Article 4 (3)

"States should take appropriate measures so that, wherever possible, persons belonging to minorities have adequate opportunities to learn their mother tongue or to have instruction in their mother tongue".

Article 4 (4)

"States should, where appropriate, take measures in the field of education, in order to encourage knowledge of the history, traditions, language and culture of the minorities existing within their territory. Persons belonging to minorities should have adequate opportunities to gain knowledge of the society as a whole".

Civil rights, such as liberty and justice, are of particular significance to minorities. There is also the right to public education that promotes a supportive climate for equality and diversity. Certain social rights such as the right to associate, certain economic rights, such as the right to participate in community development, as well as cultural and linguistic rights are also of particular importance to minorities. Political rights such as empowerment, participation and citizenship are among the most important rights, yet they are the most consistently denied. These range from participation in government to functional or geographical autonomy.

Political and Legislative Changes

The recognition of minority rights in fundamental to a truly democratic society. But the success of political reforms and legislation depends to a very large extent on the participation of both minority and majority communities, in addition to political will and competence.

Education Policy and Legislation

The following are some of the ways in which legislation can advance minority rights:

- Promoting minorities' rights and promoting the fullest participation of minorities in all areas of life;
- Setting up government departments that are actively involved in the recognition of the social integration minorities;
- Accession and ratification of international instruments relating to minorities and education e.g. Council of Europe Framework Convention on National Minorities;
- Developing autonomy arrangements for minority communities (including educational authorities) where appropriate;
- Establishing monitoring and review mechanisms such as ombudsmen to ensure coherent and positive government policies;
- Providing education in the first or mother tongue wherever possible and where desired by the community concerned;
- Curriculum reform to promote a realistic and positive inclusion of the minority history, culture, language, and identity (including any significant events in terms of minority/majority relations);
- Civil rights education of majority and minority communities;
- Entitlement to basic education for all (especially in remote areas or where minorities have low political visibility);
- Involvement of minority women in education, curriculum design, management and decision-making.

However, legislation may not fully reflect a country's international commitments. There are also problems in the political, economic and educational arena. The economic situation in many countries makes it difficult to endorse political reforms; local discriminatory policies against minorities are not uncommon. The media can often exacerbate interethnic conflicts, fear and misunderstandings. Finally, attitudes to minorities change more slowly than legislation, and legislation and majority groups can be active in opposing the progress made with respect to reform.

In many countries, the curriculum ignores or rejects the experience of minority communities within that country. Although this can be most obvious in a history curriculum or in the choice of language of instruction, it can also be detected in others parts of the curriculum, such as civil education, geography, nutrition, literature, and so on. This has a two fold effect. Firstly, minorities feel that their identity, culture, language, history and their entire sense of belonging in that country is being undermined. Members of minority communities can become demotivated, fail to attend classes and fail to learn. Education which undermines identity in such ways is rarely ultimately effective, efficient or a good use of resources. Secondly, members of the majority community miss an important opportunity through education to learn about members of other communities. Such opportunities can, if appropriately designed and carried out, help to remove barriers of ignorance and misunderstanding between different communities.

The political will to change legislation and allocate resources should therefore be matched by changes in the education system in order to help ensure a stable, long-term development. States must recognise and support the education rights of minorities and more resources should be allocated to the education of minority communities in light of their contribution to society.

Allocation of Resources for Education

- States must ensure that at least adequate resources are allocated to all regions and communities taking into consideration different levels of need and different barriers in different areas;
- The provision of education in several languages will result in additional costs; however such provision is a right and should be make available wherever possible;

- The revision of curricula to include reference to and respect for minority communities may also involve additional expenditure;
- States must ensure that the lower political profile of many minority communities does not result in lower resource allocation to those areas or communities.

Recognising Minorities' Learning Systems

In addition to states' support for the education rights of minorities (see box above), it needs to be emphasised that minorities have their own traditional learning systems based on out-of-school learning processes, compatible with their local economy, geography and social systems. Minority learning systems often build on local wisdom rather than book-based knowledge, are inextricably linked to livelihood systems, and passed down from one generation to the next. Learning systems are organic in that they take place within the community, by the community and are closely linked to a community's daily activities. Songs and music as well as other aspects of the culture of minorities often play an important role in motivating minorities to learn about themselves, their environment and the social and political context in which they exist. Adult learning systems should therefore acknowledge such informal learning systems for promoting minority cultures and identity.

Recommendations for Adult Learning by and for Minority Communities

- Allocation of educational resources reflecting the needs of different communities areas;
- A significant goal of minority adult learning is for minority communities to establish a sense of identity with their own traditions, roots and culture;
- Minority knowledge, culture, language, religion, life-style and history to be included in curricula in a way that promotes mutual respect and understanding between communities;
- Recognition of the role and value of traditional out-of-school learning processes of minorities;

- Participatory pedagogy relying on the strengths of minorities.
- Educational activities closely linked with minorities' own local economy, geography and demography, thus promoting compatible learning systems;
- Teaching through different media, including songs and music, as well as other aspects of culture with which minorities identity;
- Promoting the participation of minorities in an active learning environment, as an important way to demystify book-based knowledge and to give people a sense of confidence.

Intercultural Adult Learning

Lack of information about minority and majority communities and their respective cultures in different parts of the world is in part the result of the formal educational system. Only through cross-cultural understanding and mutual respect can the intolerance born of ignorance be overcome. The education system should provide not only information about different peoples' histories and cultures but an ethical framework as well. Civic education must address broad questions of peace and mutual respect.

Intercultural Adult Learning should Involve the following:

- the sensitisation of both minorities and majorities on minority issues;
- the collective participation of minorities and majorities for creative solutions to minority problems;
- a healthy learning environment of positive pluralism;
- review of stereotypes so that knowledge and images of the other come closer to both reality and self-image of a minority community;
- respect for other religions, as well as learning experiences about other regions;
- opportunities for the majority to learn minority languages in minority areas.

There are many ways in which intercultural education can be disseminated. Target groups should include teachers, media, politicians, local governments, public servants and police officers.

Formal and Informal Methods of Intercultural Adult Learning

- Extracurricular activities, such as guided tours;
- minority literature, publications and translations;
- media campaigns;
- museums;
- music and art;
- seminars, round tables, summer universities;
- academic studies in intercultural education;
- enhancing the role of NGOs and universities for intercultural education of adults;
- inviting sociologists and university teachers from minority groups to present their own history.

Follow-up

In the same way that women's networks started during the Mexico and Nairobi world conferences on women, it was suggested that minority networks should continue the work of the World Conference on Adult Education, CONFINTEA V, as well as act as an important lobby in future conferences. It was generally accepted that the issue of minority rights cuts across borders. The need to create a political framework within which adult learning could take place as well as the need to develop legal frameworks were crucial, as minority communities were those most lacking in opportunities.

The Areas of Follow-up in Adult Learning

1. Prototypes of curricula and materials in adult learning for any by minority communities;
2. Materials on minority rights, minority culture and history for majorities and minorities;
3. Regional networks of adult educators and members of minorities.

Part 2
Improving Conditions and Quality of Adult Learning

4

Universities and the Future of Adult Learning

Introduction

Universities are renegotiating and redefining their relations with civil society, the various economic partners and the public in many different ways. Notions of adult and lifelong learning are central to this institutional redefinition. Lifelong learning can only take place by building bridges between members of the academic community, the socio-cultural and economic realities around them and the day-to-day actions of citizens attempting to create better living and working conditions.

CONFINTEA V provided space for discussions on the links between university and society with the aim of clarifying the role of higher education from the perspective of lifelong learning.

The first session of the thematic working group dealing with the subject of Universities and Adult Education was chaired by Madeleine Blais, University of Montreal, Canada. Invited speakers were Budd Hall, the Ontario Institute for Studies in Education, Canada; Funeka Loza and Shirley Walters, Centre for Adult and Continuing Education, University of the Western Cape, South Africa; Jennifer Newman and Griff Foley, University of Technology, Sydney, Australia. The panel of the second session, chaired by John Morris from the University of New Brunswick in Canada, comprised Mechthild Hart, DePaul University, USA; Renuka Narang, University of Mumbai, India; Shahrzad Mojab, Ontario, Institute for Studies in Education, Canada; In a Grieb and Claudia Lohrenscheidt, University of Oldenburg, Germany.

The Issues and Challenges

Inequalities within Universities

Universities world-wide tend too often to replicate structural inequalities, socio-economic cleavages and sexual disparities. Female students, for example, are under-represented in natural sciences and in the teaching staff. There is therefore much lost ground that needs to be made up to ensure equality of opportunities across gender, social status and age. A major challenge for universities is to restructure and transform themselves in order to tackle seriously the inequalities within their institutions and to give access to generations of adults who were not able to enjoy their right to higher education in the first period of their lives.

Opening the Doors

Some universities are innovating: reaching out to the adult learners, adopting new admission policies for mature students, prolonging the time schedule to accommodate adults, opening information and counselling centres, establishing links between research, training and service to the community, cooperating with economic partners, dealing with issues such as gender inequalities and racial discrimination. Universities need to be opened up to people with different occupational backgrounds. New forms of continuing training need to be provided, and universities need to become more responsive to the community and active professional needs, and to the learning aspirations of the present generation of adult citizens.

Community Needs

Many women and men need new expertise and skills to be more effective in their communities as "development workers" in such domains as health, community building, agriculture, environment and family planning. They require training and intellectual support from universities, if they are effectively to play their key role in the process of forging a democratic ethos and culture of human rights and of ensuring sustainable development at the local level.

Economic Needs

A new partnership is required between universities and the various economic agencies to face the challenges of world economic competition and of new technologies. Higher education institutions are increasingly being called upon to transform their basic form and structure to become 'lifelong learning' institutions, which enable employees and unemployed people to access relevant learning opportunities at different times, in different ways, for different purposes, at various stages of their careers. Lifelong learning institutions have to be responsive to the needs of different economic sectors and able to meet the training and education needs of the economy and government in flexible and appropriate ways.

University-based Adult and Continuing Education

University-based adult and continuing education has a range of meanings. It includes:

- flexibilisation of programme delivery to meet the adults' specific requirements (time schedule, admission norms, counselling, intermediary diploma);
- university extension work;
- professional continuing education;
- university level distance education in a wide variety of methods of delivery;
- training of adult educators at both undergraduate and postgraduate levels;
- research on adult learning in all its complex dimensions;
- new partnerships with industry and civil society.

The pattern of adult participation in higher education institutions differs from country to country.

In South Africa, for example, 'adult education' in universities has mainly referred to the training of adult educators, as well as to research and 'continuing education studies'. Distance higher education institutions and open learning systems are still underdeveloped. Systems are being put in place, in line with the emerging National Qualification Framework, so as to give newly or non-formally acquired knowledge and competence a credited status. This is considered an important motivation factor for adult learners who plan to attend university-level programmes.

Adult and Continuing Education and Extension at the University of Mumbai, India

The initiatives of the Department of Adult and Continuing Education include:

- opening of a new community education centre;
- accreditation of work experience and work projects;
- linkages between business, industry and university to improve employability of learners;
- improvement of the quality of learning through training programmes and development of courses;
- empowerment of women through extension projects and establishment of a women's cell;
- special courses related to health, environment and population issues;
- short-term continuing education courses;
- management courses;
- functioning as a nodal agency for adult learning at the regional level.

Redefining the Role of the Universities

The universities, as it has been traditionally known, is undergoing dramatic changes in the face of increasing pressure to respond to market forces and technological opportunities, in the context of the competitive global economy and the consequent need for continuing education. At the same time, civil societies are becoming more active. New social initiatives are calling upon their participants to expand their competencies through learning and to increase continuously their capacity for effective intervention. This has given rise to the largest ever social demand for adult learning at all levels. Competing demands between market forces and social needs are calling for new contributions from universities.

In the perspective of life-long learning there is a shift in the understanding of adult learning toward a more inclusive definition to respond both to labour market demands and to the needs of civil society, and to meet the multiplicity of demands which come from a range of local and regional communities and organisations.

Consequently, universities are called upon to address, both in their training and research functions, urgent social issues such as health, welfare, women, and transfer of appropriate technology to the communities. New knowledge is being generated through interaction with the community, curricula are becoming relevant to the life of the people and many new learning avenues are being opened up.

The University of the Western Cape (UWC)

UWC is historically a black university, set-up in 1961 under, apartheid legislation to serve people classified as coloured' and 'black'. In the late 1970s UWC developed a history of the anti-apartheid struggle. UWC's distinctive national and international profile can be characterised by the description 'the people's university'. This profile is based on the university's commitment to support communities that were historically excluded from higher education.

Initiatives for Adults:

- establishment of the Centre for Adult and Continuing Education (CACE) in 1985 for training and research;
- second chance education;
- leadership training: 'learning to govern';
- support to trainers in social movements and organisations;
- cooperation with Human Resource Development (HRD) initiatives in the economic field;

creation of a mission to help transform the UWC into a lifelong learning institution.

The Learning Needs of Adults

The enormous variety of experience and motivations among learners shows that individual lives cannot be strictly partitioned into needs of work, home, or community affairs.

Many of the learners are playing catalytic roles in their communities and places of work. It is therefore very important that they should have access to training opportunities which take into account their daily lived experiences and their economic, social and personal needs.

Teaching and learning strategies must be as holistic and accessible as possible and be rooted in the daily reality of individual learners.

> **Examples of learners in CACE's Township Learning' Programme at UWC**
>
> Florence Dlamshe is principal of a primary school in a squatter or informal housing community. She is 41 years old. She wanted to do the course to help her develop her community, counter male dominance on her school committee, motivate women to take a leadership position and to learn more about such things as the Truth and Reconciliation Commission.
>
> Anthony Gordon works at a corporation that supplies electricity. He has a standard 8 education. He was a manual labourer and is now a trainer in Adult Basic Education and Training.

From a curriculum perspective they should:

- deal with the real issues that people are confronted with;
- enable a democratic and socially just ethos to be nurtured and sustained;
- aim to enhance the marketable skills of learners;
- induct learners into a process of lifelong learning which includes the discipline of studying, the management of time and resources.

Programmes of adult education for special communities such as minorities and indigenous peoples need to start by conducting a survey of learner needs. Particularly, minorities, migrants and indigenous peoples are linguistically and culturally embedded in their social and natural environments. Past experience shows that such programmes have taken off the ground because they have been under the control of local communities and have had community support. It is important to create a space for the university within local communities, and vice versa, a space for communities in universities.

Indigenous peoples possess and inheritance of knowledge of enormous richness and complexity, based on paradigms very different from those upheld in the universities. Indigenous knowledge is, for example, based on a close symbiosis with nature. Care should be taken that indigenous knowledge is not destroyed by attempts to impose western scientific approaches along with their tendency to exploit the environment and nature.

The Aboriginal Education Course at the University of Technology, Sydney, Australia

- There is a three years part-time programme (already running for 14 years) leading to a certificate in adult education for aboriginal learners.
- There are three Aboriginal faculty members, three members of staff.
- Two-thirds of learners are women;
- There is a high rate of completion because of strong family, work or community support when applying and during the programme, and of spaces given to cultural aboriginal manifestations;
- There is student counselling;
- Articles are published in a variety of journals.

Community-based Learning

Many universities are seeking to attract students from minority groups into adult education programmes. But this in itself is not enough. Community-based programmes are being developed which encourage students to grapple with issues of social justice. A term now frequently used is "service learning" that is to say, an "education for the common good and the creation of a just and livable society". In the planning of such programmes, workshops and debates have been held to discuss such questions as: What is the common good? What is a just and liveable society? How can learning be organised around these themes? What connections can be established with non-academic communities?

> **Services Learning Network at the DePaul University, Chicago, USA**
>
> Founded a century ago, DePaul University, with its constituent college, has set itself the mission of being a non-traditional, experienced-based and flexible higher education institution for adult working students.
>
> It provides a university access to different communities—geographically, culturally and politically distinct—to share their knowledge with faculty and with students in classes and there is a give and take on both sides.

Community-based learning is learning through working with the university to collect data from communities for the benefit of their citizens. The overall emphasis is on participatory learning. It offers courses in research techniques for gathering data and throwing light on problems relating to youth, education, economic development, health, human services, affordable housing and human capacity. The conclusions can be used to formulate policies adjusted to the community's needs. The university is used as a resource that provides tools for addressing a variety of educational issues: How does learning occur within a community? How do communities bound together accomplish their goals? How do they put aside their own needs to develop a collective voice representing all of their interests? How do they learn to find relevant data sources? How do they manage power relations in society?

Community-based Research

In community-based research, community leaders are afforded the opportunity to share their research and experience publicly and in classroom settings. It entails organising seminars, special forums, lectures and meetings that bring together diverse groups of people who are concerned with the critical issues facing society. It brings together faculty, researchers and community leaders/ activities who share similar research interests around specific community concerns, such as welfare and economic self-sufficiency, that have direct practical implications for community initiatives. It offers opportunities to discuss research results regularly in joint meetings between researchers and community activists, where ideas are exchanged and opened up for critical comment by all involved in the project.

Studying subjugated forms of knowledge presents a number of challenges for adult education researchers. University-based educators have to be able to put themselves in the role of a learner. Universities must question the taken-for-granted paradigms of knowledge and learn from people who are generally excluded from them. Knowledge can be created in very different ways from those promoted in universities. It is necessary to learn to understand the 'order of things' in other cultural contexts. At the same time universities and the academic life are a useful context for conceptualising and analysing descriptions of communities.

In community-based research there is a recognition that teaching and learning take place in both the world of the community and the world of the university. Adult educators have to learn to switch to the role of learners when they deal with people who are from different cultures and who think and theorize differently. A lot of theories need to be reinterpreted when knowledge is located and coded somewhere else rather than in the universities.

A researcher has to be a true participant in a community, or at least to be living in it, in order to learn its language and to gain access to its knowledge.

Partnerships Between Universities, Industry and Businesses

University departments are being challenged to move from being involved with only community-based learning to a much broader spectrum of university provision which will respond more directly to labour market demands. The shift is in part related to global economic development and to the growing need for increasing productivity through further training. The language of competency-based, outcome-oriented education is somewhat new to many universities, although it has become part of the normal discourse of some higher education institutions in different regions of the world.

In addition to research and development, universities are increasingly introducing continuing education courses and finding new ways to meet the rising competency requirements of enterprises and representatives of employees.

The Buskerud State College (BSC) in Norway

The BSC College, with a long tradition of international cooperation, has developed close working relationships with industry. It provides for the continuing education of graduates and other technical specialists in the field of information technology.

A Diploma in Information Technology is offered. The inscription's requirement allows flexible entry, based on previous qualifications and work experience, and also on recognition of credits taken in other institutions and of certificates of in-service programmes.

Dilemmas Posed for University Adult Education

Will national concerns to be more competitive swamp local concerns for social and economic justice? Will human capital become the new orthodoxy of life-long learning? Will the market's needs dominate at the expense of the broader social and political needs?

Paradoxically, social movements are declining in power in several parts of the world, as countries are achieving a democratic form of government. The advent of democracy in many countries including South Africa and Latin America has moved the spotlight from social movements to demands for a more formal and vocational policy oriented work.

Market forces are increasingly, expected to influence the structure and form of university provision, which may leave little space for people-centred approaches and social issues. The university courses, which will be subsidised by the state and industry in partnership, will have to encompass both the needs of the labour market and of the learners and maintain the level of quality expected from higher adult education. This means appropriate criteria for tailor-made curriculum development, inserting certificate courses into national qualifications frameworks, giving voice to the learners in assessment of their needs and seeking funding from mixed sources.

Emphasising the links between higher education and the world of work and enhancing cooperation between university and industry are needed, but it is not only work that needs to be recognised but also the other aspects of people's lives. The requirements of the employers and the needs of employees need to be balanced.

Conclusions: University Adult Education from the Margin to the Centre

Universities all over the world are faced with very similar issues and problems within their respective countries. The problems of marginality is apparent. While university adult education has tended in the past to work on the margin, it has now to develop cooperation and support from the university as a whole. On the other hand, university based adult education units need to support the university in its efforts to change and become more responsible for transforming itself into a lifelong learning organisation. Partnerships outside the institutions have to be developed. Choices need to be made. Universities should rely on co-operation with economic institutions or groups, but must also meet the needs of the less advanced groups in society.

Universities are opening their doors in various ways. There are more adults coming to university premises than ever before. Consequently, there is a need for university adult education to be present in all departments. As universities are becoming life-long education institutions, the challenge for the next few years will be, through cross-faculty communication, to support the opening of universities, programmes to all the adult population in need of university level credit and non-credit education, and of university expertise.

The "mainstreaming" of university adult learning has become crucial to this transition phase of higher education and to the strengthening of university-society relationship, which has traditionally concentrated on the education of the young generation, but must now be extended to the whole life-span.

5

The Multiplicity of Research on "Learning for All", A Key for the 21st Century

Introduction

There is a great richness in research on adult learning worldwide. It deals with different countries, peoples, cultural origins, methodologies and approaches. The workshop "The multiplicity of research on Learning for All, a key for the 21st century" at the Fifth International Conference on Adult Education (CONFINTEA V), held in July 1997 in Hamburg, proposed ways of developing international co-operation and suggested ways to preserve the diversity of research from all cultures of the world. The workshop chaired by Ramón Flecha from the Research Centre for Adult Education (CREA), University of Barcelona, featured the following panel of speakers: Hashim Abuzeid El Safi, Institute of Adult Education, Sudan; John Cummings, Harvard University, USA; Anita Dighe, National Institute of Adult Education, New Delhi; Yukiko Sawano, National Institute for Educational Research, Japan.

The Chapter presents some examples of key areas in which research is currently being conducted by various public and non-governmental agencies. It concludes with proposals for follow-up and recommendations on ways to enhance communication between researchers.

Research on Participation in Adult Education

Research on participation in different forms of organised adult learning is being conducted in an increasing number of countries using different and often complementary methodologies: quantitative analysis of survey data, qualitative inquiry and biographical research. Attitudinal studies are also being undertaken to describe patterns of learning and barriers to participation in organised adult education.

It is a question not just of determining who is participating or not, but of interpreting the cultural and social embeddedness of adult learning.

Quantitative surveys are essential to assess the situation and to reveal uneven participation (*see booklet 2d* on the monitoring of adult learning where the international project of OECD, Statistics-Canada and UIE/UNESCO is described).

Qualitative approaches should help in understanding the structural and contextual factors affecting participation and non-participation. In order to have a complete picture of adult learning it is necessary to combine qualitative methodologies, which assess communicative situations, with interpretations of cultures, communities and individuals who suffer social and cultural exclusion. Qualitative methodology is particularly useful in researching the factors that motivate adults to learn.

The tendency in the past was to interpret the marginalised individual in terms deficit. However, research has moved towards considering these persons as active players in their own lives. Participation and non-participation need to be understood in relation to other social and cultural practices and the individual's own interpretations of their daily lives.

The Research Centre for Adult Education (CREA) in Barcelona

CREA is conducting a research programme on participation in adult education using quantitative and qualitative methodologies such as surveys, life stories, case studies and comparisons. Research has shown that though there appears to be a big increase in demand for adult education, participation in organised learning is unevenly distributed between persons of differing educational and social status.

Efforts are being made to analyse the real causes of non-participation by interpreting the voices of individual. Biological accounts highlight the fact that adult attendance in literacy classes is associated with low status relative to the positive experience from attending, say, a Master's course. Reasons for non-participation include lack of time, inadequacy of timetables and insufficient access to course-related information.

Research in Gender Issues

A growing trend in research is to look at the gender dimension of adult learning: the hidden curriculum, the different learning patterns of women and men, the barriers to women's participation in adult learning, the development of gender-sensitive monitoring systems and the documentation of the best local practices on women's empowerment.

Research on gender at the National Institute of Adult Education (NIAE), New Delhi

Research projects at NIAE have focused on literacy. Emphasis is placed on the social context of literacy practices and literacy data is differentiated by sex. The questions raised are: Why do women come to literacy classes? Why do they stay? For what reasons do they drop out? To what uses do they put their literacy? How do they retain literacy?

The practice of large scale social mobilisation in literacy campaigns has important implications for women's literacy as it socially sanctions the participation of women in literacy programmes in Indian society.

Researches show that literacy classes provide women learners and volunteers with an opportunity to meet and break their social isolation. Research in South Delhi shows that women have specific personal and social reasons for participating in the literacy campaign. Literacy classes offer women learners opportunities to meet in small groups and share experiences about work, family and health.

Other researches deal with factors that facilitate women's participation in literacy classes, taking into account the constraints that poor women face in terms of time, space and social obligations.

Lifelong Learning

The concept of "lifelong education" is gaining ground, but its impact on educational systems is still unclear. We are only beginning to document the evolving relationships between initial education, adult learning and the learning environment. If there is a general trend towards lifelong education, there is also a diversity in the contexts, in the projects, in the political economy of initial and adult education, as well as in the variety of learning environments. In short, there is a plurality of lifelong educations. The challenge for researchers is to understand the empirical and transitional processes of diverse national education systems in order to see how current developments can be assessed and influenced.

Lifelong Learning Research at NIER in Japan

The Japanese Government has decided to make lifelong learning for all a major priority for reform in education. The National Institute for Educational Research has been playing a crucial research role in the field of adult education. Three approaches can for identified:

1. Gathering data on lifelong learning policies and attitudes in the different regions, mainly by compiling bibliographies.

2. Undertaking comparative studies on adult education and lifelong learning according to common sets of indicators.
3. Studying the real learning contexts and daily learning practices in a manner akin to biographical research.

Research on Teaching/Learning Processes

One current procedure of research on teaching/learning processes is to group adults according to educationally meaningful categories, and to explore ways in which concepts borrowed from the study of primary and secondary education can be extended into the field of adult learning, or substantially, revised in order to be relevant to understanding the ways adults learn. Other procedures address directly the specific learning practices of adults in different cultures.

Efforts are being made to document the everyday uses of literacy and other skills and the ways in which people recognise and share their different abilities. Such a study aims not only, for example, to help people learn to read and write better, but also to bring about changes in the culture of reading and to place adult learning in the real contexts of everyday life.

Studies are also being conducted in health and environment education to assess different non-formal teaching and communication methods.

Other research projects look at the best practices in the use of new information technologies for basic education, and for teaching/learning a second language.

Research on Adult Basic Education in Industrialised Countries

Drawing on the categories used in the International Adult Literacy Survey (IALS), most research programmes on adult basic education focus on the bottom two categories of the five step scale of basic skills. These represent the population with literacy and numeracy skills estimated insufficient to cope with the basic requirements of industrialised societies. In the US, for example, these two categories make up about 45 per cent of the population and amount to a total of 90 million people.

With communication becoming more and more complex, the required basic skills and the ability to solve daily problems at work and in social or private life are being continuously upgraded. Because of this, unskilled workers have difficulties keeping their jobs or finding new work when unemployed. Initial education of children and the school system cannot alone cope with this changing demand. Adult literacy has therefore become a priority.

In industrialised countries, research and development on adult literacy is being funded and conducted in differing ways through various agencies. Nevertheless research agencies have been trying to develop comprehensive national strategies and to advocate national research agendas. Literacy practitioners, trainers of adult educators, administrators and policy-makers are increasingly consulted to build such agendas.

The National Centre for the Study of Adult Learning and Literacy at Harvard University, for example, has adopted an agenda centred on the study of adult basic skills in the US and on research aimed at improving practice in ongoing programmes. Research includes studies on learners' motivation and prior learning experience, analysis of the teaching/learning process, evaluation and monitoring of programmes and development of projects for both training and upgrading of trainers.

Despite a high demand for learning basic skills and a growing awareness among the population concerned, there is a high drop-out rate in many adult basic education programmes. This problem has been monitored quantitatively and studied through qualitative approaches in order to find out the conditions affecting learners' motivation, which either cause them to drop out or help them to persist.

Research on Staff Development

Staff development and in-service training of adult educators are mostly done in a classroom context with formal programmes leading to formal certification. However, new non-formal and informal contexts as well as the use of distance education are gaining in importance. Research in this field aims to measure the impact of the different kinds of approach within various learning contexts.

Attempts are being made to institute a system of participatory research, where teachers do their own research as an effective way to reflect on and improve their own practices. The multiple intelligence theory, for example, is being used in a teacher/researcher project to give teachers a tool with which to understand the experiences and expertise that adults bring into the learning processes and then to build on that understanding.

The issue of professionalisation of adult education is contentious. On the one hand, most adult educators have no specific pre-service training and are afraid of losing their jobs; on the other hand, the professional status of adult educators is often only marginally recognised. In the USA an in-service approach was introduced with the aim of gradually moving towards a system on on-the-job accreditation of adult educators.

Research on Learning Attainment

Evaluative techniques with an emphasis on quantitative data tend to dominate research in adult education. The studies commissioned by governments tend to concentrate primarily on monitoring the implementation of programmes, focusing on such factors as percentage of people made literate, drop-out rate, proportion of women participants, measures of attainment.

Ways are being looked at for broadening the measures beyond pure academic standards, to embrace criteria more relevant to adults at work, in the community and at home.

Besides assessing adult learners' achievements, another important measure is the economic advantages that an adult may gain from better qualifications, both in the formal and informal economies. Such research is often directed towards informing practice in adult education and justifying funding from donor agencies.

More research and qualitative data are required on the acquisition, retention and uses of newly acquired competencies, taking into account the meaning adults attach to learning in their everyday lives.

Especially in the context of structural adjustment programmes and the shrinking number of jobs, research is also needed on the mastering of vocational skills for sustainable economic activities, both in the formal and the informal economies.

More transnational studies will help us understand how cultural and socio-economic factors impinge on learning experiences.

Despite increased participation of women in literacy, there is very little critical research on levels of literacy attainment and on the rate of relapse into illiteracy, when compared with research on literacy achievements among men. Statistics indicating the increased participation of women may conceal low levels of literacy compared to men.

Diversity of Approaches and Methodologies

Diversification is a prevailing trend in research on adult learning: diversification of theoretical frameworks, of approaches and of methodologies. But artificial boundaries are often created through isolation of disciplines and lack of communication mechanisms or inter-disciplinary documentation networks. Nevertheless, the opposition between qualitative and quantitative methodologies is giving way to recognition of the complementarity between such approaches.

Research has to embrace different processes, modalities and methodologies. Dialogue between researchers should be promoted because it encourages researchers to collaborate in the development of adult learning.

There is an urgent need to rebuild national adult learning systems, in all their diversity, along multi-disciplinary lines.

Communicative Research and International Dialogue

The aim of transnational educational research is to highlight not only commonalities but also diversities: in objectives, target groups, methodologies, approaches, learning environments and traditions.

It relies upon international networks to communicate the diverse methodologies, approaches, orientations and contexts needed as material.

Arbitrary divisions, such as quantitative versus qualitative methodologies, specialised versus participatory research and so on, make little sense. There is need to nurture diversity, while resisting a relativistic vision of diversity that might obscure the universal standard of human rights.

There are a number of prerequisites for such international dialogue:

- improved access to research reports and publications;
- translation and dissemination of research excerpts;
- multi-disciplinary and inter-regional meetings;
- support for publishing the work of young researchers.

Barriers to the Development of Adult Education Research

There are major obstacles to research in the field of adult education and to co-operation between research teams: the diverse and shifting-definitions of adult learning, as well as the co-existence of unrelated provisions and policies, often developed under different names, ministries and frames of reference.

A related obstacle is the paucity of communication between research networks dealing with adult learning and, as mentioned above, between the relevant academic disciplines.

There are many other barriers, to the development of adult education research. A commonly cited characteristic of adult education research is its marginalisation in relation to other fields of research. There is very little interaction between communities of researchers in the fields of education and social sciences, and the influence of adult education research is almost non-existent outside its borders.

Adult learning tends also to be marginalised in the power-knowledge equation. Adult education research is seldom given high priority. There is a tendency to apply mechanically to adult learning the findings developed in other fields of education and the social sciences without taking into account the different context in which these theories were originally generated.

Conclusions and Recommendations for Follow-up

New developments in adult learning need to be reinforced:

- reconstructing and co-ordinating the fragmented adult learning efforts at the national level;

- networking research in order to learn from the way problems are solved in other contexts and situations;
- shifting the vision of literacy from an instrumental to a relational and developmental perspectives;
- modifying research techniques to recognise the contribution of both quantitative and qualitative methodologies, bot separately and in different combinations;
- communicative approaches to avoid ethno-centricism;
- studying interrelationships between race, gender and classes;
- improving the quality of research and its applicability for policy development and the practice of adult learning.

The workshop made the following recommendations for future cooperation between researchers in the diversified domain of adult learning:

- to take into account the diversity of approaches and trends in adult learning research around the world;
- to avoid the imposition of research formulae;
- to make available information on research conducted in all countries in order to learn from the way problems are defined and solved in the different contexts and situations;
- to invite UIE/UNESCO to organise a seminar with representatives of existing regional networks;
- for international organisations to support international research on adult learning and to encourage multicultural research teams;
- to seek new ways to promote a debate on adult education between researchers, practitioners and institutions.

The workshop proposed, as a follow-up initiative, that an international network, bringing together existing regional and national research networks, be established using both conventional approaches and new technologies (e.g. a web site to report on research conducted in different institutions or agencies of research).

6

Global Community of Adult Learning through Information and Documentation: *Developing a Network of Networks*

Introduction

In spite of the explosion of knowledge and new media, adult education documentation and information services remain inaccessible to many people. There is very uneven access to many kinds of information and documentation for researchers, policy makers, community groups, business, adult learners, educators of adults and all those engaged in lifelong learning around the world. There is also very uneven input into adult education data banks. Most of the larger adult education documentation centres, located in Western Europe and North America, collect, analyse and disseminate predominantly mainstream knowledge without reaching to the indigenous and grassroots literature/media.

In many parts of the world resources of adult education documentation are seldom available, and many documentation services are threatened by financial cuts. Yet, the demand for new skills and adult learning is accompanied by an increasing demand for adult education documentation and information. However, no single documentation and information centre or network is able to satisfy existing information needs as well as to cope with the growing need to recognise diversity in cultural and linguistic information.

In the last couple of years, however, many centres have started networking in the field of adult education documentation or geographical region. Sharing of resources and international co-operation is a necessity and a challenge.

The Workshop on "Global Community of Adult Education through Information and Documentation" coordinated by the UNESCO Institute for Education and chaired by Terrance Keenan, Syracuse University Library, featured presentations by Martha Nghidengua, Rössing Foundation, Namibia; Eva Kupidura, International Council for Adult Education (ICAE); Rosalie Ndejuru, Centre de documentation sur l'éducation des adultes et la condition féminine (CDEACF); Alfredo Rojas, for REDUC, a Latin American Network; Susan Imel, Clearing house on Adult, Career and Vocational Education (ERIC); Justin Ellis, Ministry of Education and Culture, Namibia; Zoran Jelenc, Slovene Adult Education Centre; Judith Kalman, Departamento de Investigaciones Educativas, Mexico; Agneta Lind, Swedish Development Agency (SIDA); Shigeru Aoyagi, Asian Pacific Cultural Centre for UNESCO (ACCU); Lucien Bosselaers, European Association for Education for Adults and Flemish Centre for Adult Education; Abdulaziz Al Sunbul, ALECSO, a Pan-Arab organisation based in Tunisia; Heribert Hinzen, German Adult Education Association (DVV).

With emerged from the workshop was the need for correcting the uneven distribution of documentation centres and of networking and promoting the flow of information between both industrialised and developing countries, from South to North, from East to West and vice versa. The workshop unanimously supported the idea of developing a global network of networks, in which the UNESCO Institute for Education in playing a leading role.

The Issues and the Challenges

Knowledge Explosion and Uneven Access

The growing demand for adult learning in all sectors of economic, social and cultural development has resulted in an information explosion on adult learning. In addition documentation on adult learning is being produced in many languages throughout the world. And it is the challenge of documentation services to facilitate the dissemination of these at different levels. Electronic information sources are expanding and there have also been developments in how these sources can be accessed through a variety of information providers.

> "I discovered that there was a lot of interesting and useful documentation in Spanish, Portuguese and French which was not available in English, and, therefore, was seldom referred to in Anglaphone publications and documents. There is an obvious need for translats and dissemination".
>
> —*Agneta Lind, SIDA*

However, access to adult education documentation and information remains, limited. Educational efforts are unnecessarily duplicated because of lack of timely access to information about the work of counterparts in other parts of the world.

Diversified Nature of Information

Another challenge lies in the broad definition of adult learning and the diversified nature of information sources. One centre alone cannot cope with the increasing and multi-faceted demand for information. Better linkages need to be developed among existing information providers, and new centres need to be created in under-served regions.

> **Centre de documentation sur l'éducation des adultes et la condition féminine (CDEACF) in Montreal.**
>
> - has publications, newsletters, bibliographies, directories serving community groups, women's organisations, training institutions governmental institutions and literacy groups;
> - networks with women's groups in 30 countries;
> - there are 256 working groups working on information and documentation on topics including: lifelong learning, international solidarity, popular education, literacy, feminism, inter-cultural education, social development, community development and, information technology;
> - organises workshops;

- maintains an active electronic network of women's groups;
- moderates discussion groups on major policy documents.

Improving Communication Between Centres

Few information sources can even attempt to cover all the many fields of adult learning. The supplement their own resources they need partnerships with other complementary services, connecting with them through conventional methods or new electronic media.

There are many documentation centres on adult learning in Africa, the Arab States, Asia and the Pacific, Europe and North America and the Caribbean. Often, however, these centres operate in isolation from one another.

> "In the 1980s, in Sierra Leone, a number of projects on which we worked in the collection of traditional stories and songs as well as on indigenous learning and training were documented on radio and video cassettes as well as in written form. However, access to these documents now is very difficult due to the military and political struggle in the country. One question we must answer as researchers and documentalists is how to surmount the problems of unrest in certain regions of the world? How to talk about the Internet and networks in the face of no electricity or tele-communication?"
>
> *Heribert Hinzen, DVV*

In the development of the network of networks it is necessary to keep in mind that there are many centres that lack access to the technology necessary to participate. Another issue is the question of language in developing a network of networks. Many centres collect information in different languages. The challenge is to preserve this practice while enabling communication among cooperating partners.

The network of networks needs to be built up at different levels: at the national level, at the regional and finally at the international level.

The overall objectives of networking of documentation centres and databases are to meet the demands in the growth of adult learning, to work towards a better cooperation and exchange of ideas and towards the multi-directional flow of information between researchers and policy-makers to enable a better dissemination of knowledge for informed policy-making worldwide.

The Complementarity Between Electronic and Conventional Approaches

In the age of the computer chip and the Internet, much emphasis is placed on the need for access to electronic information. However, information is not equitably distributed, nor is it always appropriate. Access to books and other conventional information sources therefore remains crucial.

ERIC Clearing House on Adult, Career, and Vocational Education in Columbus, Ohio

- ERIC provides electronic access to practically every major article published in the field of adult education in the US as well as to much material from elsewhere;
- its functions are building the database providing user services, and knowledge synthesis—the preparation of publications which are a synthesis of collected materials and are available on their WEB Site, as well as in print and on electronic mail.

In Mexico, for example, there is a wide variety of potential users of information. Those who tend to have easy access to electronic information systems are researchers, curriculum designers, technical teams and policy-makers, because it is within the universities and government agencies that the infrastructure of modern information technology is being built up. On the other hand, literacy trainers and adult educators rarely have access to electronic information. For them it is important to secure distribution of other forms of documentation such as print materials, and in some cases, video or television.

Documentation and Research

Research in adult learning is an important input for documentation centres and data bases. The collection of data has to become more cross-sectorial and inter-disciplinary and has to tap all relevant sources. There is a need to strengthen the collection of unpublished reports and appears from all countries, as well as documents that have not been systematically disseminated, and to translate or synthesise them in many languages.

REDUC, Latin American Information Network for Education in Santaigo. Chile

- Assists in relating educational research results to policy-making through dissemination and training.
- Produces electronic educational materials for training policy-makers.
- Publishes research summaries.
- Maintains a database of abstracts.
- Operates 17 retrieval centres to collect information for a central database.

Linking Information Dissemination and Policy Making

How can documentation and information be made available to policy-makers? How can research, documentation and policy-making be linked? These are the majority challenges facing documentation services.

> "Reinventing the wheel' is a common trap that grassroots educators and organisations designing educational programmes fall into. Unaware of counterparts elsewhere in the world that have already designed similar programmes, they fell prey to repeating the same process all over again. If they had timely access to information about the work of their counterparts, a great deal of time, energy and resources could be saved and put toward other priorities for mutual benefit."
>
> *Eva Kupidura, ICAE*

In spite of the difficulties, there are many examples of documentation and information services having been useful for policy formulations, as well as for analysis and critique of educational policies. The big challenge is to be able to identify those moments when information makes a key difference in policy through being accurately synthesized and circulated at the right moment. Documentation specialists have an important role in the brokerage of information. They help officials in ministries to analyse and formulate policies from research findings. Information workshops on the most important findings of adult education research also provide useful information to decision-makers.

The Role of the Adult Learning Information and Documentation Specialists

Librarians and documentalists are becoming very active in producing documentation and focusing on key issues. Consequently their role is changing. They have become:

- documentation specialists on adult learning;
- more informed about policies and issues in their countries;
- more informed about the available facilities or technologies;
- producers of information kits for social partners;
- active members of cultural networks.

Asia/Pacific Cultural Centre for UNESCO (ACCU) and UNESCO PROAP have developed diverse materials from 18 countries dealing with:

- women's empowerment, sanitation, health education, and income generation;
- literacy rates and figures;
- literacy organisations;
- non-formal education curriculum;
- literacy publications;
- literacy glossary;
- information on donors;

- successful strategies used in working with indigenous people, respecting peoples' cultures, languages and traditions;
- information about activities being done at the local level.

Objectives:

- to facilitate an understanding of the literacy situation in Asia and the Pacific at a glance at all levels;
- to provide up-to-date key data for decision-making by governments, NGOs and international agencies;
- to share innovative literacy materials and strategies with universities, researches and students and with media covering literacy and development.

Recommendations

A concrete outcome of the workshop was the creation of a global network of information and documentation centres on adult learning, a "network of networks", the objective of which is to map and counteract the current imbalance in collection and dissemination of literature/media and information on adult learning in the different regions of the world. During this workshop, an international steering committee was formed with members representing institutions such as:

- UNESCO Headquarters
- International Bureau of Education
- International Council for Adult Education (ICEA)
- World Bank
- Centre de documentation sur l'éducation des adultes et la condition féminine (Montreal)
- Syracuse University Library and Archives
- Slovene Adult Education Centre
- ERIC Clearing House on Adult, Career and Vocational Education
- ALICE (The European Union Information Bank on Non-formal Adult Education in Europe)

- Rössing Foundation (Namibia)
- Asia/Pacific Cultural Centre for UNESCO (ACCU)
- Asian-South Pacific Bureau of Adult Education (ASPBAE)
- REDUC (Latin America)
- Damascus University, Syria
- Ministry of Education of Nepal

These documentation and information services, big and small, non-governmental, governmental and academic, from the South and the North, represent the whole spectrum of adult education work. Some of them already have experience in networking. All of them are convinced that transnational networking is a necessity in times of globalisation of knowledge and global cuts in finance and human resources.

The aim of the steering committee is to develop a long-term orientation and implementation of the network of networks, including organisation, structure, sharing of responsibilities, financing, initiating ideas and activities to establish centres, promoting access to information via new technology, overcoming cultural and communication barriers. It was agreed that surveying the adult education documentation and information scene should be the first step.

Other Important Suggestions that Emerged from the Workshop were:

- to contribute to a multi-lingual dissemination of information by increasing the number of languages available;
- to produce more documentation in local languages;
- to create a balance between regional and international databases;
- to provide conventional exchange possibilities for those documentation and information services that lack access to technological infrastructures;
- to agree on a compatible indexing format;
- to address the diversity of languages, cultures, traditions, and user profiles.

7

The Politics and Policies of the Education of Adults in A Globally Transforming Society

Introduction

Humanity is undergoing a massive transformation from the age of industrial production to the age of information and communications. History has known other transformations, but this one is taking place much more rapidly and is involving much greater numbers of people than ever before. In the process humankind is being confronted with new global risks. Adult learning is one area where these developments have important implications. While researchers, policy-makers, the media and much of the public are aware of these transformations, the profound nature of the change has not been sufficiently taken into account in adult learning policy.

The workshop session "Politics and Policies of the Education Adults in a Globally Transforming Society", held at the Fifth International Conference on Adult Education (CONFINTEA V), discussed the changes which adults have to confront, their effects on different groups of people, and the policy options available in dealing with them.

The workshop was divided into three parts. The first part addressed the nature and scope of the global transformation taking place. Chair was Eric Bockstael, Wayne State University, U.S.A. Speakers included: Harbans S. Bhola, University of Indiana at

Bloomington, USA; Sheri Hamilton, National Literacy Coalition, South Africa; Talvi Marja, Tallinn University, Estonia; Gloria Ramirez, Mexican Human Rights Academy, Mexico; Walter Uegama, University of British Colombia, Canada.

At the second session the question raised was: Is adult learning the right response? This session was chaired by Talvi Marja and the panel of speakers featured: Keith Forrester, University of Leeds; Jozsef Katus, European Symposium on Voluntary Associations; Rodolfo Martinez, Wayne State University; Daphne Ntiri, Wayne State University, U.S.A.; Rifat Okcabol, Bogazici University, Turkey; Jean-Claude Quenum, Voix d'Afrique Formation, Benin/France; Dimitrs Vergidis, University of Patras, Greece and Keith McLeod, University of Toronto, Canada.

The third part of the workshop dealt with the strategies and organisational structures required at both local and international levels. Chair was Harbans S. Bhola. The following speakers were on the panel: José Asun, University of Barcelona: Ettore Gelpi, International League of Education, France/Italy; Gunther Ghere and Karel de Witte, Catholic University of Leuven, Belgium; Pierre Leboutte and Lucien Pieret, Parthages, Belgium; Walter Temeline, University of Windsor, Canada; Mara Ustinova, Institute, for Ethnology and Anthropology, Russia; Mitja Zagar, Ethnic Institute, Slovenia; Lucien Peiret, Vocational Institute, Belgium; George Cushingberry jr. and Tony Perry, Michigan Ethnic Heritage Centre, USA.

The workshop represented all sectors of the adult community—researchers, policy makers, practitioners, the media and the public: It emerged clearly from these discussions that adult learning needs to be taken out of its previous marginal role and given a much more central place in policy-making. The growing gap between the social demand for education of adults and the resources available to meet these needs makes the question of policy central to the current discussion regarding adult learning.

Issues and Challenges in the Context of Global Transformation

The massive changes in nearly all aspects of life which people world-wide are confronted with are elements of a great transformation. Although there are a number of political, economic and social developments taking place, the deep structure of inequality persists, both within the countries of the North and the South, and particularly between the North and the South. The majority of the world's population is paying a heavy price for economic globalisation.

The impact of the global shift to a new information and communications age is everywhere influencing peoples lives but in very different ways. Given the advanced technologies involved, the transformations can have greater implications for the physical and social environment than any previous transformation. A major issue for policy and practice in adult learning is to address the human costs and benefits of the past transformations.

Taking Issue with the Development Model

The old development paradigm, which saw development as an endless upward path, is no longer valid. It is now obvious that the world is more unequal than ever, the disparities between the rich and the poor have increased, and we are consuming energy faster than we are creating it. Furthermore the majority of the world's population is paying a heavy price for economic globalisation. If human society is to find a better ay forward, a massive education process is needed—education about the limits to growth, about the threats inherent in the old development model, about possible ways of creating a more hopeful future for the world and its inhabitants. A large part of this educational effort will be the task of adult educators.

Transformation in Former Socialist Countries

Former socialist countries have had to cope with a radical transformation from totalitarianism to democracy and from command economies to the free market. This process is happening at a time of economic and political integration in Europe. In this context, adult learning policies have to:

1. safeguard the cultural heritage and identity of peoples and communities threatened by the homegenising influences of the changes mentioned above;

2. train them to be equal and active participants in the global economy.

Transformations in Work

With the world-wide swing to neo-liberal economic policies, unemployment is growing, and education is becoming increasingly privatised or subjected to the calculations of the market. Consequently, many people are being excluded from education. There is also a growing danger that migrants, refugees and other minority groups will become special categories within adult education programmes that should be meant for all. Furthermore, there is an increasing tendency to see adult learning as a matter of vocational training and human resource development.

A new understanding of education is now called for—an approach that promotes inner enrichment but at the same time develops the flexibility that is necessary in the modern world of work. Up till now, policy-making has followed the human capital development approach and has not relied on the accumulated expertise of popular pedagogy in different countries. Critical thinking and learning skills are needed more than before. Equally important is to develop awareness of ecological and cultural issues.

Processes of Democratisation in the World

Many countries, such as South Africa post-Apartheid, have chosen adult learning as one of their key strategies to reconstruct and transform their societies and to improve the human resources and vocational capacities of their adult populations.

While many of these adult education strategies are informed by democratising intentions they are being increasingly forced to adapt to the harsh requirements of the global market and to produce a workforce with the necessary skills to compete in national and global markets. This is often at the expense of the unemployed and underdeveloped, many of whom live in informal settlements and rural areas. In many countries there is therefore a tension between adult education for jobs in the competitive global context and the wider vision of adult learning for all, in all areas of life.

Erosion of the Nation State

The world is everywhere experiencing a progressive erosion of the welfare state, although with the growing disparity between the haves and the have-nots, welfare states are more necessary than ever. In order to deal with this situation it is necessary to create a new generation of political leaders able to promote civic literacy, develop human-centred social and urban agendas and create a climate in which people can deal more knowledgeably with the new local and global challenges. Civic education must start with schools and be integrated into community work and adult learning. It is important not only to have vocational skills and a job but to have the political skills to sustain a viable democracy. Above all, adult learning is a tool that can help to:

- encourage learners to understand and debate injustices in the context of the new world economic and political order;
- overcome biases and discriminatory practices;
- deal with the new technological developments;
- promote greater opportunities for women and minorities, and equality and justice for everyone;
- enhance international understanding;
- promote understanding of different cultures and economies particularly those in which a subsistence mode of living is essential to cultural and survival.

The Crucial Role of Adult Learning in Addressing the Key Issues Confronting Societies

Adult education has now firmly established itself as a separate discipline and field, complementary to initial education. The number of persons enrolled in adult learning programmes is fast catching up with the number of children in traditional school systems. This is a result of a response to the rapidity of change and emergence of reflexive societies.

Yet experience at the local, regional, national and international levels clearly indicates that this new educational reality has not yet been adequately integrated into the policy-making process.

An important task for adult learning on the threshold of the 21st century is to enable learners to see the present global transformations in a historical perspective and to understand that such periods of profound change bring not only positive developments but also dangers and catastrophes. The beginning of the present century was marked by enormous political tensions, civil war and world wars. In the same way, the changes being experienced currently are not a neutral technological process of change but run the risk of sweeping while communities aside. Recognition of these negative developments needs to inform current and future practices and policies in the education of adults.

Promoting Political Skills and Active Citizenship

There is an increasing tendency for adult learning policies to move in the direction of promoting and updating vocational skills only. While the acquisition and the enhancement of such skills is important, it is also essential to have a wider vision of adult education, concerned with active citizenship, social rights and responsibilities, work and local communities. In fact there should be no contradiction between these two approaches. Adult learning should both prepare people for the world or work and promote the development of an informed, knowledgeable and reflective citizenship.

Networking Among Adult Learning Initiatives

States are increasingly tending to withdrew from many of their welfare responsibilities. It is necessary for people involved in adult learning programmes to collaborate with others at local, regional and international levels.

New Roles of Adults

Adults are taking on new functions, responsibilities and have new learning aspirations in their capacities as workers, citizens, community workers, parents and family members. Research is showing that there are common activities, knowledge and skills that cut across all those roles. Critical thinking is not only important for the world of work but also for someone in the role of parent and community member. Adult learning should be re-conceptualised to focus on higher level transformative competencies, and not just on vocational skills.

A Broader View of Adult Learning

Education is more than the acquisition of skills, and more than formal education. It includes informal and non-formal forms of learning, enabling adults to participate in political, economic and social decision-making processes and to become active agents of change. The focus of conventional education on individuals is sufficient to deal with the immensity of change. Families, institutions, communities, societies and cultures as active learning environments are central to the transitions to the communications and information age.

Policy Strategies

Adult learning policies will be relevant only if they take into account the magnitude, depth and force of global changes. We need a multi-layered policy strategy of adult learning which has a two-pronged approach, taking into account both globalisation and diversifying tendencies. It must respond to social and economic transformations by enabling people to cope with the changes that are accompanying the introduction of new technologies. On the other hand it must empower people to become active subjects in the transformations of their own societies.

Local groups should be consulted in policy-making. For nearly two generations now, adult learners and educators in all parts of the world have been at work, developing adult education programmes and linking local groups with partners from public, private and voluntary sectors. Their experience needs to be used as a resource for dealing with the transformations and for generating new forms of policy making—both structural and programmatic. There is need to develop a symbiotic relationship between policy and grassroots action.

Adult education policy strategy should design contents which uphold basic values. These should include human rights of women, indigenous peoples and people with disabilities. Programmes, researches and networks should be built around these basic values.

Conclusion

1. The present global transformation is far from being an equitable and sustainable development.

2. The kind of issues we are dealing with are not technical or curricular ones. They deal with structural, legislative and distributive processes, at the local, national and international level.

3. The existing models of adult learning have to be reviewed to meet the new challenges and social demands. The choice is not between education for retraining or for citizenship. It is between passive adaptation and creative participation at work as well as civil and private life. For this, many kinds of training are needed—management, professional and vocational, information technology, languages, social, economic and political awareness and problem-solving.

4. Local experiences should guide practice and policy. It is the diversity and extensiveness of adult learning which is the most important resource in any future policy strategy. The involvement of local resources and local groups in a bottom-up process rather than a top-down process at the national, regional and global levels has become an urgent necessity. However the choice should not be between local and global. Both levels need to be combined.

5. It is increasingly important to share experiences and learn from others rather than painfully and slowly reinventing practices and knowledge.

Part 3
Ensuring Universal Rights to Literacy and Basic Education

8

Literacy in the World and its Major Regions

Introduction

Adult literacy for all who need it must be made an urgent priority. In all countries, North and South, all adults need continued and improved access to knowledge. They may be trying to acquire the rudiments of literacy or they may be endeavouring to keep abreast of the global explosion of information in every field. In addition, meeting the basic learning needs of adults is a key element in reducing world poverty.

Furthermore, tensions are increasing between the culture of tradition and the homogenising influences of globalisation and consequently there is a strong need for adult literacy programmes to respond to some of the adverse impacts that have been created. In this way learners can become aware of what is happening in the world, make changes and take control of what happens to them. As the world is pulled closer together it is imperative that the cultural diversity of people and pluralism of societies be recognised. Literacy is a crucial levelling opportunity and key for maintaining peace and stability in the world.

These issues were discussed at the workshop "Literacy in the world and its major regions" held at the Fifth International Conference on Adult Education (CONFINTEA V), in Hamburg in July 1997. The first part of the workshop "Literacy in the New Environment and the Evolving Society" included a review of current practice in literacy and an analysis of past experiences and new trends. Following the introductory keynote speech by Victor Ordonez (UNESCO/PROAP), short presentations of the situation in some developing regions were made by Joice Kibhati, Kenya, Maria Lourdes Khan (ASPBAE), Jules Didacus, Saint Lucia, Hacim El Safi, Sudan, Aicha Belarbi, Morocco, and Ana del Toro (INEA), Mexico.

The second part of focused on Africa where decentralisation has created new forms of self-government and empowerment opportunities for civil institutions, but which also present major challenges for adult education, the main issue being the role that adult learning and training have played in decentralisation and bottom-up development. This session was chaired by Peter Easton, Programme d'Appui au Dèvelopment Local au Sahel (PADLOS), Florida State University, USA and J.M. Ahlin, Byll Cataria, Suisse Development Cooperation. The panel consisted of Dana Fischer, Club du Sahel/OECD; Moustapha Yacouba, Project d' Appui au Développement Local au Sahel (PADLOS), Comité Inter-état de Lutte contre la Sécherresse au Sahel, Tchad; Coumba Boly (Institut Panafrician pour le Développement/Afrique de l'ouest/Sahel (IPDAOS); and Laouali Malam Moussa (INDRAP), Niger.

This workshop dealt primarily with the developing world. The complex problem of low levels of literacy in industralised countries was discussed at a separate workshop "Literacy and basic skills for community development in industralised countries", and consisted of video presentations, focusing on social, linguistic and ethnic problems of adult learners and young adults in Slovenia, France, Canada and the Czech Republic. These videos are available for reference in the UIE library.

National policies on literacy and adult learning have evidently benefited from discussions on this topic at many international conferences. Following CONFINTEA V there is also hope that as we enter the next millennium we are likely to see a more literate world.

Reconceptualising Literacy

Literacy can no longer be simply defined in terms of reading, writing or numeracy, nor can it be seen as an end in itself. People must be able to adapt continually to developments in science, technology, and to the pressures for social integration, participation and democratisation. The world is becoming more visual than before, and the ability to understand images is just as important as to understand words. Therefore, literacy has to be seen as a took for learning throughout life.

Research findings over the past several years have contributed significantly to a rethinking on the concept of literacy. The state:

- Literacy is a *positive factor in human capacity building*. It is an enabling factor, releasing people's capacities, rather than giving deprived individuals what they do not have. It is the core engine of human development and, in this respect, its impact has to be seen in terms of its benefit to communities and individuals, rather than merely in terms of whether individuals and able to read and write or sign their names. Literacy expands our scope to act, while extending our duties and responsibilities.
- As the world enters the next century, more skills are demanded. As a result the *demand for literacy* is increasing, whether functional literacy, computer literacy, of civic literacy.
- The sharp division between illiteracy and literacy needs to be overcome by *recognising the inherent wisdom of every individual,* whether he can read or not.

New information technologies are bound to separate the haves from the have-nots. The real challenge for literacy practitioners and policy makers is to see this does not happen and that *literacy reaches the marginalised.*

A new paradigm of literacy is emerging. In the rush to meet the demands of the 21st century, it is important to recognise three enduring principles:

1. Human development must be the foundation of all economic and social development as well as of sustainable development.

   The latter concept is particularly important in view of the fact that our planet has to be passed on to future generations.

2. Peace can only be attained through intellectual and moral solidarity of mankind, and by the promotion of education as a foundation for peace, freedom and democracy.
3. Literacy is a means of empowerment.

The problems of literacy relate not only to organisational structure, teaching material, languages, subjects, teaching and the training of facilitators but more importantly to the way literacy is conceptualised.

Adult Literacy and Illiteracy

Despite the increase in the world population, grate strides have been made to increase the number of literates, though there are sharp differences between industrialised and developing countries.

The growth in the number of literate men and women in the world is expected to continue for the foreseeable future. Nevertheless the number of illiterate adults has remained at about 885 million since 1980, with females still outnumbering males.

The Jomtien conference on Education for All (EEA) as well as the Beijing World Conference stressed the importance of making education a top priority of girls. Although, a consensus regarding girls' education at the level of national policy may have been achieved, at the local level, in villages throughout the world, there are still a large percentage of girls not attending school with the result that in some countries the gender gap is 20 per cent literacy among women and 60 per cent literacy among men.

Data on the distribution of the adult population by level of educational attainment also show substantial regional disparities. Sub-Saharan Africa and South Asia have large proportions of adults who either have no formal schooling or have an incomplete primary education. These adults constitute the primary target group for adult basic education.

Out of the 200 countries and territories throughout the world, about 374 million of the illiterates are located in only nine countries, which also happen to be the nine most populous countries in the world. More than half the illiterates of the world live in India and China combined, and quarter more in seven other nations.

Literacy statistics also reveal the relationship between illiteracy and other aspects of human and social development. For example, it has been shown that a strong correlation exists between female literacy, and the number of children and women's fertility. In Brazil, for example, those who left school after four years have an average number of 6.5 children, whereas those who completed more than four years of schooling have an average number of 2.5 children. Similar trends can be seen the world over. Statistics also show the correlation between literacy and longevity and infant mortality.

Literacy programmes have been launched in several countries, such as Tanzania, Cuba, and more recently India. Campaigns are also being started in Pakistan and Bangladesh. However, in some countries, these have brought only short-term rewards. In order to be successful, literacy campaigns require a great deal of support from governments for a specific period of time and the establishment of post-literacy projects and a literate environment so that people do not lapse back into illiteracy.

Literacy in Africa

Like many developing nations, illiteracy is very high in sub-Saharan Africa. Compared to other regions of the world, it is a region with the world's highest illiteracy rate (54 per cent). However, there is a considerable difference from one country to another. Whereas in countries such as Kenya, Tanzania, Zimbabwe, Botswana and South Africa the literacy rate is about 70 per cent, in countries such as Uganda, Malawi, Burundi and Rwanda the literacy rates are below 49 per cent. Nevertheless, there is a lot of enthusiasm in literacy work and a growing realisation that literacy is crucial in the context of integrated programmes for imparting messages on population, health and agriculture and in the struggle to escape poverty, and in this respect programmes are being developed in "cushioning" the poor from the negative influences of structural adjustment programmes.

Literacy is also important for creating a conducive learning environment at home for children. Women are more effectively empowered through access to literacy training and adult learning opportunities. There is also a belief that women's health, fertility and nutrition would be enhanced if female literacy rates could be increased. Advocacy groups like the Forum for African Women Educationists promote education of women and girls and see this as crucial for women's participation in political decision-making processes. Associations and organisation are also playing a key role in mobilising learning.

Although there has been a considerable number of literacy programmes through this region, a few countries have nevertheless witnessed falling literacy rates, such as Botswana and South Africa, and there is still a high illiteracy rate among women (63 per cent) compared to men (37 per cent). So there is still a lot of work to be done to eradicate illiteracy.

Literacy in the Arab States

In the Arab states which stretch from Atlantic Africa to Asia in the Arab Gulf the illiterate population has decreased to 43 per cent. For men the rate has fallen from 45 per cent in 1980 to 23 per cent in 1995; for women it has fallen from 71 per cent to 56 per cent, though several of the less developed Arab States are still encountering difficulties.

Several factors have been responsible for the decline of illiteracy in the Arab States. There has been continuing expansion of primary education in Saudi Arabia. In Egypt, a literacy campaign has been underway since 1993. Tunisia has evolved a new strategy to eradicate illiteracy. A Jordanian programme has intensified efforts in regions of wide-spread illiteracy with the hope of decreasing the rate to 8 per cent by the year 2000.

There has been a qualitative development in most Arab states, particularly in the design of new literacy programmes, paying particular attention to environment, health demographic problems, the consolidation of religious values and family coherence, freedom, self-reliance, the principles of democracy, civic education, the fight against extremism and the abuse of drugs. Special attention is also given to post-literacy schemes in formal, informal and open learning situations. Programmes for adults have a strong cultural component in them.

Most Arab states support the effort with regard to literacy under the umbrella of a commission or higher council, represented by the ministries and related institutions, universities and voluntary bodies, such as women's organisations and youth studies' associations.

Measures are being taken to create an Arab union for adult education charged with ensuring coordination of academic and voluntary efforts related to this field at the regional level.

Cooperation among Arab states plays an important role in the field of literacy and adult education. The linguistic unity as well as the geographical bonds and the common culture provide a solid base for regional cooperation.

Yet, illiteracy remains a serious problem in the Arab region, where the number of illiterate adults reaches more than 65 million people. The less developed Arab states are still encountering difficulties.

Latin America: From Adult Literacy to Basic Adult Education

Latin America provides a contrast with regard to adult literacy and learning. More than in other regions of the world the trend in Latin America is toward the very concept of literacy to mean basic education for adults, closely linked to the economic, political and social development of individuals and communities. This trend can be seen in specific areas of Brazil, Mexico, Chile, Argentina and Uruguay. Here, programmes are seeking to meet the basic learning needs of those who use them, whether it is the knowledge and skills a farmer requires to be an active participant in a rural community, political literacy for citizens in countries that have recently moved toward democratic forms of government, or diverse and flexible approaches for senior citizens with a variety of interests and activities. Particular emphasis is being given to dealing with issues of marginalisation and equity, such as those affecting girls and women, people in rural areas and the poor.

Lessons Learned from Large-scale Literacy Programmes

There are many lessons to be learned from large-scale literacy programmes. The basic requirements for promoting literacy in a sustained way are:

- the political will and commitment of society as a whole, including the media, industry and civil society;

- core funding and human resources through partnerships between government, NGOs and local communities;
- for people to understand the need for it, want it and ask for it, any campaign or effort being driven by the demand from the community itself;
- for programmes to be culturally relevant, sensitive to the diversity of learners, the learning processes and learning needs, and designed for as many special sub-groups of individuals as possible;
- a literate environment in which neo-literates can continue to operate, in order to be able to take advantage of the learning and literacy;
- for people to be helped to deal with the adverse effects of globalisation, so that can take control of what happens to them and to be proactive;
- programmes that integrate literacy with health, environmental and population education;
- participatory and interactive approaches;
- the support of other partners as it is not enough for one agency or one government to take full responsibility;
- a new conceptual framework for policy makers, designers of programmes and providers to view their mandate in a different way;
- for bridges to be built between other disciplines, other groups of people and organisations, and between formal and non-formal education;
- for it to be integrated into the promotion and support of other issues such as peace, human rights or the empowerment of women.

Literacy, Decentralisation and Local Power: Role of Local Communities, Associations and Businesses

An important question with regard to literacy, decentralisation and local power is: how do local communities, associations and businesses acquire or mobilise the competence, the skill and the knowledge required to assume new functions and new powers and to promote new activities. The Association for the Development of Education in Africa (ADEA) has funded a series of continuing research studies on topics such as the practical application of Koranic learning in African countries, how women acquire management skills in income generating activities, and on the powers for learning in the informal sector of the urban economy. ADEA is also supporting the Programme d'Appui au développement Local au Sahel (PADLOS) whose research seeks to find out how communities mobilise themselves, what skills are necessary to assume new functions, and what can be learned from that. In effect it starts with the demand side of the education equation. Agencies like the Club du Sahel are concerned with topics such as food security and management of natural resources, but in the course of their own work realise that they cannot go further without adult education and training of the local people. Thus adult learning becomes an essential component of any development project.

However, before training programmes can be designed it is necessary to ask the following questions: At what level are new responsibilities, powers and functions within communities assumed? How do people get their skills in order to exercise their new responsibilities? What role do the various training and education programmes and systems existing in these communities play in the new programmes?

Southern Mali

For the last 15 years many village communities have been taking over full responsibility for the marketing of their agricultural crops, thanks to the intervention of an adult education programme in the local language. This was followed by a stage-by-stage assumption of responsibility for management of these co-operatives. This movement has helped to generate capital savings that have enabled the people to invest in other local activities, such as water retention, grain storage schemes, and health delivery systems, and which in turn have generated employment for other people who require adult learning as their base.

Senegal

Programmes like TOSTAN in Senegal, have started offering programmes for women that also aim to promote women's self-esteem. These have been designed by local women themselves with management training. Women trained and organised in this way have initiated a move to get local authorities to ban female circumcision and have already been successful in the peanut growing area of Senegal.

Ghana

Local young people returning, after migration to the coast to their village, intervened in a land dispute between church members and adherents of a traditional religion over the drying up of a stream and a lake that had magical powers in the traditional religion, but which had been cursed by the priests of the fundamentalists sect.

These series of examples of demonstrate how local people who have either been granted additional power to carry out development functions, or have assumed it themselves, have acquired new knowledge as a result. They describe what people actually take over and do at the ground level, and how they get the skills to do it.

This movement towards local responsibility is very widespread and growing, but because it is constrained by a number of difficulties, it is uneven. Further, information on other programmes of decentralisation is very fragmentary. Although some decentralisation projects fail, the successful experiences are those that manage in one way or another to pull together three disparate but critically related elements, namely:

- *Financial capitalisation*— Some source of income generation that can be used to pay for the operating costs of the activity, reinvested in other activities or saved.
- *Institutional capitalisation*— Which means forming the structures that allow the activity to be organised, savings to be collected, decisions made on dispensing the money or the resources that have been generated, and ensure some democratic accountability.

- *Technical capacity* and its application.

All these three capacities need to be sustained, or the project will collapse unless held up by outside aid, money, support and political measures. Often, the technical and financial portion of the activity is well developed, but there is no strong institutional base that anchors it in the community. In other cases, the institutional base exists, but people do not have the necessary skills to run it. This is why adult learning is so important.

The Critical Ability in a Development Activity is Literacy

Fitting these three dimensions together is not easy. The critical ability here is that of literacy. In any development activity people need to develop these successive levels of skill and work out, with those in charge of the financial or institutional elements, a pedagogy by which people can acquire a skill, apply it and acquire the next one. For example, although local people can be empowered to take over the markets or co-operatives, providing they have enough skills and literacy to do so, the running of co-operatives and businesses relies heavily on adult educators working with credit providers and co-operative officials to analyse the market. People can take over functions and responsibilities but they have got to understand that the first level is learning numbers, registering things, regarding scales and price lists. The next level is to begin with addition and subtraction and only then can the management of stock warehouses be taken over.

The adult learning systems where people pulled all kinds of skills together included schools, hanging around in the neighbourhood, literacy programmes, Koranic schools etc. Communities drew on all these sources in diverse ways.

The lesson to be learned is that in order to support initiatives of empowerment it is necessary to think in terms of the three essential elements. The role of outside support should be the creation of the right conditions and resources. Literacy is not difficult if the conditions exist that allow people to acquire it.

Taking Over Responsibility, Autonomy and Education: The Situation of Women

The support needed for women to gain responsibility, autonomy and education is inevitably linked to the economic contribution of women and their place within the economy, politics and the labour market. On a world-wide level, 67 per cent of the working-time is covered by women, Yet women:

- get only 10 per cent of the world revenue;
- make up two-thirds of the world's illiterates;
- own just 1 per cent of the world's property;
- make up 70 per cent of the needy or poor population, i.e. one billion individuals world-wide;
- 65 to 90 per cent of all working women in the industrialised countries work part-time, combining family life with professional life;
- 45 per cent of women who are economically active world-wide occupy the lower paid jobs, aside from democratic work;
- ministerial posts concerning decisions on financial and human resources or development are rarely occupied by women.

There are however several constraints to women's education. In rural areas women are prevented from participation in education or literacy activities on account of their world load. Educational actions do not take into account the cultural contexts of women. In Niger, for example, women have asked for literacy and technical education classes to be held at night because they do not want to be seen going to public places not give the impression of idling away their time. Pedagogical methods are not linked to the needs of women. There is a lack of information and education in the local languages. Poverty of women and rising costs of education mean they cannot always afford access to education. Often they require the agreement of husbands and fathers to participate in education. In spite of policies favouring women's and girls' education, the amount spent on women's education in insignificant.

Yet, in spite of the above economic and educational constraints, women are beginning to see possibilities for their empowerment, Women have become a priority in political discourses. They have started to organise themselves, helped by the current climate of democratisation and decentralisation. Financial institutions are more inclined to lend money to women's association as women have higher credit repayment rates than men. Women take their commitments seriously. They are increasingly taking on the role as head of their families as well as taking over new functions in local development.

In this new context of decentralisation and local development, where women are assuming new functions, the main strategies should be to educate women for autonomy and responsibility for assuming their functions within local institutions: the amount of a woman's workload must be reduced and shared between girls and boys and men and women. Women need to have access to information to keep them abreast of the new developments in all fields. The knowledge and local languages of women must be valued and promoted. Local development activities must help to fight women's poverty.

Strategies for women's responsibilities, autonomy and education must include:

- personal and individual commitment in the sphere of women's education;
- information;
- participation in education programmes and projects;
- partnership: women must form partnerships between themselves, their organisations, and other groups or structures, in order to benefit from different kinds of support—technical, financial or other.

Conclusion

The workshop concluded with the following recommendations for adult literacy and local communities:

- local development programmes learning and taking advantage of other on-going projects;
- training the practitioners to enable them to recognise the problems in development;
- development agencies and educators understanding each other's language;

- creating institutions and structures in the context of initiatives;
- prioritising women;
- placing emphasis on three essential elements of local development: human, financial and institutional capital;
- local languages in administration, information dissemination and education;
- building bridges between formal and non-formal education; and between formal school education and adult learning programmes;
- imparting literacy first in the local and national languages and then in global languages of communications;
- enhancing capacity of state services to take over the role of facilitator, educator, regulator and agent for local investment in a more decentralised system. It is necessary for agents of the state to cooperate with the local communities in order to identify local needs and to satisfy these.

9

Literacy and Learning Strategies

Introduction

There has been a stagnation in learning strategies used in literacy programmes world-wide in recent years. There is needed a huge gap in adult literacy between discourses and learning strategy. Although, ideologically speaking, terms such as "self-esteem", "participation" and "solidarity" have been plentiful in adult literacy programmes, in reality most literacy programmes continue to pursue traditional strategies for disseminating reading and writing skills.

The demand for new strategies and reassessment of the notion of literacy stems from the fact that both governmental and non-governmental adult education programmes have made little impact on improving people's living conditions. In most less developed countries, poverty is increasing.

The workshop on "Literacy and learning strategies" held during the Fifth International Conference on Adult Education, had the important task of looking for new participatory strategies, learning from other methodologies and considering people as the basis of a new educational agenda The panel consisted of Catherine Stercq, Collectif d'Alphabétisation, Belgium; David Archer, Action Aid, UK; and Enrique Pieck, Colegio Mexiquense, Mexico. The chair of the session was Luis Benavides, Centro International de Prospectiva y Altos Estudios, CIPE, Mexico.

New approaches are being developed from field practices in several parts of the world. Pilot projects are being conducted and then spread to different countries through a wide range of grassroots organisations and NGOs. Even government programmes are experimenting with new approaches which are being developed by international agencies. Of course these approaches need to ensure a continuing process of innovation and renewal. This can only be attainment through networks of practitioners and exchange of information.

The workshop highlighted the need for adult basic education to start with the learners' community and environment. Rooted in their culture, learning should aim at forging links with others and broadening inter-communication.

New Convivial Approaches to Literacy

New approaches to adult literacy and empowerment are being developed through field experimentation in many developing countries. The crucial aspect of such programmes are dialogue, ownership and linking adult literacy with other development activities. Dialogue is the centre stage of such approaches. Literacy is a collective task of converting the graphics. This provides structures for dialogue, without constant intervention by the facilitator. The fact that learners construct their own materials means that they take ownership of the issues that come up—which would be impossible to achieve using set primers. Because people construct their own maps, the themes are naturally related to their immediate reality. This leads to immediate local action and a stronger link between literacy programmes and other development activities.

With respect to empowerment such programmes promote: self-realisation; increased ability to analyse; increased ability to solve problems; increased ability to articulate ideas; increased participation in community organisations; formal positions of responsibility in community organisations; community level action to improve local conditions such as constructing grain-stores, diversifying crops, co-operative buying or selling, re-garding access roads and other items of infrastructure, school repairs, water pipes, and action in the environmental or health spheres. Evaluations have shown that such programmes also result in better resource management at an individual and household level. There are marker improvements in gender relations: for example, men taking on domestic work. There is increased health awareness and improvements in education: for example, increased enrolment of children, and many parents opening new schools.

Learner-and community-based approaches involve a literacy process and an empowering process. The literacy gives people practical skills which help in the empowerment process, and the empowerment process in turn creates uses for literacy in people's everyday lives. The approach fuses the two processes through a single, well-structured participatory methodology.

The Importance of Basic Needs and Productive Work Support

The widespread poverty within developing countries calls for learning strategies which prioritise the survival needs of marginalised people.

Traditionally, emphasis has been placed on literacy and basic education as the main objectives within adult literacy. This serves to isolate adult literacy from strategies and methodologies that consider people's needs and daily concerns. This irrelevance of content explains the failure of many educational programmes. Traditional approaches are mostly based on universal educational models geared to stereotypes of the adult population. Many failures could be explained by the fact that official pedagogy bore little relevance to the way people learn.

Against a background of poverty and economic recession, adult learning presents an opportunity to foster social and economic integration, encouraging and strengthening local development. This calls for an integration of productive aspects into adult learning: to go beyond the academic rationale towards the needs of work, production and social and economic inclusion. It is necessary to link adult education to on-going activities and to develop training programmes that respect local knowledge, promote on-the-job-training and relate contexts to people's contexts and cultures. Learner's diversity must be given utmost priority.

It is necessary to understand the pedagogy of the informal sector. Adult literacy strategies should be linked to economic activity and the way people learn: people's own pedagogies, rooted in their experiences. Strategy should relate to the way people tackle their own projects. People's own learning processes should be taken into account in designing strategies, as should native and informal knowledge for meeting survival needs.

Participation is the source of a collective learning process. This entails a fostering of social and economic projects in different sectors: housing, community, shops, workshops and craft production enterprises. The projects support each other by sharing experience and valuable knowledge on which they depend.

To improve learning effectiveness means understanding people's needs. It is necessary to integrate adult learning that provides competencies for economic survival with one that provides social equipment for greater effectiveness at the local level. An integrated approaches is one which links the technical and the social competencies.

Many lessons can be drawn from these observations when considering ways to change institutions so that they respond to people's on-going activities while providing complementary educational and financial support. There is need to respect the individual and the community and encourage a learner-centred strategy.

Conclusion

The participants in the workshops came to the conclusion that it is more important to support individual and community development, and greater economic and political participation of adults, than it is to focus on standardised learning using set primers. It was emphasised that adults are motivated to learn reading and writing once they realise that these are important tools for communication, for expressing their needs and demanding their rights. Active participation in creating adult learning, own texts and graphics has been a significant factor in promoting self-confidence and self-worth—and so laying a foundation for future learning.

The workshop participants suggested four steps towards putting participatory ideology into action:

- decentralising the creation of books and programmes;
- promoting basic learning needs through non-formal strategies;
- recognising that reading and counting are not enough. Adults need functional skills to be self-reliant and productive in local economic development;
- promoting communities' own knowledge and learning traditions.

10

Literacy, Education and Social Development

Introduction

The workshop entitled "Literacy, Education and Social Development" of the Fifth International Conference on Adult Education, held in Hamburg in 1997 challenged the traditional paradigm under which adult literacy is considered primarily as an individual skill and empowering in itself. Rather, literacy needs to be seen as a part of social development. Thus, while advancing uses of literacy, it will be necessary to take into account the dialectics between local culture, societal development and the consolidation of a literature environment.

The panel featured Mamadou Ndoye, Minister of Basic Education, Literacy and National Languages, Senegal; Malini Ghose, NIRANTAR, a centre for women and education, India; Laila Kamal, Community and International Development, Egypt; Georg Elwert, Free University Berlin, Germany; and David Olson, University of Toronto, Canada, Panellists examined the types and uses of literacy in various aspects of social development, showing how the development of literacy depends critically upon its actual and perceived uses in local vernacular contexts as well in national practices and institutions.

The reason why literacy programmes and projects often fail to secure literate competencies is that they rely upon a notion of literacy that is abstracted from social contexts and cultural practices. People feel motivated to acquire literacy in situations where social relations and institutions require the use of reading and writing. In such a context, literate competencies permit individuals and communities to participate in the shaping of their development.

Social development is the capacity of individuals and communities to take upon themselves the direction of their own development. The notion of human resource development becomes central in social development. But there is no causal relationship between education and social development. The old formulation that literacy leads to development is quite different from the new notion that the workshop has tried to promote, namely that literacy is embedded in social practice and has social meanings. Approaching the questions of literacy from this perspective is not to consider education as an independent commodity, but to analyse carefully the literate competencies needed in a specific society and to link education and literacy to the social practices people are involved in. Only by approaching literacy in this manner can adult literacy be seen as integral to the development process.

The Making of Literate Societies

In order to understand the relationship between literacy, education and social development, it is necessary to raise the following questions:

- How do societies become literate? How is literacy, related to the growth of social complexity and the emergence of institutions? What kinds of social practice create a demand for the acquisition of literacy? Under what conditions does literacy become irrelevant?
- What is the relationship between individual learning and societal context? In what way can the acquisition of literacy contribute to social processes like empowerment, economic development, political and legal accountability?
- What is the role of languages, local knowledge and different types of scripts in the making of a literature society?

The New Literacy Paradigm

A new literacy paradigm is emerging out of research and practice in adult literacy. It has been shown that, in order to bring about cultural and social transformation, literacy must be seen as an activity embedded in social and cultural practice. Literacy acquisition is concerned with participation in a literate environment at the individual, local, national and regional levels. It is therefore no longer appropriate to regard illiteracy simply as a deficit or to speak of "eradicating" illiteracy". The acquisition and use of literacy has to be seen as part of a long-term process, in which a community or a society seeks to effect its own cultural and social transformation. Thus there is a need to revise the traditional paradigm which considered literacy as input for development and which tended to see the issue primarily in terms of measurable literacy skills to be attained and the numbers to be made literate.

The new paradigm is based on the assumption that it is possible for even small communities to begin their own process of literacy, making it part of the fabric of their own way of life. Furthermore, this new approach implies the participation of both literate and non-literates in a textual community.

Societal Literacy

Central to the new paradigm is the notion of societal literacy. This means that reading and writing become meaningful social practices when they are backed by social institutions that give legitimacy to written documents. The use of writing and reading has consequences for the way economic relations are formalised. In a literate society, written contracts are legitimised by legal institutions and procedures. Therefore literacy should entail making written laws accessible and transparent so as to promote accountability.

Literate practices in institutional contexts contribute to the evolution of a written language that is structurally different and more complex than oral language. Written language is also an important tool for fostering the rapid circulation of information, enhancing the exchange of ideas and promoting social networking. It also enhances to communication of innovations, technical knowledge and individual and social creativity in general.

Examples of Societal Literacy

A district officer took someone's land for his wife's business. *A protest note was written* and sent to a legal institution. The arbitrary action of the district officer was reversed and he was fined.

Someone took an advance payment and signed a receipt, but did not deliver the commodity. *A letter was sent to a legal authority,* which ordered the man to pay back the due amount.

These two examples of societal literacy show that a simple letter can have a considerable effect. They show that writing does make the difference. Accountability and the effective functioning of a legal state depend upon societal literacy. Societal literacy implies empowerment for those who want to communicate. It could mean, for example, posting a printed information bulletin for peasants in their own language in the local market.

It is not sufficient to organise lectures, ask for more campaigns, more teachers or better pedagogy. All this misses the point about literacy. Only if the demand exists and there are institutions to sustain this demand, do literacy campaigns, and improvements in pedagogies make sense.

It is often assumed that interaction with power structures is only possible through personal contact rather than by means of the written language. Consequently people often resort to bribes or persuade influential relatives and patrons to interact with officials on their behalf. All this has detrimental consequences for enterprise and business. Many people have been inhibited from starting an enterprise because of lack of access to the power structures and institutions when in fact they could have applied in writing.

It is important to recognise the role of institutions that create and reinforce societal literacy. Institutions are needed for developing languages and enhancing them to the status of a literate medium. Institutions consolidate literate languages by promoting their use in all spheres of human activity, by encouraging intellectual exchange and disseminating information about matters and events of social concern.

Societal literacy can be sustained only when institutions of the legal state work without corruption. Institutions reinforce but are also reinforced by societal literacy. There is a continual process of mutual feedback.

To promote these institutions is less costly than investments in physical infrastructure. But they require empowerment and freedom for action. For example, if societal literacy is to flourish there needs to be a free market for books and periodicals.

Literacy is Embedded in Social Practice

The extent to which a community uses literacy as an integral part of life varies greatly—depending on the local, national and the international contexts. In the case of many traditional communities, written documents play a very small part in social organisation or activity. There are also many communities, particularly those linked closely with markets, who need numeracy more than writing. Thus regardless of whether or not communities are predominantly literate, they should be given the opportunity to bring into any literacy situation their own knowledge and their own way of constructing reality. Literacy is more than just reading and writing. There is a mistaken but common belief that being able to read and write in itself is the key to all progress. The ability to participate in politics, for example, does not necessarily require the mastery of reading and writing. Rather it demands being part of a literate community and engaging in a debate with that community.

It may also be a mistake to think that rationality is bound up with writing and reading. Among the ancient Greeks there were few people who could read and write. Their real pride lay in the fact that they could think, argue, debate with each other, and honour rules of procedure which allowed other people to express their points of view. There is therefore a need to rethink the concept of literacy as embedded in social practice.

Reading and writing become a meaningful and important part of the dynamics of a specific community or society which people acquire these competencies and are part of an institutional environment which promotes their use, whether it be for highly personal reasons such as writing letters to friends or in more formal situations, such as when dealing with legal matters.

Literacy work with illiterate communities in India shows that women in these communities need numeracy more than reading and writing skills in order deal with authorities. They have developed skills in order to deal with authorities. They have developed intricate methods of keeping accounts, using embroidery stitches to record relevant information.

Contexts of Literacy Acquisition and Use of Literacy

Literacy provision in the past has been characterised by centralised control and a one-way transmission of skills. In future it must reflect the specific and diverse contexts in which literacy is acquired and used. From the learners point of view, these include:

- what the learner already knows, wants and brings to the learning experience;
- the mother tongue of the learner: a critical, factor, because through it the learner's own identity and knowledge systems are formed;
- the cultural background of the learner, including family culture, local culture, oral traditions and indigenous knowledge;
- the identity of the learner in terms of gender, class, religion and race;
- the social, economic and cultural context of the learner; for example, where women and marginal groups are concerned it is important to recognise that it is not just illiteracy that is keeping women or marginal groups powerless, but a whole range of factors, such as resources, land and uneven land distribution. Literacy needs to be seen in this context.

All of these contextual factors must be taken into account when delivering or designing programmes or working with communities.

One reason why some campaigns have failed is that they have been carried out without proper regard to the language, prior knowledge and learning needs of the individuals and communities involved. Linguistic diversity must be acknowledged by developing literacy programmes in local languages. Research has shown that learning to read and write in the mother tongue facilitates not only the acquisition of literacy but also the learning of a second language.

Acquiring literacy in the mother tongue or in the language of one's community also helps to foster a sense of cultural identity. An added complication is that people in many countries face a trilingual situation; first, the local language, second a more widely spoken language of the country or region, and third a former colonial language such as English or French. As English grows as the global language through the explosion of information and communication technology, pressures to learn it increase, creating both opportunities and dangers for communities whose language is not spoken by a large population.

Sustainable literacy is the maintenance of literate practice. A key factor in this is the provision of adequate published material, from local newspapers to academic books and from poetry and fiction to history and folklore. What is important is that people should continually have the opportunity to read, write, interpret and use textual materials. Sustainable literacy therefore requires support to local, national and regional publication and training networks for the exchange of materials and information. It also depends on the establishment of a political climate and institutional structures accountable to learners and communities. It is also important that there should be an adequate supply of materials in local languages to meet the needs and demands of the readers.

The overall message is that adult literacy is not a commodity to be delivered but something that has to be an organic part of social practice and cultural meanings. Any developmental policy must make this perspective an integral part of its programmes.

11

Literacy Research, Evaluation and Statistics

Introduction

The area of literacy is one domain is the broad field of education where relatively little attention has been given to research, evaluation and statistics. There is now a critical need to build a more effective knowledge base, to facilitate the design, planning and implementation of literacy work.

The issues concerning research, evaluation and statistics in relation to literacy were discussed at a workshop held during UNESCO's 1997 Fifth International Conference on Adult Education (CONFINTEA) in Hamburg. The discussions covered a wide geographical and thematic range. The panel was chaired by Dan Wagner, Director of the International Literacy Institute, University of Philadelphia. The speakers on the panel were: Maki Hayashikawa, UNESCO; D.J. Daswani, Professor of Linguistics, NCERT, India; Sissel Volan, Norwegian Development Agency (NORAD); Scott Murray, Statistics Canada, Ottawa; Claudio de Moura Castro, Division of Social Policy, Inter-American Development Bank, Washington; Ila Goksal, Director of the Mother Child Education Foundation, Istanbul, Turkey.

CONFINTEA attracted a very large number of organisations dedicated to research and action in adult literacy. It is not enough to say that governments do not take or support adult literacy seriously enough. The spadework of providing them with research, evaluation and statistics upon which they can base their policies is a key task if adult education is to reach those it is most intended for.

Stating the Problem

Although there are adult literacy programmes in almost every country of the developing world, there is a serious lack of comprehensive information on their capacity, performance and impact. This has direct consequences for the effectiveness of national policies. Government and official adult education agencies use statistics of adult illiteracy which are often not very dependable and which tend to be out of date and too general.

Evaluation is normally one of the formal requirements for running a programme. Every programme should provide an evaluation report on completion. Very often the commissioning or government agency is interested in obtaining value for money. In this respect, literacy evaluations have tended to be rather limited in their criteria. In addition, each evaluation is based on its own methodology, hypothesis and theory, with the result that evaluation reports seldom lend themselves to comparisons.

With regard to research, there are many universities offering courses in adult learning, from undergraduate to post-graduate and doctoral research programmes. But often there seems to be little interface between the programme and the regular university system. University graduates seldom become involved in the implementation of adult literacy programmes. Consequently, research at the university level is largely academic, is treated as a course requirement, and seldom deals with field level problems that are faced by implementing agencies. While there have been a number of research projects on infrastructure and profiles of learners and teachers, these are sporadic and unconnected with each other.

In view of the inconsistency in the collection, analysis and dissemination of information on literacy, it has been very difficult to demonstrate the efficiency of literacy programmes and the quality of the output. Policy makers and donors agencies have not been getting the data on which to base policies, projects and advocacy.

Analysing Facts

One of the reasons for this lack of data lies in the popular character of adult literacy programmes with their grassroots, bottom-up participatory approach. Well analysed facts to support them have not been there. For example there has been little comprehensive testing of participant achievement of other research that would help to plan and implement programmes elsewhere, or academics to deepen theories of effective adult learning. The situation is further complicated by the fact that in some countries, the private sector has taken over adult literacy, with a strong reliance on media. It is too early for any reliable indicators of success of these efforts.

This situation is amply demonstrated by the three large-scale literacy movements in Brazil. The first cycle of literacy programmes was driven by a peasant social movement. The second cycle came from a military regime. The third cycle is being promoted by employers and their associations.

In the first cycle, the literacy drive was connected with wide mobilisation of peasants. It used a method developed by Paulo Freire to educate poor peasants and was part of the process of creating political awareness. Literacy was expected to help people become aware of their situation, and the idea behind the mobilisation what that, in order to make the population literate, it was necessary to make people conscious of their situation.

The second cycle came during the 70s, when Brazil had a growth rate of 11 per cent but 30 per cent illiteracy. Economists were hired, and a lot of money was spent on creating an extremely well-trained staff of teachers and instructors. But this technocratic approach did not work because it was too short-sighted, and the emphasis was more on showing results rather than producing the right outcome. It failed to consider the real difficulties at hand. There was a lack of visibility of the results of the many large scale literacy programmes.

Since the late 80's, Brazilian firms have become learner and more worried about costs and efficiency. This movement has generated a third cycle of literacy programmes in the form of a spontaneous development inside business and in employers' associations. Although there is no master plan, nor a broad consensus, there appears to be a tacit agreement on the need for more education and the provision of this by employers. This tacit agreement has generated a number of solutions.

These include:

- Workers returning to school with financial support from their employers.
- Associations of employers creating programmes like FIEMG (The Federation of Industries of Minas Gerais) which has made concrete plans to eradicate illiteracy from the State's work force by the year 2000.
- Payment of 35 million dollars by the Federation of Industries of the State of Sao Paulo to a television network to create a televised course to prepare for the equivalent of primary- and secondary-school leaving examinations as well as offering a course on mechanical technology. All lessons take place in factories and offices, and involve workers and managers rather than the traditional classroom teachers and pupils.

Need for a Better Knowledge Base

We need a much wider knowledge base and better research data upon which to base adult literacy programmes. The questions that need to be addressed are:

- Who participates in literacy programmes?
- How do adults learn?
- What knowledge do they bring with them when they came to the programme?
- What is their motivation?
- What is the communicative repertoire of the learner?
- What is their mother tongue?
- What is their second language?
- What are the uses of literacy in society?
- How is literacy retained?

- How much literacy is retained?
- How is literacy diffused?
- What are the challenges in literacy requirement?
- What is the impact of literacy on productivity, quality of life, and on society?

The purpose is to understand the context, grasp the learners' felt needs and to discuss the effectiveness and relevance of programmes by capturing the continuum of literacy abilities that goes beyond the simplistic literacy/illiteracy dichotomy.

Ensuring Quality of Adult Literacy Programmes through Effective Monitoring and Evaluation

Providers of information on literacy can be individual persons and literacy centres/institutions. Data on individual persons can be obtained from population censuses, household surveys, and literacy surveys. The type of data collected through population and household surveys would include data on the illiterate and literate population, educational attainment, school attendance, household and personal characteristics. Household and literacy follow-up surveys could include more detailed questions on perceived relevance and quality of literacy programmes attended, retention, use, spread, improvement of acquired skills and finally outcomes and impacts of literacy.

Data channels for monitoring literacy institutions and programmes are regular surveys or administrative records and reports. Such data focus on the availability, location and timing of adult literacy programmes by type of institution, capacity, participation, level of resource inputs, quality of personnel and facilitators, relevance and impact of the programme and level of achievement of participants through participatory learner assessment.

Literacy information management systems, including practical assessment methodology, will provide information on three levels of programmes and a continuum of literacy abilities. These programmes are:

- Non-formal basic education for out-of-school children and youth.

- Adult basic literacy programmes.
- Continuing education.

In terms of the subsequent analysis of the information, it will be particularly valuable that the following issues be clarified:

- learning achievement in individuals;
- outcomes/impacts on learners' everyday lives;
- programme level efficiency and accountability;
- in-country and international comparisons.

The coming years will witness the development of broader strategies for monitoring literacy, by:

- making coordinated use of different approaches;
- introducing a participatory approach;
- promoting the creation of national directories/databases;
- fostering a culture of information for literacy;
- developing practical literacy assessment methodologies and tools.

To do so, the countries may have to adopt the following measures and policies:

- building in-country monitoring capacities;
- maximum use of existing monitoring channels;
- establishing universal literacy criteria and norms;
- adapting the assessment methodology to specific social and cultural contexts;
- applying the methodology to specific countries;
- mobilising appropriate partners, such as NGOs and community organisations.

Surveys on Literacy Skills

The International Adult Literacy Survey (IALS), based on an initial survey in Canada and a subsequent survey in the United States, and which has now been carried out in many countries, is a good demonstration of how to use the best of education assessment technology to gather data on a broad range of individual literacy skills and to look at basic skills from a continuum or scale perspective, rather than reducing literacy research simply to categories such as *literacy/illiteracy*. The survey has shown that:

- Factors which make reading more or less difficult for adults are common to many languages and cultures.
- The conditions and causes of literacy skills are becoming clearer.
- Such studies offer a normative base, against which all other statistics can be compared.
- They give a coherent framework for thinking about literacy development.
- They inform choices at both the individual and the governmental policy level. Individuals need to make choices about what they want to do with their lives; governments need to make choices about resource allocations.

There are several myths about literacy which the literacy survey has tried to demystify. It is often assumed, for example, that literacy is very high in the industrialised countries. The literacy survey has been able to show that in every country studied in the IALS survey there is a high percentage of adults without the required skills for effectively participating in the society and economy. Low levels of skills limit the social and economic participation and opportunity of adults.

There is the myth that literacy is a product of formal schooling and that initial education gives everybody a standard quantum of literacy competency. Data is now available indicating that this is not true. There are many people who are illiterate despite their formal qualifications. On the other hand, there are a great number of adults who do not have formal qualifications, yet have literacy skills at quite high levels. This indicates that there are other forces in society besides formal education that are responsible for a person's level of literacy. It also raises questions about equity and quality in the educational system and the role of literacy environments, workplace literacy and family literacy.

Information from highly-developed economies shows that literacy skills are to some extent independent of formal qualification: only 30 per cent of literacy can be attributed to formal education and qualifications, while a further 30 per cent is acquired in out-of-school situations. The same is true of the workers who are past the credential stage in our economies.

Literacy has a strong influence on who gets access to adult continuing learning, particularly at the workplace. Literacy skills can thus by a key marginalising force, leaving governments with the problem of what to do with those people who are marginalised in the process.

Literacy is not just a matter of the supply of skills, but also of the demand for skills in the economy. This is important to recognise because it is often held that the workforce is over qualified and does not use the skills that it already has.

Many economies pride themselves on having an equitable system—educationally and economically—with fairly reasonable equality of opportunity. But, contrary to this view, analysis from the survey shows that children and adults from disadvantaged backgrounds who live in provinces with severe social and economic problems perform more poorly on literacy achievement than adults and children from other provinces.

The major problem in the world today is not one of absolute illiteracy but of low literacy skills which are insufficient to meet the demands of a changing economy.

The Importance of Research on Adult Learning and Literacy

A research project conducted in Turkey has been developed into a full-fledged programme of parent and early childhood education, called the Mother-Child-Education programme. It is a multiple-pronged programme, which not only underlines the potential of academic research, but also attempts to create a more literate family environment, for both parent and child. It sets out to assess the socio-economic, socio-emotional and cognitive development of pre-school children and the impact of training given to a random sample of mothers for over two years. There were two components to the mother training projects: (i) A cognitive component, which was designed to foster cognitive development of the child; (ii) A mother support component, which was designed to support the mother in fostering the socio-emotional and personality development of the child.

The cognitive component was designed to create a more literate home environment for mother and child. It was found that the implementation of the cognitive programme for children contributed to significant differences in children's cognitive development and in months' literacy skills.

This programme, implemented in 50 provinces in Turkey, has been extended to include reproductive and family health, aiming not only to upgrade the pre-literacy and numeracy skills of a child, but also aiming to further the literacy of the mother in order to support a more functionally literate society.

Literacy needs to be supported by other institutions in society, the family being one of the most important. People need to be reached in the context of their environment and positions in society. Mothers are being reached and drawn into the programme by telling them: "You can help prepare your children for school, or you can help them to become more successful in school". This is found to be a better approach than saying: "Your skills are not enough for the society—let us try and upgrade them".

The three main aspects highlighted by the study on mother-child literacy are: (i) The importance of research which guided the programme and enabled it to reach a wide range of people; (ii) The importance of multi-purpose programmes in literacy, with an emphasis on adult education rather than on adult literacy alone; (iii) The importance of conducting evaluation at different levels and for different stakeholders.

Donor Agencies and Literacy Programmes

In assessing requests for assistance, donor agencies are interested in research, evaluation and statistics in the planning and implementation of adult literacy programmes. In planning such programmes the following considerations are important:

- Planning needs to be accompanied by systematic research or solid evaluation.
- A closer contact needs to be made between academic research in universities and literacy programmes.

- Official agencies should provide reliable statistics on literacy, emphasising both quantitative and qualitative data.
- It is necessary to take into account the growing role of industry in providing literacy education.
- Improved tools are needed to enhance the knowledge base on literacy. It is not literacy or formal qualifications *per se* that make people literate. It is more a question of providing equitable opportunities for continuous learning.
- Learners need a supportive literate environment for sustainability of literacy skills and for developing themselves into holistic personalities.

Effective action depends on adequate knowledge. The very sustainability of literacy work in an increasingly competitive educational environment will require adult literacy and adult learning to build a better knowledge base on initial education.

12

Literacy in Multilingual/ Intercultural Settings

Introduction

Multilingualism is the norm rather than the exception in the majority of countries today. Language has been a crucial factor in the history of both industrialised and developing countries. It is therefore self-evident that language must play a key role in adult literacy today. Language, literacy and power are closely linked.

One of the major constraints in the implementation of an effective literacy programme is the lack of recognition given to realities of language usage. Almost all multilingual and bilingual countries face this situation. How are international languages to be used to teach literacy in local contexts? Do they simply serve as languages of cultural imperialism? What are the advantages of standardising local languages? Should we be concerned at the disappearance of local languages and cultures?

These and other questions were discussed at a workshop entitled "Literacy in multilingual and inter-cultural settings" by a panel consisting of Enrique Camargo, Bolivia; Gloria Lara Pinto, Honduras; Maurice Tadadjeu, National Research Project for Language Education in Cameroon, (PROPELCA); and Isabella Buagbe, Ministry of Education, Ghana. The chair of the session was Luis de la Torre, Ecuador.

Speakers raised important questions on the issue of literacy in both the mother tongue and in the national languages, in Africa and Latin America.

The CONFINTEA V Agenda for the Future states that "Literacy enables individuals to function effectively in their societies and to fashion and shape individuals. It is a process in which communities effect their own cultural and social transformations in the context of their personal, local and global identities". The workshop made an important plea that local and indigenous knowledge, culture and language need to be integrated with western knowledge into the educational processes, so that adult learning can not only enhance educational capacity but also make learning a joy while respecting peoples' cultural identities.

The Situation

A large proportion of children in developing countries are either completely illiterate or have had only rudimentary instruction for just a few years in their mother tongue, before a second, usually, international or national language is introduced as the medium of instruction. Lack of proficiency in the second language has been shown to be a key reason for high drop-out and repetition rates, as well as poor achievement in primary and secondary schools. This has negative consequences for employment.

The situation for adult literacy is equally complex. Almost all adult education programmes are voluntary, and language choice is often subject to the varied motivations of learners. Some of them are interested in job promotion, where a global language might be an asset, while others are motivated by a desire to write letters to their families, where a local language might be more suitable.

Because of the significant political implications of first and second language policy, many decision-makers have been reluctant to review language policy in the context of literacy work. It goes without saying that issues of politics and power are inclined to usurp the primacy of language and literacy. Several issues are at stake here:

- whether mother tongue literacy should be a precondition for the introduction of a second language in school-based and non-formal setting;
- under what conditions should mother tongue precede second language literacy;

- how the policies regarding the language of instruction affects literacy after schooling.

The Latin American Situation

Most Latin American countries are multicultural and multilingual—implying coexistence of a diversity of languages, cultures, and world views. A basic characteristic of Latin American cultures is their oral tradition. In the past this oral culture with its rules and practices had a place in indigenous communities and societies, until, through conquest and colonisation, the medium of writing was introduced. This led to a tense confrontation and relationship between oral and written traditions. In time, writing became dominant as a new medium of instruction. The transmission of local languages takes place mostly orally, although some religious texts are studied in the local language.

The general attitude today in Latin American countries is that writing is an effective tool for achieving dynamic social and cultural development. But it is also felt that their societies must retain oral knowledge integral to their cultural heritage, and necessary for the survival of indigenous communities. Oral language has been an important factor in ethnic identity and history consciousness, and it is very much evident even today.

The educational situation in Latin America in ridden with problems. In the period between 1945 and 1965 Latin American education systems greatly neglected native culture and languages as governments promoted an active integration policy. The modernisation paradigm held that education was a key prerequisite for modernising and thus for economic growth. Since the idea of modernisation included rapid spread of new technologies and ideas through education and mass media, a common language was considered necessary. This integration through modernisation and the promotion of universal values led to the destruction of language and cultural diversity in Latin America.

Education through a foreign language is one of the main pedagogical and socio-cultural causes for illiteracy. Many school pupils consequently regress into illiteracy because:

- they do not use their literacy skills;
- literacy skills are not useful in their daily life;
- higher value is placed on oral tradition;
- non-formal learning is of poor quality;
- content is not related to the child's world;
- methodologies are not problem-oriented.

This means that illiteracy will not be eradicated unless local languages are developed, to some extent, as languages of literacy.

There is however very little statistical data on mother tongues of illiterates. Nor is there information on the percentage of illiterates among populations obliged to accept instruction in a second or foreign language if they were to attend schools or non-formal courses. In Ecuador in 1990 there were 681,000 illiterates recorded, some 13 per cent of the population, although the actual number of illiterates could be as high as 40 per cent. The percentage of illiteracy or insufficient literacy among indigenous adults is particularly high. In Honduras, indigenous people make up 5 per cent of the population, i.e. 250,000 people. Whereas the literacy figures for the general population is about 48 per cent, it is form 72 to 100 per cent among some indigenous communities.

Although there seems to be a consensus that learning to read and write is most effective in the mother tongue, many Latin American Indian societies are ambivalent in this matter and feel that they should not be denied the chance to learn Spanish to quite a high level. Spanish is exerting increasing influence, particularly among the young. This is coupled with the fact that, for many people, the stigma attached to illiteracy means rejecting the local language. Further, because of the lack of standardisation of local languages, many people find local languages difficult to write.

There is also the problem that indigenous languages are fast becoming obsolete because parents, particularly mothers, do not use the mother tongue with their children anymore. With the neglect of their languages these minority indigenous populations are also losing their cultural identity. Mother tongues provide a link between the first important learning phase (family or intimate learning) in a child's life and the second basic education phase.

Women and children among the Indian populations have the highest incidence of illiteracy. For indigenous women illiteracy and poverty are closely intertwined. Women also lack proficiency in the Spanish language, and are less likely than men to be bilingual. This is an acute problem and, on account of this, a potential for early learning and cultural self-confidence, normally acquired in the family, is being negated or devalued.

The success of children in the basic education phase depends on the mother's competency in the second language. Therefore women, as transmitters of language and culture in society, should be included in adult learning with a strong intercultural and bilingual component. This is crucial for the literacy of future adults.

Since the 1970s cultural identity has become an ever present factor in improving people's life conditions. In Bolivia, the question of inter-culturality and the right to bilingual education is now officially recognised. In Guatemala also the constitution states that literacy should be bilingual. Literacy in the mother tongue is taken seriously and almost everybody learns to read and write in it. Mother tongues strengthen people's capacity to learn other languages. However, it is generally felt that though the mother tongue is very important and should be protected by law, this should not deny the right to choose how far people wish to study in an international language.

Indigenous organisations have played a key role in education reforms in Latin America as well as in bilingual adult education programmes. The participation of local communities has been crucial in the promotion of bilingual education. They have served as experts, strengthening the recognition of local languages.

The "assamblea del pueblo" (Village council), founded in the late 80s in Bolivia, plays a crucial role in the revitalisation of ethnic cultures and languages. It is also established important networks with organisations addressing cultural identity and bilingualism in Latin America. Its major endeavours are:

- promoting the participation of local communities in the design formulation and execution of literacy programmes;

- utilising to the fullest human capacities available in local organisation;
- pressing for constitutional reform to give indigenous people greater power of expression;
- the permanent negotiation of communities with the government and official agencies;
- in particular, elders in the organisation have examined key words in the local language, recognising them for use in the educational process.

The right to associate and participate actively in organisations has been crucial for local organisations in promoting local languages. International organisations and governments should recognise the importance or indigenous organisations and should work directly with them.

Another factor in adult learning programmes in Latin America is the importance give to bilingual post-literacy. Guatemala, for example, sees itself as being in a post-literacy phase, the focus of which is to consolidate literacy skills, to further and sustain literacy. Bilingual post-literacy is recognised by the state as an essential part of adult basic education. Guatemala is promoting literacy in 15 local languages. The Academy of Maya Languages (all 24 languages in Guatemala are of Mayan origin) has the aim of establishing a universal Maya language, by unifying various local languages. This is done by interpreting the meetings between languages.

In Latin America there seems to be a plethora of very interesting debates, ideas and experiences on language and literacy. In the design of programmes a great deal of attention is given to:

- recognising the value of the native language and culture;
- promoting the value of culture in bilingual literacy;
- integrating local languages and cultures into the educational process;
- strengthening and enhancing individual and cultural identities through bilingual literacy.

The African Situation

The downgrading and degradation of indigenous African languages in Africa during the colonial period and through neocolonialism and its ideology has produced a situation where African languages are in grave danger, and extra support for them is needed in the schools.

The low level of literacy in many African countries is closely linked to the poor quality of basic education. Basic education services are not universally available; rural schools are poor in quality; basic education is low in impact and sustainability; basic education is ineffective in imparting knowledge, skills and habits appropriate for full social and economic participation in society; poverty as well as poor transportation to schools, especially in urban areas, hampers participation in basic education; education is through the medium of a foreign language.

Governments in many African countries are promoting the development of indigenous languages in both formal or non-formal literacy programmes. This, is in Ghana, is seen as fundamental for learning other languages. Local languages are used for teaching from pre-school up to the third year. Only in the fourth year is the shift made to English. This is often a problem for pupils unable to understand English, as well as for teachers forced to use local language to explain the new English terms. At the senior secondary level, pupils choose from 11 local languages, which are being encouraged at the teacher training level, the tertiary level and the literacy level, as well as by radio. Only seven of the 60 local languages are used in radio programmes. The reason given for official recognition of only 11 out of 60 local languages is a lack of learning materials for each of these languages, and the lack of trained teachers of facilitators to teach these various languages.

In the attempt to foster local languages, governments have established special university departments to study indigenous local languages and to train teachers in them. However, it is not enough to teach trainers the language, they should know the social context, literacy theory and the culture.

The government philosophy is to support literacy in the mother tongue, the assumption being that literacy skills can best be learned that way. For most Ghanaians, the mother tongue is the most effective channel through which to relate to their environment.

Some Aspects of the Ghanaian Functional Literacy Programme

The government of Ghana piloted a functional literacy programme in 1987 with the support of the World Bank, DFID and the NORAD, Ghana is a multilingual state with approximately 18.3 million inhabitants using over 60 different languages. English, the official language, is mastered by only a few. Many of the local languages have never previously been written. The literacy programme was conducted on a nation-wide basis in 1991. Some aspects of this programme are as follows:

- About 80 per cent of the learners are under the age of 45;
- 30 per cent of them are below 15 years;
- The literacy classes are being held in 15 Ghanaian languages, spoken by 95 per cent of the population;
- 91 per cent of the learners enrolled in 1995 cover 8 of these 15 languages, and a meagre 9 per cent cover the remaining seven. This makes the unit cost in the minor languages higher than in the major languages;
- Instructions pivot around a literacy primer which contains 28 themes geared to the relevant need of the target group;
- Language diversity is greater in bigger towns than in smaller towns;
- Because of migration, it has been difficult to find enough teachers for the northern languages in the south, and vice versa;
- The choice of the language often depends on emotional links and individual ambitions;
- Very often learners refuse to learn a language because of local conflicts;

- Since English is the official languages, there is often a very high demand to have literacy classes in English. Currently, 20 classes are held in English.

The pedagogical and organisational burden for implementing adult literacy programmes in 15 languages is massive. It exceeds the state financial allocation to basic education of adults. However, policy guidelines as to whether literacy in Ghanaian languages is to be seen as end product or intermediate step to literacy in English, are still not clearly defined. If literacy in the local languages is to be an end product, then a literate environment for these languages must be established and developed.

In the discussion about literacy programmes for adults it needs to be clear whether the object is to transfer technical skills—how to encode and decode the sign/sound relationship—or whether it is to be address deeper notions of self, of identity and the nature of knowledge. Adult literacy programmes should be clear about the cultural and ideological implications of transmitting literacy practices from one cultural group to another.

A major problem is that indigenous people are often forced to learn other languages for the simple reason that their own languages were never previously written. As a result many indigenous people are familiar with other local languages as their second mother tongue even before they start formal schooling.

In many, African countries, if the education system is to meet the demands of the changing economy, then there is no alternative route to adult literacy than through bilingual education.

Cameroon Literacy Education and Development Project (CLED)

A new approach to adult literacy was initiated in Cameroon in 1995, within the institutional framework of the National Association of Cameroon Language Committee. This institution includes a centre for applied linguistics, providing expertise in multilingual education and literacy, and is part of the effort of finding new ways of making Cameroon society literate.

> Cameroon is the most multilingual country in Africa, with a population of 134 million people and 250 languages. The National Research Project for Language Education has developed a model for teaching a mother tongue plus a first and second official language. 12 languages are being taught in the school system.
>
> In 1992 this knowledge was applied to the adult literacy programmes, giving birth to the Cameroon Literacy Education and Development Project (CLED) in 1995. Under this project 40 languages are being taught. The philosophy behind this approach is to put basic human needs before economic growth, giving communities a greater opportunity to develop their own language. Two elements have contributed to the success of the Cameroon literacy programme. The first is the grouping of village communities into municipalities for coordinating activities, including literacy programmes. This is the smallest governmental structure, not exceeding 10,000 people. The second is the establishment of the African economic community embodied in the Treaty of Aboudja, June 3, 1991 and effective from May 12, 1994. This treaty provides formulae to integrate all sectors, including quality education in African within 34 years.

Compared to the prevalent approach to adult literacy, the new elements in the CLED model include:

- multilingualism;
- the central role of local languages and local language committees;
- bridging mother tongue literacy and national language;
- linking adult literacy and local development projects.

Following this model, a literacy programme is normally:

- bilingual in a mother tongue plus English or French;

- the first official language is preceded by literacy in the mother tongue;
- those who are already literate in French or in English get involved in literacy in the mother tongues;
- trilingual literacy is considered to be the ideal.

This new approach is a long term project which is mobilising forty other language committees through a variety of nationally coordinated activities. These include planning, training, materials development, implementation, evaluation and partnership development with governmental and non-governmental organisations.

Language and Adult Literacy Policy

Language and literacy policy in many developing countries follows a model in which literacy in the mother tongue is seen as a bridge to learning a second language. However, even at the technical level, the decoding skills of mother tongue literacy do not transfer straight-forwardly to a second language. The situation becomes more complex when social meaning and cultural notions and uses of literacy are transferred from mother tongue to say, English literacy.

The policy of maintaining the mother tongue may well be important for political and cultural reasons. But this should involve mother tongue literacy in its own right rather than simply as a channel to second language literacy.

Policy-makers need to be clear that diversity is a vital part of globalisation. Diversity is the social reality. Dealing with this diversity will demand difficult policy choices.

In a rapidly changing world, values and perceptions of language also change. In a period of revolutionary change resisting or unlearning a second language in favour of the mother tongue may take high priority. On the other hand, in a period of rapid economic globalisation, communication in the broader global market, and accessing information sources crucial to that market, require global languages of communication; of these English appears to be establishing itself as the leader. Economic security depends upon such languages for practical communication, say, tourism, soliciting foreign investors or donors and acquisition of commercial information. By being restricted to their mother tongue, adults are either excluded from these important areas or depend on expensive translation and interpreting services.

Adult education in the mother tongue thus must be linked with at least one global language of communication. If thus is already provided in primary schools, then it should becomes an essential learning objective of any emancipatory adult learning system.

The didactics and methodology of imparting language skills in a global language of communication have to address the following issues:

- they must be directed towards the very learners who will use language skills;
- the learners should immediately experience the applicability of the newly acquired language skills;
- the development of simple language units requires cooperation in international research. This must analyse the respective learning requirements and environments as well as the uses for the languages;
- new didactics and methods have to be developed that give equal consideration to everyday use of the language of communication and learning environments outside the school system;
- both old and new media should be deployed. Research must address the difference between oral and written communication, their different skills and learning techniques;
- new approaches should be developed—such as workshops, conversation groups and specialist publications—for imparting language skills.

Follow-up

Follow-up to the workshop will include meetings and discussions on how experiments in introducing local languages into adult literacy processes have been conducted, their successes and failures, the performance parameters and reasons for success of failure, including:

- degrees of acceptance among the target population;
- methodologies employed;
- the issue of language status;
- procedures and criteria for choice;
- problems engendered by such choices;
- where choices are arbitrary, how can they be rationalised?
- what activities need to be carried out to further this?
- how can language management become a reality?
- what is the future of the relationships between local and foreign languages, when the latter are official?
- if the methodology led to failure, how can it be a "state of the art"?
- a summary, being a thorough examination of the current situation, with the aim of improving it.

What will be at issue is no longer the relevance of using local languages, but the ways in which they are used in adult education, and thus to promote a literate environment in those local languages. Following on these issues it will be necessary to revise the various methodologies and lobby the decision-makers.

If the development of bilingual or multilingual literacy programmes, the participation of target groups, their interests and expectations must be taken into account right from the planning stage through to their final implementation.

13

Literacy and Technology

Introduction

Many changes are now taking place throughout the world and they are of enormous concern and relevance to adult learning. Adults are under pressure to develop and utilise new knowledge frameworks, skills and value systems. It is time for literacy provides to have the courage to experiment, to try out new alternatives and renew the assault on illiteracy. Innovations in technology can improve literacy programmes and accelerate the spread of literacy. This forges an inevitable link between the use of technology and literacy.

This chapter presents results of a panel discussion on "Literacy and Technology", held during the CONFINTEA V (Hamburg, 14-18 July, 1997). The term technology here embraces educational technologies such as the Internet, TV, interactive video and radio. The aim of the panel discussion was to explore the relationship between literacy and technology, and the potential role of technology as a tool in literacy provision. The important question was not whether, but how technology can adapt to changing demands.

The panel was chaired by Jan Visser, UNESCO LWF, Learning Without Frontiers (LWF), UNESCO, France. Mohamed Maamouri, International Literacy Institute (ILI), Tunisia, served as discussant. The remaining panel members were: Alan Tuckett, the National Institute of Adult Continuing Education, England and Wales, (NIACE), UK Minda Sutaria (INNOTECH, Philippines) Shigeru

Aoyagi, Asia Pacific Cultural Centre (ACCU) UNESCO, Japan, Sibiri Tapsoba (IDRC, Senegal), and Christopher Hopey, National Centre on Adult Literacy, USA.

An important conclusion was that technological innovation, the costs of technology and the introduction of technology into literacy teaching are not the main problems. The real concern is how to ensure that literacy providers have the capacity and political will to apply the technology appropriately.

Technology, a Tool for Improving Literacy Programmes

Today's world is moving towards a more open and global society. In order to deal with its changing demands, people need to learn how to cope with change and at the same time to interact constructively with it and retain control of the processes involved. Alternative strategies need to be identified to ensure greater learning effectiveness and meet the literacy needs of masses of people in a timely and economical manner.

Technology is a useful tool to improve to quality and the efficiency of literacy provision. It helps create learning environments ideally suited to the needs and interests of previously unreached populations and offers new learning opportunities. It stimulates learners to be more creative and innovative. In fact, it revolutionises the way we handle information-with the focus moving from teaching to self-directed learning, from learning as a one-time event to a lifelong learning process.

Technology is introducing radical changes, with non-formal and informal education assuming an important place in addition to formal education. Non-formal education is already improving because of the advantages of technology. It has proved to be effective in reaching out to vast unreached school-age populations. In fact, the distinction between those categories is becoming increasingly irrelevant.

Technology is not an end in itself nor an answer to all educational problems. It is a tool to improve literacy programmes, raise awareness about the literacy problems and reach a vast number of unreached illiterates. Technology deals not only with textual literacy, but also with visual literacy.

Adopting technology demands also a process of selection and decision-making regarding which technology is appropriate, by and for whom it is to be used, and for what kind of communication and content. The process is itself useful because it helps to crystallise ideas, create visions, and motivate greater numbers to pursue literacy through technology. It encourages participation.

Technology does not Operate in a Vacuum

It is important to view technology in the wider political, social and economic context, rather than merely defining it in terms of hardware and software packages. By considering all of the interrelated components, technology can create learning environments suited to the needs of the learners and be made highly relevant to literacy programmes.

Technology offers the possibility of quality education for all in less time than required by traditional strategies provided that it deployment is well thought out planned and subject to continuing evaluation and renewal.

The following are some of the principles in planning the integration of technology into literacy programmes:

- Depart from existing strategies and structures. This might require using a combination of old and new technologies.
- Focus on affordability of initial investment in setting up the system.
- Include a training programme in the use of technology. This often requires the largest investment, yet it is most crucial to successful implementation of technology.
- Include issues such as:
  - — commitment to a long-term plan for maintenance and support;
  - — commitment to periodically upgrading the system;
- Be flexible about time schedules. There should be no definite deadline for introducing technology. It is more important to seek the best solution.

In this context, it is important to think about the possible marginalisation of people, and the creation of new zones of power depending on the advantages being created for some through technology. For technology to play its full role it should be accessible to those who have been deprived of it in the past. If all societies in all their diversity are to be motivated and persuaded that reading and communication matters really, then their voices must all be heard. Technology should be for people's empowerment.

Types of Technology

Different types of technology can be used to promote literacy, either independently or in combination. The main selection criteria are the appropriateness and affordability of the technology.

TV and radio are important sources for life long and life-wide learning. Huge numbers of non-literate or marginally literate individuals, for whom formal education has little practical applicability, with little or no reading material in their homes, have regular access to radio and often TV as well. The educational uses of television and radio include:

- generating awareness of the literacy problem
- developing consumer demand for learning
- retaining learners in a programme
- reaching a large number of individuals

National broadcasters are also involved in educational broadcasting as well as specific educational initiative. Positive feedback on high quality educational broadcasting has shown that people for whom the education system has failed do not trust educators as much as they trust broadcasters. Educational broadcasting often has a motivational function, rather than an instructional function.

Experience with the use of computers and other technologies, such as interactive video, suggest that they can contribute to the development of thinking skills and make instruction more individual. They also provide ways to collect and evaluate information efficiently as well as help learners to communicate what they think and feel.

The Internet is another tool that can be used in improving literacy programmes. Through it adults can be provided with higher quality materials and access to information in homes, workplaces and public libraries. It also provides adults with greater choices which is the key to motivation, retention and enriched learning experience. Using the Internet in literacy promotion means learning faster what is happening around the world and having access to almost unlimited resources for the sharing of professional ideas and problem-solving.

Technologies based on Internet do not need to be expensive. Many people in developing countries, as in industrialised countries, already have the technology, but they lack extra phone lines or faster modems to allow effective and extended networks. In fact, the problem of introducing technology in literacy programmes lies not so much in its cost or the rate of innovation, but rather in the human factors of reinforcing human competence and political will.

Does Technology Increase Inequity?

Technology often raises the rear of inequity. There are also fears that technology may be a new form of colonisation, resulting in reducing diversity. The use of technology can widen the gap between those who have access and those who do not. The dilemma is that introducing new technologies requires an initial level of technological competence. The crucial question is: who will be the user? Will it be an experienced user, or a learner who was deprived of technology in the past? Or should technology-based literacy programmes initially target professional educators and policy makers? Government and non-governmental agencies should be aware of this problem and must address the issues of who will be the users and who will be controlling, constructing and policing the technology.

To address the issue of inequity is a need for:

- trust, political will and devotion to the people, if the gap is not to widen;
- respect for diversity of language and culture;

- promotion of technology for two-way communication. Information should flow from top to bottom and visa versa, as well as horizontally;
- reliable information on beneficiaries in order to identity clearly how to disseminate information and to whom, who developing different strategies for different contexts. This information may include literacy materials, statistics, relevant organisations, curricula, literacy, publications, and a literacy glossary.

In the short term, it may be true that technology can widen the gap between those with access and those without it, but in the long term, it is worth remembering that radio and television were once instruments of the rich. It may perhaps be wise to take a time horizon into account when talking about these fears.

Summary of Existing Experiences

Below are some of the conclusions from the panel discussion on "Literacy and Technology" during CONFINTEA V:

- Technology has transformed many literacy programmes, by providing access to information especially in areas of public policy, and by advocating rights of adults and learners. It has made a big difference to the level of funding and resources that flow into literacy.
- Technology encourages adult learners to be much more creative and imaginative. It offers new learning opportunities for adults, such as instruction online, video, audio and other tools.
- Technology provides adults with greater choice which is the key to motivation, retention and enriching learning experience. New technologies also provide new places to learn. Through the Internet and other new technologies adults can have access to higher quality material and more learning opportunities from homes, workplaces and public libraries. This is turn extends resources from local literacy programmes into those places.
- Technology does not need to be expensive. The crucial point is to make the optimal use of time, energy and staff.

- Through technology such as the Internet, teachers themselves become adult learners. They learn how to use the computer, how to integrate in into the curriculum, how to organise the resources, how to be creative and imaginative.
- Teachers training in technology use is absolutely essential for the successful integration of technology into literacy programmes.
- Interlinking technology and literacy makes sense when it deals with technology not only as a vehicle, but also as an important content area for the promotion of adult education.
- The real issue behind literacy and technology is about adult educators taking a lead in the field of education and providing new ways of learning, rather than waiting for others to tell them what to do and how to do it.

Conclusion

New technologies are not necessarily the whole answer to the problem of delivering literacy programmes. There is room for both old and new technologies. Technology must be appropriate and should help people to learn as quickly, as economically and as effectively as possible. Technology properly used, i.e. in a way appropriate to the communities that learn through them, can facilitate the learning of new higher level skills needed for a world which is becoming increasingly global and which is therefore more and more in need of local empowerment. Technology should be well thought out and planned for that context. There should be a continuing evaluation and revision process to promote the best mix of technologies. It is no longer cost-effective to ignore technology. In particularly, adult education, the least well funded area of education, just cannot afford not to use the technological opportunities that exist.

14

Literacy for Tomorrow

Introduction

A world-wide debate on literacy has been taking place for almost half a century. This debate covers many questions and issues. The very definition of literacy involves a number of conflicting interpretations. There are questions about ownership and gender perspective. There are inter-related operational issues. There is the problem of balancing demand and provision. There are different learning styles to be taken into account. And there are questions of the social uses of literacy and the choice of language. The creation of conducive environment, what is sometimes called the ecology of learning, is also of crucial importance. The overriding question is now to promote literacy on a large scale and how to create literate societies.

These issues were debated and discussed at the workshop "Literacy for tomorrow" held at the Fifth International Conference on Adult Education (CONFINTEA V), in Hamburg in 1997. Agneta Lind, Swedish Development Agency (SIDA) chaired the panel discussions, which featured: Rosa Maria Torres, Kellog Foundation, Latin America; James Page, Loteracy Secretariat, Canada; James Kanyesigye, ACTIONAID REFLECT, Uganda; and Denzil Saldhana, National Literacy Mission, India. Various themes were dealt with in the workshop: analysis of past trends in adult literacy in developing countries; the link between and adult and child literacy; implementing large-scale literacy programmes; literacy and the empowerment of learners; and the rising requirements of literacy. Each theme was introduced by one of the panel and commented on by two other speakers.

Large-scale Adult Literacy

A review of past trends in adult literacy in developing countries shows that, from the point of view of achieving large-scale literacy results, the following factors have been crucial:

- the state as the prime mover, but not the sole actor;
- political will or national commitment;
- a favourable development context;
- continuous mobilisation activities;
- a broad conception of literacy;
- a broad collaborative involvement;
- central co-ordination of all major stakeholders and actors;
- post-literacy and other follow-up efforts, such as the development of literate environments;
- a dual strategy, combining universal primary education and adult literacy.

Other key issues needing careful planning and consideration in each context were:

- timing and duration of instruction;
- the choice of language of literacy instruction;
- mobilisation and support at local level;
- motivation and training of teachers, including in-service training and a network of pedagogical and organisational support services;
- a curriculum adapted to a realistic learning process, avoiding too many themes or topics;
- methods within the reach of the teachers;
- treating adult learners with respect and patience;
- the allocation of sufficient resources to minimise problems such as irregular attendance, drop-out among teachers and learners, relapse into illiteracy etc.

A number of arguments have been made against large-scale adult literacy campaigns by NGOs and international agencies. One argument is that literacy should be directly linked with income-generation, other development activities or practical skill training. It has also been argued that literacy is often an imposition of the modern world which damages traditional culture. A further objection is that centrally designed programmes and materials are inefficient and irrelevant.

Nevertheless a few exceptional cases of well-resourced and planned large-scale national adult literacy initiatives have taken place, notably in Equador, India, Namibia, Ghana, Egypt, Eritrea. In all cases, the state has been the prime mover, but with the organised involvement and collaboration of multiple partners. Some lessons from these experiences are:

- Literacy campaigns are quite possible to organise without departing radically from the formal structures. In India and Ecuador the formal education sector was the major partner, contributing volunteers from among teachers and students, and back-up from local education committees and central administration. The impact was reciprocal and revitalising and boosted the formal system of education for children.
- In Namibia, literacy teachers have had to be paid, trained and guided through regular in-service support. Follow-up stages needed to be prepared from the beginning. A second mother tongue stage was followed by a basic English stage. Systematic and continuous monitoring and evaluation was built-in.
- The Ecuador campaign showed that human rights was highly relevant overriding theme and motivating factor.
- The experiences of both Namibia and India show very large internal regional differences in motivation, participation and results. There were better results in rural regions with a history of social and political activism, than in urban areas and deprived rural areas without such a history.

The Namibian Literacy Programme (NLP)

The majority of participants are women, often about 35. More men than women drop out. A neglected gender issue is the need to motivate illiterate men, who for reasons of status are often reluctant to join literacy classes. The individual empowering impact of participation in adult literacy classes has been strongly manifested and well documented. In the programme, the powerful inter-active links between literacy for adults and for children have been highlighted and recognised as a critical issue. It was found that external funding was crucial to begin with but internal resource mobilisation and state budget allocations are necessary for the sustainability of a large-scale adult literacy programme such as this one.

It can be easily said that the features disclosed by the analysis of current innovative and successful literacy programmes are recurrent in most of them and will prevail in the next century. The making of literate societies is more complex and requires a conjunctions of different societal and institutional interventions.

Learner and Community-based Approaches

The view supported by the World Bank that the state should limit its services to formal education is still having an impact on adult literacy provision. NGOs and civil society are thus coming to the forefront on account of their capacity to adapt to local circumstances and initiate decentralised programmes. Although adult literacy has not been very high on the agenda of most NGOs in the past, NGO programmes in the field of adult literacy are increasingly filling the void created by large-scale state programmes. A few of these NGO programmes have been well documented. The example of REFLECT in Uganda is an illustration of the current trend.

REFLECT (*Regenerated Freirean Literacy through Empowering Community Techniques*) was piloted in Uganda, Bangladesh and El Salvador from 1993 to 1996 by ACTIONAID, and funded by DFID

(Britain's Department for International Development, formerly ODA) and the World Bank.

In October 1993, a two year action research project aimed at developing a new approach to adult literacy was started. The new method was to draw on the visualisation techniques developed by practitioners of Participatory Rural Appraisal (PRA) who established that non-literate communities can construct elaborate local maps, calendars and matrices. In other words, then can construct their own learning materials.

It was in the field, in Bundibugyo, Uganda, that the REFLECT literacy method began to take shape. The pilot project situated 400 km from Kampala, the capital city, was a long-term integrated rural development programme. Physical isolation is one of the most striking characteristics of the district, which is divided into Ntoroko and Bwamba countries. The literacy rate in Uganda is officially 55 per cent. The three main language groups are Bantu, Nilotic and Central Sudanic. The official languages are Ugandan, and English.

The REFLECT Approach and Impact

Introducing the new literacy programmes involved the need for an interactive, practical and participatory literacy methodology to empower people to take control of their own development. In designing the manuals, reading, writing and numeracy work were woven around maps and matrices dealing with key themes such as gender inequity, isolation, prevention of illness, agriculture, savings and credit. The language used was the main local language, and one most widely demanded by the learners—Lubwisi, a previously unwritten languages. However, the project them also felt that the learners in each circle should retain the final choice over language and they might want to chose other local languages. A manual was produced in the main local language, with an index of words in the two other local languages—Lukonjo and Rutoro. Facilitators had to transfer graphics from ground to paper. Facilitators' initial training consisted of experience in participatory rural appraisal techniques, followed by practice with the units. Groups of facilitators exchanged experiences. Support from ACTIONAID consisted of a manual, a set of cards with visual images, a blackboard and some large pieces of manila paper for each facilitator. Learners received an exercise book and a pencil. Reading materials have also been provided.

As regards the learning outcomes, in all the sample classes visited, evaluators looked carefully at the maps and calendars drawn from each unit and asked learners to interpret their work. Learners were able to interpret the graphics sequentially and with clarity. They could look objectively at the advantages and disadvantages of specific aspects of their environment, and represent these in a visual code. Before taking any actions, a collective view or decision was made. The people could read and write using annotations to the graphics and thus generate their own form of language. In the discussion, they were able to use the graphics to illustrate particular points, irrespective of their level of literacy. They could mark months in a calendar and count off different categories of people in a household. It was found that the participants showed more interest in graphic construction and discussion than in literacy and numeracy skills. However, the average learner after one year can read a paragraph aloud and understand it, write a letter on a familiar topic such as a request for a loan, and calculate.

> As regards the issue of creating a literate environment, surveys of learner-and community-based approaches have shown that people were creatively using their skills to read the Bible as well as lables, signs, directions and instructions, often in other languages. However, considering that the language of literacy was not previously written, the main reading activities were in the literacy class itself. The future provision of reading materials presents a serious challenge.

If literacy skills are to be consolidated into literate habits in local communities, much depends on the creation of a literate environment. The use of local notice boards can help in this regard. Notices of meetings and other events can be posted. People, should be encouraged to write letters for both personal and official purposes, to participate in the preparation of local project proposals and to writing down oral histories. Organisations working in the field should print the local histories written by learners in a newsletter, translate texts on health, agriculture, politics and law into local languages. Maintaining the momentum and the demand for literacy will depend on people's attitudes towards literacy and how they define it. Most significantly it also depends on pride in the language of literacy. It is not only literacy, but the local language, previously unwritten, which needs to be promoted. Government agencies need to start to recognise local languages and accept their use in the first three years of primary schools.

With regard to empowerment, literacy learners have gained in self confidence and in the respect that they command from others. They have acquired new knowledge and skills in problem-solving which serve them in their daily lives. They have strengthened their skills in planning and projection, thus contributing to more effective management of scarce local resources. Discussions in literacy circles have led directly to collective action at community level. There are also indications of a change in gender roles in cases where circles have addressed health issues. The wider impact on children's education is particularly notable in Uganda.

Methodology must learn from the mistakes and successes of the pilot projects and should in future lead to more successful future projects. Methodology needs to be adapted according to the local situation. The process should be seen as more important than the product and the process of literacy is something that primarily concerns the community. It is the community, not the teacher, who produces the maps and matrices.

A key point is the need for adequately educated facilitators. A basic literacy level is necessary for the facilitators to be able to use the innovative approach effectively, to read the manual, prepare lessons and benefit fully from the training. Every effort should be made to simplify the manuals and cards. Regular contact between facilitators is essential in order for them to review their experiences. The facilitators must determine the agenda of their own training themselves. There is a need to have a mix and a balance in the focus of themes, so that everyone covers a range of core themes.

Intergenerational Approaches to Literacy

The link between adult and child has been rather weak. Adult literacy and child literacy have developed as specific and complementary fields. In fact two quite different specialisations have been shaped around initial basic education and adult lifelong learning.

Important though non-formal programmes are, the formal education system is the most important and widespread means of initial education. Learning to read and write is central to future success or failure. Therefore, ensuring the school's capacity for effective literacy teaching and learning must be a priority. An important way of improving the literacy of children is through the involvement of parents. It is parents who decide whether children should go to school and it is they who provide the support and the appropriate environment needed to learn. Finally, parents are best able to demand quality and accountability from the school.

Thus the effort to raise the quality of school education, especially primary education, can only be made in conjunction with a corresponding effort in the area of adult basic education. This implies that adult educators must consider children's education and formal schooling as an integral part of their work.

They must recognise that dealing with illiteracy means dealing not only with the remedial side of the problem, but also, most importantly, with its prevention.

According this two-track approach to literacy means accepting that the term literacy applies to both children and adults and includes both school and out-of-school education. This implies building bridges between the two rather than increasing the gap between them.

While literacy for children through formal primary education, and to some extent through non-formal primary education, was boosted by the 1990 Education for All (EFA) conference in Jomtien, Thailand, the same cannot be said for adult literacy programmes. The conference failed to acknowledge that adult basic education is a key factor in improving the quality of formal primary school education. In addition, in the context of economic crisis, growing national debt, structural adjustment programmes and deteriorating social services, there is a danger that governments may become even less interested in adult literacy than before. In the context of the educational policies of the World Bank adult literacy has been more or less removed from the area of state responsibility, the latter concentrating mainly on formal school education. All this has had a detrimental effect on efforts to link adult and child literacy.

Levels of Literacy

Although the need for literacy teaching is greater in the developing countries, the issue is also concerned in the industrialised countries. In many industrialised countries, literacy has long been a key element in the development of education and training policies. It is becoming increasingly important in the development of policies relating to youth, language, employment, rural development, social development, administration of justice, crime prevention and health.

There is an increasing appreciation of the interconnection between literacy and adult learning on the one hand, and the health and well-being of individuals and society on the other. Governments promote the positive benefits of literacy rather than the negative consequences of illiteracy. The reason for doing this is to "de-stigmatise" the issue in order to be able to reach out successfully to the adults who have less than adequate literacy skills, to motivate them and encourage them to get involved in literacy and learning. The question asked is not: "Can you read to write," but: "How well can you read or write?" Literacy is defined as the ability to understand and to use different types of information in life's daily activities at work and in the community.

This approach is backed up by a substantial amount of research. The International Literacy Survey (IALS), led by Statistics Canada in co-operation with the UNESCO Institute for Education and the OECD, assessed three forms of literacy:

1. prose literacy, which means understanding different kinds of text, such as editorial pieces, news stories and poems;
2. document literacy, which tests the respondent's ability to locate and use information from documents such as time tables;
3. quantitative literacy, involving simple calculation and comprehension of numbers embedded in texts.

Levels of Literacy Skills in Canada

To take Canada as a fairly typical example of a country covered by the International Literacy Survey, people at level one have great difficulty in reading, have few basic skills, available to interpret and work with texts, and are generally not aware that they have a problem. Some 22 per cent of adult Canadians are at level one.

Those at level two have less limited skills. They can read, but not very well and can deal only with material that is very simple and clearly laid out. They often do not recognise that they have limitations. About 26 per cent of adult Canadian are at this level.

People at level read competently, but they might have problems with more complex tasks. Level three is considered by literacy specialists to be the minimum desired level and represents 32 per cent of Canadian adults. Levels four and five are the highest on the scale. These are people with a very high level of literacy skills and make up 20 to 25 per cent of the Canadian adult population.

This survey shows that over 40 per cent of Canadian adults do not have the required literacy level 3 to participate fully in daily activities. As citizens they risk being marginalised and relegated to the fringes of social and cultural life. As workers they have difficulty in being part of the new economy.

Literacy should be an integral part of a person's life experience. It should be both lifelong and "lifewide", that is to say, it should be present in all aspects of all—the home, the community and the workplace.

Literacy is important for different reasons depending on the stage of life. For pre-school children, literacy is a critical formative skill, and holds they key to vocabulary building. For young people in school and colleges, literacy is important for development skills; higher-level literacy is required for the acquisition of analytical skills. For mature adults, literacy is important for a variety of life skills and workplace skills. In retirement, literacy is also important. Seniors require levels of literacy to handle the complex demands of life with dignity, assurance and self-reliance.

The Literacy of Tomorrow

The literacy of tomorrow should not be a static condition. The level of literacy required to function in everyday life is constantly shifting upward. Furthermore, basic skills like learning to write and read require constant use in order to be maintained.

The key policy question is how to help all citizens to develop, maintain and continuously advance their literacy skills in order to live and learn in a knowledge-based and information-intensive society. The challenge is to enable all citizens to have lifelong access to literacy and learning-rich environments and meeting this challenge successfully will require that the word "remedial" be removed from literacy vocabulary. Such a term would have little meaning in a culture and an environment that allowed people to progress and learn throughout life. A shift is needed from the industrial age paradigm of learning as an activity which ends on the completion of school or college and which is separated from work, family and community. There is also a need for coordination between hitherto, separate fields of education. Pre-school learning, literacy practice, the formal educational system and adult learning must become components of a comprehensive and integrative learning system. Progress towards a more literate nation should be made through a collaborative strategy involving individuals, communities, social and cultural agencies, employers and governments at all levels.

This notion of convergence means sharing research and policy agenda, and enhancing the communication between the academic and the practitioner. It also means the recognition of non-formal and informal learning, in addition to formal education.

The workshop issued the following conclusions and recommendations:

- Literacy for tomorrow has to build upon the experience of the past half country.
- A commitment must be made to literacy as a human right.
- The discourse of the market should not be allowed to undermine the concept of literacy as a social good.
- Appropriate resource allocations must be made for adult literacy promotion in all societies without expectation of merely economic returns. Cultural and political consequences must be taken into account as well.
- Sustainable mass mobilisation will depend on local initiatives. This must be taken into account in the development of methodologies.
- Political leaders and social activists must actively undertake mobilisation efforts on a regular basis and not expect such efforts to arise spontaneously.
- Institutional arrangements for the delivery of literacy and adult learning must receive due attention and should be established from the global to the local level.

- It should be ensured that relevant institutions at various levels are participatory, allowing all parties involved to make their voices heard and have their interests taken into account.
- An intergenerational approach should be adopted, linking child and adult literacy, and built on organic relations much more strongly.
- In the crucial field of methodologies, there is a very disturbing standardisation. There is need to have a serious methodological debate and draw on best practices from a wide range of programmes. It should be recognised that methodology *per se* is not the whole answer. Teachers and adult educators must understand the principles of learning before developing methodologies.
- Voluntary as well as salaried agents should be harnessed in the promotion of literacy work, depending upon the social and economic context.
- Due effort should be made to enable new literates to use their newly-acquired literacy skills in their life and work.
- Resource allocations to adult literacy and adult learning have been too often denied on the grounds that no hard data were available on the social returns from adult literacy. Recent research points to the fact that the social impact of adult literacy on communities is considerable.
- New research on the social impact and cost-effectiveness of adult literacy should be both replicated for greater reliability and validity and should be widely disseminated for use by policy makers in governments, in development banks and other agencies.
- A culture of literacy and a literate environment need to be developed.

Part 4
Promoting the Empowerment of Women

15

Women's Education: *The Contending Discourses and Possibilities for Change*

Introduction

This chapter is a reflection on the issues raised at a workshop on women's education and empowerment, held during the 1997 Fifth International Conference on Adult Education (CONFINTEA V) in Hamburg. It focuses on promoting empowerment for women in a variety of educational contexts ranging from formal education systems to literacy and poverty alleviation programmes.

It is often assumed that schooling for women will automatically bring about their political advancement. However, there is evidence that schooling on its own does not enhance women's political voice. The radical agenda of education for empowerment, however, presents a contrast to the conventional conception of adult education and training. It encourages participants to work collectively, and develop strategies for use in areas of political and societal transformation.

The panel was chaired by Nelly Stromquist of the University of Southern California at Los Angeles. The other members represented a wide spectrum of expertise. Sara Hlupekile Longwe from FEMNET, the African Women's Development and Communication Network, opened the discussion on contending discourses in women's empowerment. Anne Marie Smith, Centre for Gender and Development Studies, University of the West Indies, Jamaica, talked about how educational opportunity is not necessarily translated into personal, social and economic gains for Caribbean women. New radical discourses in adult literacy work dealing with the issues of violence were brought up by Jenny Horsman, literacy educator and researcher from Canada. Malini Ghose from NIRANTAR, a centre for women's education in India, described an example of empowering women through participatory adult learning.

CONFINTEA V demonstrated that feminist educators are increasingly influential in shaping international agendas on education, asserting the need for women not only to gain access to learning, but to participate fully in determining the content of the learning opportunities on offer.

Perspectives on Women's Empowerment

In recent debates on women's empowerment through adult learning different perspectives on women's advancement have been expressed. One perspective advocates improving women's position and equity without radically altering the existing structure of gender relations. This perspective includes the so-called self-reliant model of empowerment. In this context self-reliance means achieving the best one can for oneself within the present system. From this point of view, a women is "empowered" when she is literate, educated, and has productive skills, has access to capital and self-confidence. This view of empowerment as individual self-reliance is considered not to recognise nor question how a woman can gain increased access to resources if the hurdles of gender discrimination remain in place. It leaves out the political and ideological dimensions of women's struggle.

The other perspective sees women's advancement as necessarily involving the transformation of an excessively male-dominated society. This involves collective action and working as a team towards the goal of ending discriminatory practices and gender inequality. Advocates of this view use the term "gender equity" to denote their ambition for a new form of gender justice within an egalitarian society and are interested in structural transformation to create more justice. They hold the view that women can achieve an equal footing with men only if there is equality of opportunity, which is not the case, as women continue to face systematic discrimination. The unique educational situation of Caribbean women amply demonstrates that, even when women reach high levels of educational equality, they do not attain commensurate economic and political equality.

Are Women Empowered through Education?

Women's marginalisation shows that participating in male dominated institutions, including education systems, benefits only a tiny percentage of women who are able to succeed with the odds stacked against them.

> **Trends in women's Education in the Caribbean**
>
> Since the 1970s, the trend in the Caribbean has been for women to take greater advantage of education. As a result, women have been demonstrating higher levels of achievement compared to men. Educational trends show:
>
> - Equal education opportunities for males and females in terms of access at the pre-primary, primary and secondary levels;
> - Enrolment in favour of females at the primary level in Bahamas and at the secondary level in St. Lucia;
> - Girls perform better in school on average;
> - More females sit for the most sought after Caribbean Examinations Council Exam.
>
> There are perhaps two main reasons for the unique educational situation of women in the Caribbean. First, Caribbean women are socialised to be independent and to prepare for shouldering family and other responsibilities, independent of male support. Secondly, education of women tends to result in lower returns than similar investments in the education of males: a woman needs to be more qualified in order to occupy the same job as a man.

However, this impressive educational achievement is not automatically translated into better jobs or into personal, social and political power for women, who remain at a disadvantage when compared to their male counterparts. Income disparities are considerable, and women have less access to political and economic power. For example, they are under-represented in parliament, local government and the judiciary.

In other words, the positive development for women in the educational field over the past three to four decades have not been matched by greater empowerment. This situation is aggravated by economic globalisation processes: women in the adult education system are increasingly being threatened by younger graduates, equipped with new skills. A women's family responsibilities very often prevent her from taking advantage of the opportunities for continuing education. They also have less time to dedicate themselves to adult continuing learning.

A persistent problem in education is the segregation of the curriculum according to fairly strict and traditionally accepted gender boundaries:

- Women are still concentrated in the so-called "soft-subjects", qualifying them for low paying and low status jobs.
- Women with so-called "soft-skills" such as sewing and hospitality management form the bulk of the unemployed labour force.
- Within the academic track, men predominate in physics, while women prefer biology, integrated science, the humanities or the arts.
- In the vocational training institutes women are usually clustered in non-technical areas.

One of the tasks of adult education is to address the limitations and contradictions of formal education and to foster a critical re-examination of the social, political and economic system, as it affects the situation of women. This is being done through an array of innovative strategies in adult learning which go beyond the conventional definitions of empowerment.

Community Participation in Adult Learning

Women's adult learning can play an important role in making women aware of the many forms of disadvantage they suffer, pointing out their rights and helping them to shape their own lives. Often this kind of education is combined with the teaching of literacy, practical skills and community participation.

Community participation is now an accepted intervention in development. It means involving the beneficiaries in the planning and implementation of programmes. In the case of programmes for women, this entails women increasing their level of control over the allocation of resources and combating discriminatory practices which stand in their way.

Empowering Women through Participatory Adult Learning: Mahila Samakhya

An example of empowering women through participatory adult learning is the women's programme Mahila Samakhya which is currently being implemented in the Banda district of India. The project has to be understood in the context of the hardships suffered by rural women in India. They are mostly caught up in the daily struggle for survival—fetching water, collecting firewood and securing a livelihood. Women are kept out of the decision-making process, denied access to information, and there is little or no recognition of their productive capacities. Power relations work against women at all levels—in the family, in the community and at the governmental level. Female illiteracy is very high and some villages do not even have a single literate women. Violence and poverty are inextricably intertwined.

Mahila Samakhya is run by women activists and mechanics who have been trained in specific skills. It aims to build upon and support the experience of non-governmental organisations in working with women in the field of education to initiate a process of change whereby poor rural women can more from a situation of passive acceptance of their situation to one of actively shaping their lives and environment. A key feature of such programmes is the combination of literacy teaching with training and practical skills such as water pump maintenance.

The community participation approach first takes into account the women's experiences in their own communities and then gradually introduces them to basic education and literacy teaching. Thus instead of offering education and literacy as a panacea for their problems, it begins by:

- affirming women's existing knowledge and skills;
- initiating a process of critical questioning and analysing with regard to issues such as survival or discrimination within the family;
- promoting the new role of women as activists in their communities.

Adult learning is not just a matter of transferring skills but also of enabling women to use their skills to negotiate more effectively and to deal with structures of power. The training of women as hand-pump mechanics, for example, has led to building confidence and mobility and breaking stereotypes. It has enhanced competencies in:

- dealing with structures of power;
- lobbying government for change;
- demanding basic necessities from the power structures;
- demanding information.

Such projects illustrate how women's education and empowerment can be complementary processes. The demand for reading and writing skills as well as other basic educational skills follow social, cultural, political and economic demands.

Another innovative empowerment strategy involved encouraging groups of newly literate women to bring out a bi-monthly newsletter. The women were trained in the basic principles of print production, and they themselves decided the content of the material. They were given in-depth training in writing, language, editing and layout, so that they could be responsible for all stages of the production of the newsletter.

This had a number of empowering aspects other than just strengthening literacy skills. It helped to break gender stereotypes. It allowed women to control the content, thus giving women a voice in what they wanted to read and how they wanted to see themselves. The newsletter, published in the local language of the women, made possible a broader exposure of incidents of violence.

The idea was to create a group that could train other groups of women in the community. It meant decentralising the innovation. It made learning and training not a one-time activity but a crucial process of improving capacities and developing new abilities, procedures and processes that could sustain learning.

Empowerment cannot take place without an empowering methodology. The creation of knowledge and information through material production takes into account women's experiential knowledge in various fields, such as health, water, forests and agriculture. Some aspects of empowering methodology are as follows:

- using women's own knowledge as critical to social development;
- locating literacy is social practices and lived realities of women;
- involving women in determining their needs, their issues, what they want to learn, and how they want to develop their own strategies at various levels;
- enabling women to transform, negotiate and challenge the structures of power, both at an individual and a community level;
- creating structures and institutions for sustaining the adult educational process;
- establishing partnerships with collaborating agencies and local government departments as crucial to women's role in the planning and conceptualising of projects, as well as in the actual implementation of them;

- making women responsible for managing and providing services such as hand-pump repair;

The literacy camp method is another strategy for coping with women's chronic problem of low and irregular attendance at non-formal educational centres. The literacy camp method organisers residential training courses in which a conductive and supportive learning environment is encouraged through group learning, ensuring a high teacher-student ratio, encouraging women to generate their own texts as well as promoting a continuous learning environment including games and songs with an educational purpose.

Creating Safe Adult Learning Environments for Women

Closely connected to the issue of creating conductive and supportive learning environments is the need to understand the difficulties and constraints experienced by women learners who come to literacy classes. It is necessary to ask why they often lack concentration, drop-out, attend infrequently and have low motivation.

Research has shown that many adult learners are victims of violence. They are afraid to speak about their experiences, feel unsafe in classroom environments and struggle beyond their capacities and energies while attending classes. Literacy workers are seldom aware of the fact that many of the learners may be in a state of crisis and conflict—even trauma. In such a state of mind it is difficult for them to summon up the necessary motivation and concentration to benefit from a class.

It is crucial therefore to design adult literacy programmes that take into account the situation of women who have experienced trauma and violence. There is also a need to become aware of the varieties of knowledge that come from these experiences and to examine thoughtfully how such knowledge can be included in adult learning.

Asking the following questions may help adult educators to understand the situation of learners who have been through violent situations:

- How attentive are the adult learners?
- What are the barriers to their attentiveness and concentration?
- What is the atmosphere needed in the classroom to help adult learners to feel safe?
- What changes need to be made in the classroom to create such an atmosphere?

Paying attention to these points can encourage learners to attend literacy classes and stay present, motivated and attentive.

The Challenges for Adult Learning

In the light of the above issues, the workshop concluded with the following challenges that adult learning will have to face if it is to empower women.

For many women violence is so embedded in their everyday lives and the culture surrounding them that they have difficulty in discussing the problem openly. Education for adult women should include an examination of the patterns of subordination to which they have been conditioned through cultural socialisation reinforced by schooling.

Adult learning should give a voice to women who have suffered violent experiences whether of a private or political nature. It should understand what a woman may be going through internally when she attends a literacy class and makes the effort to learn. In short, it should recognise that many and perhaps most women learners are survivors of violence, and take this into account in every aspect of a programme.

In designing curricula, it is necessary to focus on the learning methodology and learning environment. In the learning environment a safe space for women? The learning environment also has to take into account informal learning situations, as a lot of important communication happens outside the classroom and does not form part of formal teaching. A genuinely participatory form of adult learning supports and promotes the learner's role in determining the curriculum.

Empowerment can give women a new perspective enabling them to reject things that they once accepted as part of their culture. This often results in conflicts within the family or the community, which have to be anticipated and addressed through adult learning.

Since discrimination against women is institutional in nature, breaking those barriers will also need some kind of public institutional legislation and governmental support such as affirmative action.

Although formal education has several limitations, it has nevertheless an empowering element. It is through formal education that people enter the professional or political elite, albeit in small numbers. On the other hand non-formal education is in a better position to challenge the status quo. The challenge for women's adult education is to connect the formal and non-formal systems within the perspective of lifelong learning. Adult education should deal with gender issues in the context of a whole package that goes from infancy to adulthood.

It was mentioned earlier that there are different perspectives regarding women's empowerment. It is necessary to build bridges between those who choose the "self-reliant" way and those who take the path of more radical transformation. Only by encouraging a dialogue will it be possible to bring about a genuine transformation.

16

Raising Gender Issues in Formal and Non-formal Settings

Introduction

This chapter highlights the main issues raised at the workshop "Raising gender issues in different educational settings" at the Fifth International Conference on Adult Education, held in 1997 in Hamburg. The aim was to review the current situation of women's education in different formal and non-formal educational settings, in different regions and contexts. The panel featured the following speakers: Vimla Ramachandran, ASPBAE, India; Lean Chan Heng, Malaysia; Alejandra Valdez, The Women's Institute of Chile; Elsie Sutherland, Forum of African women Educationalists (FAWE), Ghana.

While considerable gains have been made in women's access to education, which have benefited some, their participation continues to be lower than that of men. Although political leaders, administrators and policy-makers are aware of the magnitude of the problem, the education of women is not being raised as a major issue in the context of the political agenda. Where policy exists, it has not been translated into concrete action. The workshop's main message to policy-makers was the need to have a strong advocacy in education, particularly in the South Asian and African regions. It was also held that this advocacy would be possible only through in-depth research on gender issues in the area of education.

Fortunately, there are more effective non-formal adult educational initiatives coming from outside governmental offices and from social movement organisations. These seek to empower women through activities, such as leadership and gender-awareness training. In discussing these non-formal programmes, participants expressed the view that current education for women needs to pay more attention to women's subjectivity, their diverse cultural identities as well as their emotional well-being. These aspects of empowerment are particularly important for women in countries in transition to democracy, as well as in situations where increased economic competition among people, groups, nations and regions are resulting in discrimination against women workers.

Gender Gap in Educational Participation

Women's participation is formal education continues to be lower than that of men. Statistics reveal the low value of education in women's lives in many countries. According to UNESCO sources (1996), there are an estimated 556 million illiterate women in countries of the South, compared to 315 million illiterate men. There are also 73 million out-of-school girls, compared to 37 million out-of-school boys. In sub-Saharan Africa alone 27 million girls are not in school. There is a big gender gap in women's participation in formal education for South Asian women too. African and South Asian countries therefore have a long way to go in closing the gender gap.

A study sponsored by UNESCO (PROAP AND ASPBAE) has examined the reasons for this imbalance in South Asia in the past 50 years. One of them is the little attention being paid to implementing reforms. Despite a subsidised education system professing equal treatment for both sexes, there have been few attempts to implement reforms aiming to promote the education of girls and women. Girls seldom get scholarships. In rural areas, parents are reluctant to send their daughters to school because of the low recruitment of female teachers in schools. In rural schools in India only 20 per cent of teachers are women. Administrators seldom view girl's education as being important, despite numerous policy statements to the contrary.

The strategies developed in the 1970s to promote women's adult education focused on setting up separate women's departments, projects and programmes. Although the women's movement argued for a special status for women's programmes, this in fact has inadvertently resulted in their isolation from the rest of the system and has often reduced women's influence in other departments and sectors. It was difficult, for example, for women's departments to influence the World Bank's programme on the vocationalisation of secondary education, which fell under the jurisdiction of the education sector. Women had little say in demanding courses geared to the labour market. They continued to receive a training in predominantly non-technical subjects. Similarly, literacy programmes have often been run as women's programmes, separate from other adult education programmes.

The tension between the allocation of a special status to gender issues and the integration of these issues into adult education is both a major problem and challenge for adult education. A different approach is being attempted in the case of women's health, in which reproductive health programmes are designed not only for women but also for men. Reproductive health is to a large extent about male responsibility for preventing disease and controlling family size. In short, the need to integrate gender issues into adult education still remains a big challenge.

Comparable to the situation in South Asia, in Africa literacy programmes are seldom linked to women's and girls' multiple roles outside the educational field. Insufficient attention is being given to the social and cultural barriers which prevent girls and women from entering the educational mainstream. Women's participation is also hampered by poor curricula, inadequate text books, ill-trained teachers and badly managed programmes.

The negative perceptions of girls' and women's education often discourage them from continuing their education, or undertaking further education. Limited resources for education cause parents to make decisions in favour of the education of boys. There are hardly any policies worth the name dealing with marginalised disabled girls or girls who leave school on becoming pregnant.

Often, adult learning is implemented in a ahphazard or ad hoc manner, and in many countries it suffers from limited funds. It is widely synonymous with literacy education and often has to make do with part-time staff.

Advocacy for Girls' and Women's Education

Although political leaders, administrators and policy makers are aware of these problems, it is often the case in developing countries that education in general and women's education in particular, are not a major political priority. Even where adult educators have been trying to promote gender issues, and even where the education of women is an important part of policy, that policy has seldom been implemented, as the South Asian case study in this booklet has shown.

There needs to be strong advocacy for any education movement. It is necessary to mobilise public opinion, the media and people in power and to bring education onto the political agenda.

A good example of effective lobbying and advocacy is the Forum for African Women Educatioinalists (FAWE). It brings together African women in high-ranking government or university positions to support the educational concerns of women. It has had a significant impact on policy reforms in Africa in a short period of time. The work of the Forum is based on in-depth research into gender issues, particularly in the area of education. Among other things, the Forum:

- provides research data for targated policy and practice;
- proposes alternative paradigms of education for African girls and women;
- consolidates evidence on women's education, making people aware that gender discrimination is unacceptable in the educational system;
- sensitises policy-makers and administrators of programmes on the centrality of women's and girls' education;
- trains policy makers and decision makers;
- sensitises teachers and instructors;
- is critical of text books that often portray women as helpless;
- promotes affirmative action, especially for disabled girls;

- brings pressure on governments to bear more responsibility for the continuing, post-basic as well as higher education of women.

FEWE promotes a holistic view of education and the "generation" of education policy and practice, concentrate on human rights and social justice. It does research on the relationship between empowerment, development, education and gender. The essence of FAWE is to network with people who are doing similar kinds of work in different countries. Its approach is to use women in privileged positions to help other less privileged women and girls to succeed in education.

Adult Education in Non-formal Settings

In the 1980s the women's movement in many Latin American countries was striking in its extent and variety, and the feminist movements in those countries were remarkably successful in bringing their perspectives to bear on the core issues of de-legitimising military influence and reconstructing civil society. With the return to democracy in many Litin American countries, the women's movement is redefining its role in relation to governments. Many of the organisations active in the 1980s have disappeared. New groups have emerged. There has been a rise in governmental organisations working with women and supporting women's studies programmes. Women's group have also moved in the direction of becoming more professional adult learning organisations. They are no longer characterised as mere grassroots activist initiatives.

The Women's Institute in Chile, developed during the period of transition to democracy after 18 years of dictatorship, introduced a new educational practice for enabling women to take an active public role, and to deal with social and political issues. There was a big demand for training women candidates for public functions, and for enhancing the competencies of those already in important decision-making areas. Women demanded training in organisational skills for the management of their organisations.

Although women were largely united against dictatorship, their response to the new situation of democratic transition revealed diversity and difference. Cultural, political and social difference among women began to be articulated in a positive way.

The Women's Institute, Chile

Its aims were to:

- bring about changes in social, cultural and political institutions;
- elaborate and articulate political issues such as women's rights as well as issues linked to the women's private sphere;
- establish a network of political support for women in all fields of life;
- promote female leadership, emphasising at the same time cultural diversity;
- define leadership in terms of the complex nature of identities, taking into account the different roles which women occupy as mothers, workers, urban citizens, activists, daughters, wives, consumers or patients in the health system.

Adult learning in such organisations deals with women's issues in an inter-dependent and interdisciplinary way. Topics range from issues of gender, power, women's rights, to issues of conflict and women's invisibility. A free association of themes is encouraged as a way of constructing new meanings and of creating new knowledge. Emotions and feelings and a participatory approach play an important role in knowledge construction. Attention is drawn to the diverse kinds of discourses, imaginations and collective projections that affect women's lives. Emphasis is placed on family histories, personal memory, and accounts of the country's history—each theme being explored in its symbolic context—and on deconstructing the ideology of the past. The aim of these learning processes is to promote empowering capacities such as individuality, eloquence and creativity among women. Another very important aspect is the emphasis on project ownership: women are given the opportunity to distinguish themselves from the collective identity and yet be a part of it. Another aim is to promote useful capacities which relate to the immediate needs and interests of women. Women are encouraged to evaluate their situation and circumstances in a creative way and to air rather than suppress conflicts. A final objective of such adult learning is to promote the capacity for visibility. This includes disseminating competencies that help women in building a public presence and taking over public tasks. At the same time women are helped to recognise their interests, ambitions and personal wishes in different political environments.

The aim of such adult learning practices is to relate educational processes to women's identity and individuality. Women are being helped to overcome their invisibility, not only through participation in public institutions but also through the construction of discourses and through the development of their personalities and personal identities.

Connecting the Local and the Global

Adult education should recognise the experiences of women at the local level, taking into account the forces of globalisation that are creating more competitive relations among people, groups, nations and regions. The global economy often exploits the traditional subordination of women at the local level. One example is the use of women on global assembly lines. These women work under very poor conditions that barely allow them and their families to survive. Women's work as global assembly line operators is tedious, repetitive and menial. They are non-unionised, often unskilled shift workers, and are subjected to discipline, pressure, verbal abuse and intimidation from supervisors and male co-workers. Their environments are both hazardous and stressful. Gender relations at work are a common source of subordination as well as work-related stress for women.

Although working conditions have improved in the past 20 years, the subjective experiences of women have not. Society continues to view them disparagingly. Male-dominated organisational practices and pedagogical mythologies tend to deny women workers to space and authority to talk about their gender experiences. In fact women experience further subjugation and often internalise the stereotypes about themselves through the kind of educational work that they undergo. Adult education for women workers has centred very largely in the past on their objective material situation, their employment conditions and their rights. Hence consciousness-raising about women's exploitation an the importance of workers' unity have been important parts of the agenda. The focus has been on "gender practical needs" of women.

However, women's subjectivity and their personally lived experiences are rarely taken into account. Even in situations where gender agendas are covered, women's unspoken thoughts, feelings and emotions tend to be overlooked.

Importance of Subjectivity in Adult Learning

Subjectivity means how women relate to themselves and to others. It is made up of emotions, modes of understanding the world, a personal sense of being, individuality, uniqueness, gender identity, continuity, an awareness of the other as well as conscious and unconscious thoughts.

It is vital to recognise the centrality of emotional well-being of women in adult education work. Adult education needs to address the following aspects of women workers' subjectivity: their emotional experiences and subordination, their feelings of powerlessness, inferiority and subjugation in workplaces and in homes.

How should these feelings and emotions be addressed in educational work? They should be a methodology of adult educational work that emphasises the use of reflective talking, story telling and sharing experiences in small groups. This process of articulation, naming and reconstructing, gives women a sense of worth and self-confidence.

Conclusion

A political agenda is needed to respond to women's needs in the context of the global economy. Although there is a great deal of talk about women entering the global economy, there is very little being done in the development of their education to meet the challenges of the global markets. The vast majority of the women are unable to complete in the global market without education.

There is no point opening more schools unless the question of women's participation in educational processes is resolved. Literacy alone is not enough; the issue of proper quality and relevance at all levels of the educational system has also to be addressed. Education for women has to be a multi-pronged and multi-faceted approach.

Part 5
Adult Learning and the Changing World of Work

17

Work-related Adult Learning in a Changing World

Introduction

We are experiencing tremendous changes in the area of work and witnessing major shifts from the industrial age to the world of new technologies, including information and communication technologies and biotechnology. At the same time, conventional technologies continue to be used alongside the new. This co-existence is a necessity if major social disruption is to be avoided.

In this period of change and transition work-related adult learning needs to respect the unity of humans beings as citizens, individuals and workers. People's competencies cannot be reduced simply to their vocational skills. Social relations, personal development and cultural and human values are important too, because the internationalisation of work is leading to greater integration of labour markets across national boundaries and this has strong implications for economic, social and cultural identities.

This chapter highlights the main issues raised during the workshop "Adult learning and the changing world of work" at the Fifth International Conference on Adult Education, held in Hamburg in 1997.

The first session dealt with the most significant changes taking place in the world of work. It was chaired by Abrar Hasan, OECD and Karamat Ali, Pakistan Institute of Labour Education and Research, Karachi, Pakistan. The panel of speakers featured Renate

Peltzer, International Confederation of Trade Unions (ICFTU), Brussels, Belgium; Prof. B.W Kerre, Moi University, Kenya; Lurliene Miller, Vocational Training Institute (HEART), Kingston, Jamaica; Maria A. Ducci, Training Policies and Systems Branch, ILO and John Lawrence, UNDP, New York, USA.

The second session, dealing with the implications for adult education programmes, was chaired by H. Müller-Solger of the Federal Ministry of Education, Science, Research and Technology, Bonn, Germany and Prof. B.W. Kerre, Moi University, Kenya, Speakers were: Ikhyun Shin, Korean Educational Development Institute (KEDI), Republic of Korea; Barry Hobart, former UNESCO/UNEVOC consultant; The Working Group within the Committee on Educational Research in Co-operation with Third World Countries of the German Association for Education Research.

At the third session, chaired by Lurliene Miller, Kingston, Jamaica and Tony Greer, Department of Employment, Education, Training and Youth Affairs, Canberra City, Australia, policy implications were discussed. The panel speakers consisted of: Mr. Karamat Ali, Pakistan Institute of Labour; Helga Foster, Federal Institute for Vocational Training, Berlin; Ettore Gelpi, consultant, Paris and Tony Greer.

While acknowledging the changing nature of work the workshop reaffirmed the importance of the right to work. It also examined the contribution which adult learning makes to the individual's creative potential and to equal employment opportunities, thereby allowing men and women to participate in the decisions affecting their work, their lives and their livelihoods.

Although adult learning is becoming more and more an individual effort, this will have to be counterbalanced by provisions and opportunities and imparted in clear regulatory frameworks set by governments, counteracting any market distortions and addressing equity issues.

The workshop highlighted the importance of adult learning to those who have neither access to regular work nor the promise of permanent jobs in future. It was held necessary to design adult learning more thoughtfully, so as to place more emphasis on the diversity of experience, information on human rights, the vulnerability of individuals to change, and to spread of technology to support communities. Serious concern was also expressed about unemployment and precarious employment, gender inequalities, displacement of labour and dislocation of peoples. In many countries the concern is not simply on of employment but also of partaking equally in the processes of globalisation and democratisation. The workshop stimulated discussion on the role of adult learning as a tool for promoting gender democracy and for integrating all active populations, including the unemployed and those working in precarious occupations.

The Changing World of Work

The changing world of work is a many-sided issue that affects all spheres of economic, social and cultural life and has tremendous relevance to adult learning. Globalisation and the dramatic innovations in technology are affecting the lives of individuals as well as societies. While global competition, communication networks, rapid investment flows and technological innovations have brought success to some enterprises, inequalities have widened and poverty persists in vast segments of society. Competition around the world is intensifying, bringing a new level of insecurity. Already in many countries active populations are expressing their dissatisfactions because of lack of jobs, poor salaries, growing disparities and increasing costs of basic social services. The future scenario suggests that hundreds of millions of people will be moving from one part of the globe to another, from one continent to another and within countries, to find food and work opportunities, the non-earning populations will in future demand a greater share in the world of wealth.

Currencies, technologies and information will be exchanged from one end of the globe to another. The implication of these transfers will be enormous. At the same time, the regulation of financial exchanges and common labour market policies are being discussed as the international markets no longer appear to be self-regulatory.

Employment patterns are also changing throughout the world along with their official definitions. Some countries will consider a person with less than 20 hours of work a week as "employed", others only if he or she has a full-time job in the conventional sense. Statistics of employment and unemployment are becoming a very important political issue.

Although globalisation may offer unprecedented opportunities to several countries there are concerns about its affects on human and social progress. All major global conferences since 1990 have given warnings about the inherent unsustainability of current production and consumption patterns, for despite economic growth there are nevertheless global and environmental constraints as outlined by the Brundtland Commission, UNCED and the Commission for Sustainable Development. A sustainable proportion of the world's labour force has never had a job in the contractual or regular sense of the term. The increasing urbanisation of the world will change the patterns of life for the better and for the worse. Labour force growth in the 1990s in Africa in exceeding 5 million new entrants annually. Although new jobs are being created, there are also new concerns regarding the environment. It is no longer possible to draw up linear scenarios.

While a section of the population in the South is starting to share sectors of modern production, parts of the Northern populations are becoming increasingly marginalised within their own national labour markets.

The majority of the world's active populations are finding other solutions to the problem of work, such as participation in the so-called informal sector, the traditional or popular economy. Within these contexts work structures and processes are characterised by employment relations that lack legally-based protection, social security and opportunities for personal development. Two-thirds of informally employed people are women. Most of them, especially in developing countries, operate often under acutely competitive conditions, at subsistence level and have few marketable skills, and little access to credit or proper marketing outlets.

The diversity in the conditions of active populations in the productive system is becoming greater, with different career paths leading from unemployment to employment and vice versa, as well as from house-hold work to productive work. Women's participation in the formal labour market will increase, while more men will be active in household work. The ageing populations in the North and South will influence the culture of work and leisure as their numbers rapidly increase. The culture of work will also be strongly influenced by the integration of new information and communication technologies into work and education. But at the same time, work will be related to traditional culture, values, practices, codes of conduct and behaviour, especially in agriculture and craft-work. For many societies, culture including the preservation of their natural environments is an essential part of their economic survival now and in the future.

The organisation of work is rapidly changing. New information technologies have created communication methods, which ignore traditional boundaries between people, countries and religions and which are influencing the rate of production and the delivery of goods and services. The home is becoming an important place of work. The place and time of work are scattered across space and time. Managers will be obliged to take into consideration the internal and external reality of work. While new technologies can contribute to the autonomy and self-sufficiency of a part of the active populations, they are also causing another part to lose independence and autonomy through exclusion.

Work-related Adult Learning

At the present time work-related adult learning is a continuous and recurrent learning process. The competencies of a worker depend not just on technical knowledge and basic skills, but on attitudes, values, and behavioural patterns as well as personality traits such as initiative, creativity, adaptability, responsiveness and innnovativeness. Basic skills, comprising literacy, numeracy as well as cognitive and problem-solving abilities, show the relationship between general education and work-related adult learning. General education provides the foundations for a continuing learning process throughout the entire working life.

In order to be employable or to create their own jobs people need to have skills and competencies. Employable workers mean enterprises can be supplied with the qualified, motivated and committed work-force they required to compete. In a globalised economy the competitive advantages of every country will consequently depend on having and maintaining a labour force with the necessary knowledge, practical skills and innovation. These skills will, in turn, allow people to create, keep, find, enrich and change jobs, and to obtain fair personal, economic, social and professional rewards in return. Adult learning is therefore closely linked with employability.

In this competitive environment, enterprises have to flexible. Leading employers have shown that investing in the adult learning of workers is essential for competitiveness and growth. Training and establishing a culture of learning within the enterprise and in the community, enhances job security of employees. Learning organisations thus become a link by which employers' interests in improving performance converge with a long-term commitment to be well-being of workers.

Firms and companies are now learning that people should be working in a more meaningful way. It is increasingly being recognised that the greatest value of work is its potential to offer human beings the chance to express their creativity and identify with a product or piece of work.

Knowledge-based investment is being given equal priority to that of capital. Building the knowledge society of the future calls for a different kind of learning as well as a commitment to training and provision of employment opportunities. New markets for continuing adult learning and gradually being opened to private and public institutions as well as to NGOs, and performance incentives are being introduced for training institutions that link training with the labour market and use enterprises as training places.

However, the impact of these new attitudes is twofold: it values competent workers, but at the same time, excludes others by drawing a distinction between those who have "learned how to learn" and those who have not. It also means that employability and job security will increasingly depend on performance an that workers will have the additional responsibility for acquiring skills and pursuing their personal growth in order to remain in employment. While some workers will be privileged to have a good foundation of general education upon which to build vocational skills, others will have to rely on narrow vocational skills. For the latter group, work-related adult learning will be necessary to remain in employment.

With adult learning becoming increasingly integrated into the productive process, it is now being regarded as an important commodity itself and one capable of making a profit. Public or private institutions may therefore alter the nature of adult learning because of profit motive. Education policy-makers will therefore have a very important function to keep at least some of the adult education activities for the personal and collective development of people in general.

Adult Learning and Sustainable Livelihoods

The majority of the world's working population is in the informal sector. Here, starting one's own enterprise represents a chance for overcoming poverty and offering possibilities of employment and income to others. Given the size of the informal sector and its importance for the survival and development of hundreds of millions of people, there is no doubt that a system of adult learning linked to it would sustain its development.

Informal Avenues of Work-related Adult Learning

Almost 85 per cent of the world's working population acquire the necessary skills for conducting an economic activity outside the formal system of education, mainly through informal avenues of adult learning. A large proportion of young adults who work in the formal sector receive their vocational training within a framework described as "informal apprenticeships". Young people are integrated into daily working life at an early stage. Learning takes place through imitation and identification. Learning processes are directly linked to production and sales and the skills taught are necessary for the local market. However, informal apprenticeships are very often associated with the exploitation of trainees as a source of cheap labour, though this very condition perhaps provides the master with the incentive to "train".

Non-formal education, or organised education outside the formal system, is particularly effective in terms of its accessibility, participation and lost cost. In contrast to the top-down approach, non-formal educational schemes attempt to carry out education at grassroots level, and aim towards greater relevance to learners and communities. It also has an identifiable clientele and sets clear learning objectives.

Informal learning may be described as the lifelong process whereby all individuals acquire attitudes, values, skills and knowledge from daily experience and from educative resources in their environment, whether in the family, the community or on the street. This form of learning often overlaps with socialisation processes. Learning is characterised by a lack of structure, absence of an underlying curriculum and a particular timetable and takes place primarily by doing and through experience i.e. by active acquisition, rather than by receptive learning.

Work-related abilities in the informal sector are closely related to economic survival in the context of family, community, work, physical location and social relationships. They define how someone will be able to earn money and secure a livelihood, and to market and service his products. One of the most important characteristics of the informal sector is the household-based enterprises which combine different trades with various sources of income, credit and human resource to secure daily subsistence through periods of weak economic activity. Entrepreneurs working in self-help groups generally do better than those operating individually. They gain information though their networks about new technologies, new markets and about opportunities for subconstracting.

Educational bodies operating in the formal sector must therefore be aware that learning takes place not only during the process of production, but through such activities as negotiating, searching for new markets and becoming aware of the potential of groups, network or organisation for solving problems. This means that they will have to look at the whole concept of production, including the production of ideas.

Diversification and Reform of National Training Systems

The demand for lifelong learning for the entire labour market and all active populations, dramatically increases and diversifies the demand for training. This, in turn, requires the urgent reform of national vocational training and education systems. Three issues are at stake in this:

Reforming National Vocational Training and Education Systems

1. Devising flexible and continuous adult learning and training systems to meet the learning requirements of the entire labour market, including the informal sector and all active populations;
2. Mobilising greater investment by building partnerships;
3. Ensuring equitable access to adult continuing training.

1. Devising Flexible and Continuous Adult Learning and Training Systems to Meet the Learning Requirements of the Entire Labour Market and All Active Populations

In ensuring the labour force can adapt to the demands for new skills, the past distinctions between education, training and work are becoming less relevant. Reform in the workplace in leading to the development of continuous, lifelong learning which integrates what people do in the workplace with processes for developing skills and learning. Competencies required in the world of work include general knowledge and techno-professional skills, combined with a sound foundation of aptitudes, attitudes and values. Therefore the platform of solid general education is essential for subsequent training and work.

In lifelong learning formal, non-formal and informal learning are equally valuable aspects. This learning process which goes on is as many situations as possible, does not distinguish between work and learning. A lot of it takes place on the job, either in training schools set up by employers or, at the other end of the spectrum, by schools setting up their own enterprises for students to gain hands-on experience. Viewed from this perspective, the concept of adult learning becomes broader than literacy development or remedial education.

Recognition of the Competencies in the Informal Sector

Adult education needs to build upon the abilities which people in the informal sector often have in abundance—their own knowledge, values, skills, attitudes and resources. Starting from the knowledge and experiences of the participants themselves, it should help adults to become aware of their own potential, and gain a more positive attitude to their own abilities. This is crucial if they are to have sufficient motivation to influence their working and living conditions.

In most approaches to training for the informal sector there is a tendency to neglect general abilities. Social skills which include the ability of micro-entrepreneurs to establish and maintain contracts are central to conducting a business in the informal sector. The social skills include the art of communication, empathy and willingness to co-operate. Organisational abilities include analysing and planning. Micro-entrepreneurs often attribute their success to their own ability to work hard and to a range of personality factors, dispositions and orientations (readiness to compromise, tolerate frustrations etc.) Literacy and cognitive competencies facilitate the organiation of economic activities and are used to develop communicative skills such as giving advice, convincing and negotiating. General abilities must be related to institutional and economic influences operating in the informal sector (raw material acquisition, infrastructure and marketing, for example). They must be described and analysed in relation to their application, rather than to imported theoretical concepts.

The basic educational abilities of people in the informal sector are, at present, full of shortcomings. Adult learning should provide remedial help where such basic abilities are lacking. Instruction in the mother tongue, for example, should be complemented by one of the global languages of communication in order to promote access to avenues of further education and social resources.

Community-based Adult Learning

Community-based adult learning is becoming an integral part of university adult education departments, where university-based adult educators have a chance to learn more about the socio-cultural realities around them by their involvement with migrants, minorities, indigenous communities and other groups. They can then identify the needs of causal workers and micro-entrepreneurs and help improve their employability by promoting links between business and industry, and through project work. Inducing learners into a process of lifelong learning which includes the discipline of studying and the management of time and resources is also of importance.

Supporting Sustainable Livelihoods

Adult learning which aims to support a sustainable livelihood should introduce the concept of vulnerability and risk management when dealing with survival strategies. It should promote the management of self-help organisations, encourage participation of groups in political decision-making and increase negotiating and bargaining positions of disadvantaged sections and strengthen the goals of existing groups. It should take into account the economic unity of household and enterprise: appropriate skills in the basics of business management are needed to improve the ability of small enterprises to withstand crises. It should give due consideration to traditional and informal methods of acquiring vocational competencies. In addition, new information technologies should bring information to the most remote communities so that people have equal access to information on their rights, to participate in policy dialogue, to legal recourse, to protection of assets and entitlements, and to basic social services. The Human Right's education effort has provided a base for initiating these kinds of approaches, besides pointing out some of the difficulties.

Adult Education and Training for Women

All these efforts will go down the drain if we do not take women into account. Non-formal programmes of adult education and training for women should support their training in a wide range of programmes, including those which are aimed at empowering women, such as gender awareness training and leadership training. Trainers and teachers of women should be trained in different teaching and learning methods that promote independent and critical thinking, in addition to social and marketing skills. Lack of these skills can often be blamed on social attitudes towards women as well as a school education, both of which demand that they follow fixed norms rather than creative ideas, and memorisation of text books rather than critical thinking.

Building Bridges Between Formal and Non-formal Education and Training

As it becomes increasingly clear that the formal education and training systems do not always reach large part of a population government departments in many countries are turning towards "de-formalising" the formal education system by integrating innovative and attractive components of non-formal education into formal education and training schemes.

Building bridges between formal and non-formal education is necessary in order to make formal education and training more attractive for persons and groups involved in non-formal and informal learning. On the other hand, non-formal education and traditional forms of training should be more strongly subjected to a process of certification.

2. Building Partnerships

If adult learning is going to respond to the changes in the world of work, then new and complementary roles for the state and the private sector need to be defined. The goal is to bring about a culture of learning, involving government, enterprises, individuals and other stakeholders. Learners, educators—both formal and non-formal—the media, the different producers and consumers of goods and services will be actors and authors of education related to the future of work. The organisation and implementation of adult learning policies will be the result of integrated action of the above actors and designers of policies.

The World Bank's 1997 Report which deals with "The State in a Changing World" accepts that the state has a role in market-led development by providing the right environments of rules, institutions and core services. Full employment needs an enabling environment of economic and financial policies, an appropriate legal and institutional framework, a competent, effective and accountable public administration, and clear policy priorities to create and expand employment. Government-sponsored adult education schemes are often the only available choice for the vast majority of disadvantaged persons.

Governments are increasingly decentralising their responsibilities towards continuing education by sharing responsibility with regions and local authorities in many transition economies. This is necessary because it is only at the local level that trends in economic development as well as the needs of the labour market can be adequately analysed. It is also easier to organise the cooperation of stakeholders at the local level.

Sound industrial relations and well-functioning tripartite systems for consultation are the best methods for ensuring that the labour market responds smoothy and efficiently to change, ensuring that steady growth and competitiveness may be achieved, and making difficult choices about the distribution of scarce resources. Tripartite governance will include government, unions, and enterprises and partners.

Unions are demanding the inclusion of basic labour standards in international trade agreements. Every working man and woman and every child anywhere has the same rights that need to be respected, and working people need to be equipped for being at the forefront of technological and structural developments. For unions it has become urgent to protect workers who do not enjoy the security of a regular employment relationship.

3. Ensuring Equitable Access to Adult Continuing Education

Equity concerns are based on solidarity and social justice, and emphasise equality of opportunity for all citizens to realise their potential as human beings, and to participate actively in economic and social development. At a time of rising inequalities and increased vulnerability amongst workers, it is imperative that measures be taken to redress equity imbalances. Training should become part and parcel of a comprehensive set of broader measures geared to create and expand employment and improve its quality. The social protection of all workers should become an integral part of the opportunities for adult learning.

- Young people and new entrants to the labour market need specially designed training programmes which should include greater exposure to and familiarisation with the work environment.
- Displaced workers need to be retained to facilitate their reintegration into the labour market.
- The unemployed, and particularly the low-skilled long term unemployed, require adult education integrated into a package of support services which will enhance their employability. The cultural and ecological dimensions should not be ignored in their adult learning.
- Home-workers, part-time workers, and those in insecure, short-term jobs should be covered by adult learning programmes.
- A significant part of further education should aim to ensure access to new technology in rural areas.
- Adult learning must address the question of gender inequalities: the majority of the world's poor people and the ones that have the most difficulty in entering the labour force are women.
- Workers in micro-enterprises and other informal sector activities, as well as small farmer and causal rural sector workers, face even greater constraints. Small productive units need training to become competitive, to link with larger enterprises as clients, suppliers and sub-contractors, thus entering into the stream of development and growth. An essential requirement is to link the training for apprentices and instructors with business development programmes. There should be a balance in micro-enterprises between learning and the striving for profit.

In several countries government policy is being directed towards compensating for this historical disadvantages of certain groups such as indigenous peoples, migrants and social disadvantaged peoples, and to developing strategies by which the position of those groups can be improved. A special form of income support is made available to indigenous. Australians, for example, to improve their access to further education. The long tradition of part-time and distance learning recognises that some students have employment or family commitments or are located in rural and remote areas which makes access to tertiary education difficult.

Conclusion

Work-related adult learning offers the individual a greater potential, equality of employment opportunities, security and personal development. It will give all active populations, including women and migrant workers the skills they need for work and for democracy. Adult continuing learning is absolutely necessary to raise standards of living and increase individual freedom in transition economies and it is vital for the success of the process of transition from planned to market-oriented economies, and to democracy. Furthermore, it has the advantages of being able to respond quickly to the needs of, and being accessible to, local and regional communities.

Work-related adult learning courses are particularly important for women, frequently providing support for women returning to the workforce following periods of full-time caring. They also provide a wider range of language, literacy and numeracy training critical for many educationally, disadvantaged people to access formal vocational training. Young people, who often have difficulty with more formal education, find that the informality and flexibility of adult learning courses ease the path into the education and training system.

All in all, work-related adult learning has vocational, cultural, social and political dimensions and to ignore any one of these would mean an improvishment of adult learning as well as of the workplace.

Part 6

Adult Learning in the Context of Environment, Health and Population

18

Adult Environmental Education: Awareness and Environmental Action

Introduction

The central aim of the workshop "Adult environmental education; awareness for environmental action" was to discuss the present state of environmental adult education, its major difficulties and shortcomings and to develop recommendations for the further development of this field. The fifth International Conference on Adult Education provided a unique opportunity to create a dialogue between policy-makers, educational planners, practitioners, and between governments and NGOs.

The workshop was jointly organised by the International Network for Sustainable Energy (INFORSE), the Learning for the Environment Programme (LEAP) of the International Council for Adult Education, the University of Lüneburg, and the UNESCO Institute for Education, Hamburg. The panel discussion, chaired by Walter Leal Filho, University, of Lüneburg, Germany, featured the following speakers: Ruth Kiwanuka, Joint Energy and Environment Projects, Uganda; Angele Fatou Sarr, FOPEN Solaire, Senegal; Zareen Myles, Women's Action for Development, India; Pierre Foulani; Adoum Ngaba-Waye, CREFELD, Tschad; Raul A. Montenegro, Fundación Para la Defensa del Ambiente, Argentina. The Minister of Education from Lower Saxony, Professor Wernstedt, opened the session.

A poster session showing examples of adult environmental education in difficult regions of the world was also organised. This featured fuel wood saving and clay stoves in households in Uganda; education and information programmes for peasants in Senegal; household bio-gas systems in India; teaching adults about the environment in Argentina; and desertification in Africa.

Adult Environmental Education: Learning for Action

According to a working definition provided in 1992 by UNEP/ UNESCO/OECD Paris, environmental education is "a permanent process in which individuals gain awareness of their environment and acquire the knowledge, values, skills experiences, and also the determination which will enable them to act individually and collectively to solve present and future environmental problems...as well as to meet their needs without compromising those of future generations".

Adult environmental education should disseminate knowledge about the environment's direct and indirect physical and related social impact. It should also transmit knowledge on the interaction between local activities and their effects which may occur further away. Direct impacts, such as deforestation and diseases caused by polluted water, are visible and tangibly affect daily life. Solutions to them can be found in the short term if appropriate measures are taken. Indirect environmental impacts may include increased soil erosion, a disproportionate workload for women, general depletion of resources such as food, animal fodder and water, reduction of numbers and diversity of wildlife and increased risk of bush fires and flooding. Indirect effects take longer to be felt. They occur over a wider geographical area. Their solution requires long-term planning, commitment and global approaches.

Adult education has often included a political and socially transformative perspective. Since Paulo Freire's work on literacy and its emanicipatory potential, the social and political role of adult education has become a central pillar of much of today's practice in this field. With his motto "from reading the word to reading the world", Freire invited people to explore the social and political as well as the physical environment. The environmental factor is now becoming increasingly important and can hardly be ignored in education efforts committed to social and political goals. With the links between changes in the physical environment and current social and political problems becoming more evident, environmental education is assuming an important social function. It is developing into a more holistic education project similar to the education envisaged by Freire. However much remains to be done. Much environmental education is still purely science and technology oriented rather than addressing environmental and social issues in an integrated way.

Liking environmental and social issues and locating environmental problems within the context of our daily lives and action are important challenges for adult environmental education. In fact, as one speaker said: "There are no such things as environmental problems, there are just a lost of social problems".

Current adult environmental education is experimenting with different ways to bring about changes and initiate action. Such projects go beyond creating understanding and awareness. They aim at developing skills, creating a sense of commitment and stimulating individual and collective action. Environmental education has the potential to bring about action at individual, community and governmental levels.

However, environmental activists and educators are becoming aware of the kinds of situation that create barriers to participatory action for the environment, such as:

- Situations where marginal communities face grave economic and social problems.
- Where there is a lack of environmental awareness and of commitment to environmentally friendly policies among governments and industry.
- Where local initiatives do not achieve their aims because of lack of support from the institutional sector, and because of lack of co-ordination with other initiatives.

Environmental education therefore needs to address all sectors of society: people, communities, public institutions, the private sector, governments, policy-makers and international organisations.

Strengthening Collaboration

Adult learning is a central took in the process of raising environmental awareness and promoting environmentally supportive action. Many environmental organisations disseminate information, organise community initiatives and practise non-formal adult education. Environmental educators and activists recognise the need to strengthen and innovative this educational dimension of their work. Environmental groups often seek the collaboration of adult educators, and in this sense they are trying to change their educational work from mere information sharing to more participatory and creative ways of learning.

Environmental issues are becoming more and more important for other fields of adult education too. Given the negative effects of environmental degradation and pollution on people's health, environmental questions can be dealt with in health education programmes.

Environmental topics can also be an important component of community education programmes. Such programmes can provide a frame, for linking environmental issues with social and political problems of the community. In a community education project in Northern Ontario, the two most important issues identified by the community were youth violence and soil erosion. At first sight it seemed doubtful how such apparently disconnected issues could be linked to each other. However, it soon became clear that the two problems had a lot to do with each other.

Collaboration between environmentalists and adult educators should be strengthened. They could, for example, join efforts in planning and implementing activities at the community level and promote local capacity building. At the same time adult educators and environmentalists should work together in influencing policy, at both national and international levels. National and international NGOs can be important partners in this process.

Environmental Education: A Central Theme for Adult Education

The integration of the environment into general and vocational **adult education can provide a range of new opportunities for an** environmental education which is more relevant to learners' concerns. This is particularly important for developing countries which are today experiencing serious environmental problems that directly affect people's lives.

Environmental education, if it is to be meaningful to adults in their daily lives, needs to address ecological questions in terms of the social, political and economic factors involved. In industrialised regions, for example, environmental education entails dealing with the crisis of modern production systems and their consequences for employment. In developing regions, on the other hand, it deals with issues relating to global production structures, national economy, international trade, local agricultural, development aid and foreign debt.

Kutch Mahila Vikas Sangathan, Gujrat, India

Kutch Mahila Vikas Sangathan (KMVS) is an organisation of rural women living in the arid border villages of Kutch District, Gujarat. The organisation, which was founded in 1989 and includes more than 1200 members, provides a range of projects aiming at supporting rural women, articulating their concerns and initiating new action to improve their lives and economic situation. A major focus of KMVS is ecological degradation and income generation. In Kutch, women are most affected by the negative consequences of ecological degradation. There is water scarcity and soil salinity. KMVS has initiated an education programme including a water harvesting programme. The programme met with serious resistance from the men of the village. Women are traditionally responsible for fetching water, while resource management is a male task. Addressing water scarcity resulted in a complex situation where the women also had to deal with the question of rights to land holdings. This is a politically sensitive and touches on issues of caste and gender.

One of the big challenges for environmental adult education is to change the widespread belief that what happens to the environment is not caused by our own actions, but by someone somewhere else. Yet adult educators are aware of the fact that, although community action is a powerful tool, there are clear limits to what can be achieved at this level, especially when local political and social conditions are taken into account.

The Fisherfolk Environmental Education Project

Tambuyog Development Centre (TDC) has developed an environmental education and training programme for coastal communities. Fishermen and women learn to understand the political, economic and biological factors which lead to the growing destruction of the marine ecosystem. Several factors are involved:

- the exploitation of resources through the fishing industry;
- the fact that the fishermen and women have no property rights over the sea and the mangrove areas;
- the support given by power structures to the fishing industry;
- the deteriorating income of fishermen and women;
- the use of dynamite to catch fish.

The project helps fishermen and women to understand their own complex situation. At the same time it provides them with the necessary insights into the existing power structures. It creates an awareness of the effects of the use of dynamite on fishing resources and the status of the mangroves. TDC's environmental education project includes holding workshops and the use of educational comic books to reach a larger public.

But awareness-raising activities alone cannot lead to sustained change. TDC is now providing resource management training for the fishing community, helping them in establishing local organisations and supporting alternative fishing techniques.

Economy versus Ecology?

Although the negative effects of modern production and agricultural techniques on soil fertility, for example, and beginning to be recognised by many governments and aid agencies, yet there appears to be a continuing contradiction between the interests of economic growth and sustainable resource management. Technological progress is still considered a positive factor in economic development, even though it has many negative consequences for the natural environment. As a result, environmental education often receives little attention and financial support from policy-makers. This is especially the case in countries which already have few resources for education.

In poor an marginalised communities, environmental education is often regarded as a luxury. Even in many industrialised countries, environmental issues re being given less attention than, say, 10 years ago. Very few countries are willing to experiment with radically new political solutions. In view of the present unemployment situation, solutions which aim at transforming the economy towards more ecologically sound patterns of production and consumption often clash with policies for short-term economic growth.

Environmental adult education often suffers from this mistaken conflict between economic growth and sustainable development. At times when economic needs are a priority, it might seem absurd to propose the integration of environmental dimensions into educational programmes. Yet this is a concern of many educators, social workers and development workers, in both developing and industrialised countries.

Environmental education has the urgent task of overcoming such misconceptions. It needs to stress that environmentally friendly technologies can be an opportunity to modernise and improve production systems. More importantly, such as education needs to reveal to its participants that an ecologically sound production strategy does not automatically imply higher costs and lower revenues. The use of renewable energy sources is a good example to show how such measures can help people improve their incomes.

Environmental Education and Women

Many women's groups and environmental organisations focus their work on household production and consumption, as this affects the lives of women directly. One of the main issues that women's projects address is the consumption of fuel, principally wood, for cooking and heating. Some projects and promoting a combination of methods of food preparation, cooking, heating and fuel substitution. Since women are often the primary collectors of wood and do most of the cooking themselves, many initiatives in this area focus on lowering their workload and improving their situation. At the same time they promote the use of environmental-friendly energy resources for the whole community.

The use of firewood or charcoal for cooking and heating is widespread. In many communities in Africa cooking is traditionally done in large fire-places which consume great quantities of firewood. These traditional hearth can also lead to serious health problems, because women inhale large amounts of smoke as a result of spending many hours of cooking at the hearth daily. The use of wood also seriously depletes local forests. The resulting soil erosion has a negative impact on local agricultural production. However, as people seldom have an alternative to firewood, they continue to rely on wood despite their awareness of the negative consequences of wood cutting. In Uganda, a local organisation has developed an education programme to introduce clay stoves in the villages. It aims to equip communities with the skills and knowledge needed to manage their natural resources in a sustainable manner. People are also trained in new methods of charcoal production which use considerably less wood than traditional methods. Moreover, the production and sale of charcoal provides families with an additional income. The project also supports the replanting of trees in communities, in which a group of villagers is trained which then disseminates its skills to other community members.

Many local associations and NGOs are promoting the use of fuel-efficient stoves. These come in many different designs and use different materials. Solar cooking and heating are also being promoted. The savings in fuel consumption range from 0 per cent to 40 per cent depending upon the quality of the project, funding, the extent of local initiatives and participation as well as on cultural acceptance of the innovation.

In some places people are supplied with supplementary fuels, the consumption of which is less damaging to the natural environment than wood. Among the substitutes being tried are charcoal, peat, crop residues, kerosene, bio-gas and carbonaceous briquettes.

Projects, such as the one from Uganda, often combine the introduction of energy conservation methods with strategies to protect and restore trees and other vegetation. This is done through the promotion of domestic tree-planting, shelter belts, live fencing, agro-forestry and organic gardening.

What is chosen as the focus of environmental action depends much on local conditions. Firewood consumption is a crucial problem in Uganda. For the fishing community in the Philippines the biggest issue is the state of the mangroves and over fishing. In arid and semi-arid regions of Senegal, to access to water is the major environmental problem.

The Global Dimension

"Thinking globally and acting locally", which has been a frequently heard slogan since the 1992 UNCED conference in Rio de Janeiro, is one of the guiding principles of most environmental adult education programmes. While community initiatives are vital, it is evident that the local level cannot be the only focus of change. It is also necessary to create greater awareness of global environmental problems, through networking, advocacy and lobbying at all levels, from government to the factory floor.

Because of the global dimensions of current problems, environmental education for one region must include environmental education elsewhere. For example, environmental education for Africa must start with educating people in the North, because as long as industrialised countries continue to take large quantities of timber from Africa, Asia and Latin America, deforestation and desertification in these regions cannot stop. At the same time environmental conditions—water, energy, climate and soil—are different in each region and each local context. Educational tools therefore need to take into account the specific cultural, political and environmental contexts.

Local Knowledge

Environmental learning encourages participation. It builds a vision in which the contributions of women, men, persons of different colours, abilities and creeds, indigenous people, the young and the old are equally respected. Environmental education explicitly draws from the knowledge of indigenous people and those who are closest to the land.

The need to promote and build on local knowledge and indigenous traditions has been repeated time and again. That communities often possess immensely valuable knowledge and mechanisms for coping with often harsh environments is widely known and acknowledged. The expertise of the learners, who have a first-hand experience of the changing environmental balance, is regarded as an important source of knowledge. Similarly, the role and authority of local communities in protecting their own environment is stated in many policy papers and reports. But in reality many indigenous populations today have been deprived of their rights, including property rights over the land they inhabit. Backed by national governments, international companies make enormous profits by exploiting national resources on a large scale. In Malaysia, for example, communities' livelihood is seriously threatened as their lands are being destroyed by logging and plantations.

In these contexts, local concepts of resource management and conservation techniques have lost their meaning. Traditional knowledge, which functioned as part of a system of governance, no longer exists. It is often claimed that environmental education needs to include traditional knowledge and has a specific responsibility to revive and promote such traditions. However, in a context which is characterised by economic exploitation and political domination, local systems of preservation, which rely on local authority ad control over resources, may no longer be effective.

It is nevertheless possible and even necessary to use traditional knowledge in environmental education, provided that local traditions are reassessed in the context of the present conditions. This process of analysis and comparison of different strategies should be carried out in conjunction with and under the control of local populations. A process of critically assessing the value of local experience and avoiding externally imposed solutions should form the core of any environmental education programme. Otherwise such initiatives face the risk of becoming mere folklore programmes.

Wainimate—Save the Plants that Save Lives, Fiji

Wainimate is an association of traditional healers, nurses, environmentalists and community educators living in Fiji. It promotes the use of safe and effective traditional medicines and the conservation of medicinal plants. It has established demonstration gardens growing medicinal plants and dealing with traditional medicine. Workshops focus on traditional medicines used to treat common diseases, such as skin diseases. Participants are invited to carry out ethno-botanical surveys to analyse how plants can be used in the treatment of diseases and for assisting people to record information about useful plants. In this way it promotes the preservation of important knowledge. Another important area of the association's work is finding ways of generating income from traditional medicine.

Conclusion

The experiences presented during the workshop have highlighted a number of problems facing current adult environmental education.

- Government and donor polices with regard to adult environmental education are in a precarious state.
- Environmental education is less developed in adult and non-formal sectors than in schools.

- Teaching practices in environmental adult education often tend to be limited to the transmission of knowledge rather than to promoting a critical examination of environmental problems.
- Practical solutions are seldom promoted in environmental education for adults.
- Environmental education is seldom linked to the immediate environment of the participants.
- There is often a bias towards promoting 'expert' knowledge and scientific and technological approaches.
- There is still the pervading notion that science is neutral, progress linear and growth unlimited. In other words, rather than critiquing dominant models of development and economic growth, adult environmental education remains locked within ideologies which have caused many of our contemporary environmental problems.

In addition to discussing the many difficulties facing the current adult environmental education, the workshop proposed a range of possible solutions and approaches. These include a close collaboration with the community and a democratic approach to project planning and implementation. Other strategies proposed were the integration of social, political and environmental issues into adult education programmes, identifying problems and the use of experimental and creative teaching/learning methods. The active involvement of non-govenmental organisations and local associations has been an important factor contributing to the growing prominence being given to environmental adult education.

19

Health Promotion and Health Education for Adults

Introduction

Health has always been an important topic in adult education. It features in the curriculum of many adult education, as well as general education programmes. Health-related education projects offer courses on general health, nutrition, healthy lifestyle, as well as on specific diseases and their treatment.

Improving people's knowledge about health is a major component in many literacy and basic education programmes. Many of these programmes focus on women and include nutrition, hygiene and family planning. Health education is often combined with other measures to improve well-being and promote community development. Such programmes usually include micro-credits or skills training for income-generating activities. In addition to the structured learning opportunities in formal institutions, adults also learn about health in local self-help and community groups, at the workplace or in non-formal organisations. They also receive information about health informally from television or advertising, or from their parents and peers.

Education is a major determinant of health. It is well known that those who are most likely to suffer from ill health are not only the poorest, but also those with the lowest level of education. What is more, experience in both developing and developed countries shows that literacy and non-formal education programmes can lead to significant improvements in health and general well-being.

Although there have always been close links between health education and adult education, the relationship between the two has not always been systematic. Recently, however, the two fields have been drawn more closely together. The concept of health education, which now embraces a wider notion of health promotion and a new emphasis on prevention, is increasingly focused on learning and empowerment. New methods of teaching in health education have gained ground in accordance with concepts of learning in adult education. Within adult education, the major changes reflect the recognition that adult education has high relevance to current societal issues. As a consequence, adult education is encompassing more and more factors and is increasingly taking a central role among diverse policy sectors—health being one of them.

As a result of these changes, new strategies have been developed in areas where health and adult education overlap. As new connections are forged, the need for a systematic approach to collaboration between the sectors is felt. The growing importance of health in adult learning and the interest in joint action is reflected by the fact that health education and health promotion were included for the first time in a UNESCO conference on adult education. The workshop clearly underlined the desire from both sides for greater co-operation.

The workshop, chaired by Mercedes Juarez, Royal Tropical Institute, Netherlands, featured the following speakers: Ilona Kickbusch, Division of Health Education and Promotion, WHO; Kris Heggenhougen from the Harvard Medical School, Chij Shrestha, World Education, Nepal; Gerlinde Zorzi, Volkshochschule Hamburg, Germany.

The Context

Since the Alma-Ata Declaration on Primary Health Care (1978) and the Ottawa Charter for Health Promotion (Ottawa 1986), which identified the essential role of health education, substantial progress has been made in improving global health. Infectious diseases and infant mortality have declined. More people are better nourished. Access to clean water has increased and people are living longer than before.

But these gains have not been evenly spread. They have been accompanied by major setbacks for many sections of the population. The majority of the world's population still lives in poverty, with poor housing and sanitary conditions. Many people still have no access to basic health care. Despite progress in controlling certain diseases, many contagious diseases, such as malaria, are on the increase. At the same time new epidemic diseases have emerged. There are vast inequalities in access to treatment of certain diseases, with drastic consequences for people with HIV/Aids in particular. In industrialised countries, increases in non-communicable diseases, such as cancer, as well as increases in chronic health problems, stress and drug abuse, have slowed progress towards the goal of "health for all". Developing countries are also experiencing an increase in life-style-related health problems, on top of their already high incidence of infectious diseases. Lifestyle-related diseases are responsible for 70-80 per cent of deaths in developed countries and for about 40 per cent in the developing world.

This situation not only demands sustained investment in public health infrastructure, but also necessitates new approaches to prevention and health promotion, these include providing access to health information, encouraging participation in the control of health measures, and supporting communities in the development of their own health systems. All these strategies rely heavily on adult learning.

However, despite the urgent need to develop such strategies and to continue the struggle for "health for all", there is an unwillingness to invest in public health infrastructure, basic health prevention services and education. In industrialised countries, health budgets are being cut significantly and health systems are becoming increasingly privatised, making access to health care more difficult for large sections of the population. In developing countries, the economic crises, structural adjustment programmes and a reduction of foreign aid have negatively affected health and education services.

The Social Aspects of Health

"Health is essentially a social construct: it is created in the interaction between people and their environments in the process of everyday life: where people live, love, learn, work and play".

Ilona Kickbusch, Promoting Health Through Adult Learning. CONFINTEA, Hamburg, 1997

What is defined as health or sickness, as well-being or disease, depends not only on individual and biological factors, but on the social and cultural environment within which we live, work and interact. Different cultures and sub-cultures have their own understanding of health and sickness. Western biomedical science, although dominating much of diagnostic and therapeutic practice in many parts of the world, is not the only way to fight disease. Health education needs to take into account such different concepts and recognise different medical traditions and local ways of healing. Today, much adult education in the area of health emerges from a growing awareness of the limitations of allopathic medicine and an interest in alternative medicine. People no longer uncritically accept the dominance of one model and the role of the medical expert as the only provider of knowledge. Increasingly, they ask for information on specific diseases and want to be informed about different therapeutic options.

If health is a social construct and a social process, medical factors alone cannot explain what makes us sick or how we can be cured. The physical and social environment within which we live is equally, if not more, important. Basic requirements include access to clean water, housing and food. Other factors, such as economic resources, social situation and political participation are equally important.

It follows from the above that health problems cannot be solved by medical intervention or behavioural change alone. It is crucial that health education take into account the social, environmental and economic factors that determine people's health. Health education needs to enable people to change these conditions. In this view, health education is essentially a social and political process, and a central component of human development.

Health Promotion

The concept of health promotion builds on a social and cultural understanding of health and illness. Health promotion is the process of enabling people to increase control over their health through advocacy and inter-sectoral action. Health promotion is a dynamic and evolving concept which involves people in the context of their everyday lives, e.g. home, school, workplace, etc. and promotes the achievement of the highest level of physical, mental and social well-being for all.

Health education can be understood as a component of health promotion. Health promotion and health education both aim at improving access to health-related information and services to give people more control over their own health and well-being. The knowledge referred to here deals not only with the dissemination of simple health facts, but also other information and skills, such as negotiation and coping skills.

A key component of health promotion policies is community action. Local initiatives are supported through the provision of relevant knowledge, information and training. Recognising the role of environmental and social factors in achieving and maintaining health, community initiative often takes the form of advocacy or political action for creating an environment conducive to health. Such initiatives focus attention not only on models of disease or curative services, but on the social and institutional factors in everyday life.

Although community action implies that communities take on responsibility for their own health, this does not mean that attention is directed away from the political level and the professional health sector. Advocacy and lobbying for better health and more effective health policies is a major objective of health promotion. Public health education is the government's responsibility.

Health Education and Adult Learning

Adult learning plays an important role in current health promotion strategies. At the same time adult educators increasingly recognise the importance of health, including environmental health. There is growing interest among adults to learn more about health issues and this trend is reflected in the growing number of programmes offered in this area.

The closeness between these fields is reflected in the similarity of goals and principles which characterise both contemporary adult education and health promotion policies. Both are being developed to empower people and encompass individual and societal change.

Just as adult education is a process of enabling people to improve their own living conditions and general welfare, including health status, so also is health education/promotion a process of enabling people to take control over their health.

Community participation and learner involvement are shared principles of health education and adult education. Both health educators and adult educators are aware of the importance of the community setting its own agenda. It is considered extremely important to build on local initiatives and people's own experience, e.g. by involving local health specialists and community committees. The role of the health educator or the adult educator is to be a facilitator, a resource, a catalyst for action and sometimes a link for communities to approach other structures, such as government services.

Recent developments in both health and adult learning have brought the two sectors closer together. In the area of health, major changes in policy have been seen since the end of the 70s. The Primary Health Care (PHC) strategy based on the integration of social and economic development, requires community involvement and emphasises people's own capacity to make decisions and manage their health problems. In a similar way, adult education in the 70s and 80s developed towards its current focus on participatory learning which starts with people's own knowledge and experience, and puts control of learning into their own hands. Increased recognition of different forms of knowledge, including 'alternative' or local forms of healing, and a shift away from the expert or the teacher as the only provider of information, have a strong influence on teaching practice in both fields, health and adult education.

In the health sector, the change in the concept of health education and the emergence of the new health promotion strategy has been the most important development in adult learning. Health education has moved from a sole emphasis on transfer of information and individual life-style changes to health promotion that focuses more on the social, economic and environmental factors which are conducive to healthy lifestyles and self-reliance.

With the emergence of this new social understanding of health, adult learning has become increasingly important in health policies. Health professionals and health educators today acknowledge the relevance and usefulness of the methods and strategies developed by the adult education profession.

Health as a Basic Human Right

Like education, health is a basic human right. It is also a prerequisite for the full enjoyment of all other human rights. Respecting this principle requires that national and international human rights instruments be adopted and applied.

> The States parties to the present Covenant recognise the right of everyone to the enjoyment of the highest attainable standard of physical and mental health. The steps to be taken by the States Parties to the present Covenant to achieve the full realisation of this shall include those necessary for the provision for the reduction of the still-birth-rate and of infant mortality and for healthy development of a child; the improvement of all aspects of environmental and industrial hygiene; the prevention, treatment and control of epidemic, endemic, occupational and other diseases; the creation of conditions which would assure to all, medical service and medical attention in the event of sickness.
>
> (Article 12, *International Covenant on Economic, Social and Cultural Rights*. Adopted by the General Assembly resolution of 16 of December 1966).

Health Literacy

"Health Literacy" implies confidence in making one's own decisions relating to health. Health literacy includes knowledge and skills needed to participate in joint action for sustainable health in the family, as well as advocacy in local groups and community organisations.

Health literacy implies more than the ability to read health information; it includes the capacity to use this information, thus turning it into knowledge. Better educated people have better access to information about HIV, its treatment and how it can be avoided. Making information and services available and improving health literacy are therefore crucial to any attempt to combat the disease.

The concept of a learning society implies a broad understanding of education: including non-formal, informal and self-directed learning in different places and settings. Learning about health is a process which can take place in a variety of ways over the course of one's life. As living conditions change and the body becomes older, risk factors keep changing. Thus the continuous need for new health knowledge.

In the field of health, knowledge is changing at a rapid pace. Access to relevant, up-to-date information is critical for informed decisions and choices. Health literacy also takes the form of advocacy. It is no longer just the professional teaching the laity, rather patients and lay people can equally teach the professionals and decision-makers about their health needs.

The most effective education is in helping people to be more confident about their decisions and to widen choices. Being "health literate" includes being autonomous in everyday life, allowing people to be more confident.

Health literacy is a new concept. In order to further the idea as a tool for policy development, it is necessary to identity indicators for the health literacy of individuals and society. Strategies to increase health literacy need to be developed. This is an important area for collaboration between the two sectors.

Projects for Adults

During the workshop many examples of education projects, from countries as diverse as Nepal, Germany and Bolivia, were reported and discussed to illustrate the links between health and adult education. All projects followed an interactive and participatory approach. Adult education was seen as a key element, enabling people to make informed choices and actively participate in improving health conditions at the individual and collective level.

> **Health Education and Adult Literacy in Nepal**
>
> This initiative builds on collaborative work between five Nepali, NGOs, a US-based NGOs, and an international NGO, World Education. The project addresses neo-literate women in Nepal. It imparts literacy, numeracy and health education in the area of health, nutrition and family planning. Learning materials have been developed, taking into account the social and cultural environment of women. The texts are adapted to the literacy levels of women participating in the programme.

Many health education projects focus exclusively on women. Even programmes that are open to both genders have a majority of women participants. Many projects for women combine health education with literacy and income-generation activities, taking into account the fact that women's poverty, lack of education and ill health are closely correlated.

In Bolivia, women have the right to health education. This helps them to learn more about their own health, reproductive rights and sexual health—all issues of immediate concern and relevance to women.

In a project developed in an adult education institution (Volkshochschule, Hamburg) the main concern was dieting and overweight. The project helps women to free themselves from societal expectations and male-dominated images of femininity.

> **Learning in Setting, WHO**
>
> A major part of the World Health Organisation's (WHO) work in the area of health education and health promotion focuses on the idea of "settings for health".

This concept was based on the premise that people are most likely to be interested in organised learning when they can see the link between health programmes and daily life situations and circumstances which create or impede health. In fact if we look at these "settings" where learning about health is most likely to occur, then a range of new entry points for health promotion and health education can be identified. The concept is based on the assumption that all organisations and communities have a health development potential which can be fostered. Promoting health in settings combines health "learning for the individual" and "learning for the organisation". Through this process, individuals can increase their knowledge about health and well-being. A whole range of health promotion projects is being developed in different setting: in universities, villages, schools, work-places and hospitals.

The WHO "Health Cities Projects" has already expanded into a large network of cities all over the world, to make big cities a better and healthier place for their inhabitants to live.

A New Health Policy

Collaboration between adult education and health education has always existed and there have been many joint projects, particularly at the community level. Yet, there is a need for more conscious partnership between the two.

We need to establish grounds for such collaboration. The concept of health promotion, with its focus on inter-sectoral activity and learner empowerment, provides the ideal umbrella for such policies. Health promotion needs education to be effective. Knowledge and skills are needed to enable people to participate actively in health promotion. Ability to participate means empowerment—the power of individuals, organisations and communities to support new approaches to health improvement.

Combined strategies—including education, training, advocacy and organisation building—are needed if real empowerment is to take place. To that end, adult and health educators should collaborate. Public and private partnerships are needed to complement these approaches.

Policies can be effective only if they are implemented at several levels and with the support and participation of stakeholders. The promotion of health at all levels—local, national and global—through an integrated approach is imperative. But the complex interactions and growing international interdependence of our world can also work against the creation of supportive environments for health.

If health promotion is to be understood as empowerment, then projects need to involve the critical examination of social, cultural organisational and environmental conditions and their effects on health and disease. This includes a careful analysis of changing health conditions and how they affect different sectors of the population.

Adult education programmes for health promotion should include the following policies and aims:

- protect the environment and ensure sustainable use of resources;
- put a limit on the production of inherently harmful goods and substances such as tobacco and armaments;
- discourage unhealthy marketing practices;
- safeguard individuals in the marketplace and the workplace;
- promote a dialogue between Western biomedical systems and other medical approaches;
- integrate equity-focused health impact assessments into policy development.

Conclusion

The workshop was an important step towards the goal of combining health education and adult learning. There is both the need and potential for collaborative action at levels from the community to the international.

Education and public health share a vast range of interests, objectives and approaches. Experience in both areas shows that the most effective learning is that which starts from people's own concerns, builds on their own initiatives and brings them together for collaborative action. Understood in this way, participation is more than just assessing people's needs: it implies participation of communities in decision-making.

The right of individuals and communities to health education is well recognised. However the political reality in many countries is different. Health education and health promotion lack vital financial and political backing. Therefore, although appropriate declarations about the importance of health education are included in national and international policy documents, there is little real support for translating these statements into concrete action by governments and member countries.

The Hamburg Declaration includes the important formulation that "Health is a basic human right. Investments in education are investments in health. Lifelong learning can contribute substantially to the promotion of health and the prevention of disease. Adult education offers significant opportunities to provide relevant, equitable and sustainable access to health knowledge".

20

Adult Education and Population Issues in the Post-Cairo Context

Introduction

In the context of the workshop jointly organised by the UNESCO Institute for Education and UNFPA on Adult Education and population issues in the Post-Cairo Context, an international group debated and discussed the future directions of adult education in the field of population issues. The contributions were varied and reflected the multi-faceted nature of population education throughout the world. The chair of the session was O.J. Sikes, Chief of Education Division UNFPA. The keynote speaker was María Josefina Bilbao, Minister for Women, Chile. Panellists at the workshop were Babatunde Osotimehin, the Social Sciences and Reproductive Health Research Network, Nigeria; Jacqueline Pitanguy, Cidadania, Estudo, Pesquisa, Informacao o Acao (CEPIA), Brazil; Wanda Nowicka (Federation for Women and Family Planning, Poland. Commentators were Ansar Ali Khan (UNESCO/Bangladesh); and Pramilla Senanyake, International Planned Parenthood Federation; London.

Particular emphasis was placed on the continuing need to interpret the post-Cairo paradigmatic shift, from a strictly demographic focus towards a new vision of development and gender rights, which was reflected at the 1994 ICPD meeting in Cairo and which had been preceded by many years of preparatory work, both at the level of international civil society represented principally by the women's movement, and at the level of the UN and national governments. The need to interpret went hand in hand with the demand for these agreements to be translated into practical policies particularly in the field of adult education. In this sense, the discussion in Hamburg was seen to be crucial for the development of adult education policy in relation to population and development.

Reproductive Rights in the Post-Cairo Context

At the very centre of the new population discourse is the notion of reproductive rights, applying to both men and women. Reproductive rights come within the arena of human rights as a whole. They involve control and ownership of the body and focus particularly, although not exclusively, on the rights of women to make decisions about their reproductive futures. However, in order to make effective decisions regarding reproductive rights, women and men need to receive information about their options and the implications of these. This is where adult education should play a key role. If the new post-Cairo discourse is to have any meaning over and above the level of verbal exchange, people need to participate in educational processes which will empower them to make reproductive choices. Here we are dealing with the key issue of how to move from written agreements to concrete policy implementation. The role of adult education should be to provide information, promote discussion and debate on the new focus and create a context for moving from global agreements to local and people centred initiatives.

The 1994 Cairo conference brought about a paradigmatic shift in the way that we now deal with population issues, moving from a Neo-malthusian perspective, centred on population control and geared towards demographic goals, to a perspective centred on human rights, and more specifically on reproductive rights. Before the Cairo Conference the issue was seen in terms of reducing global numbers. Little attention was paid to the needs of the individual. Nevertheless some achievements from the pre-Cairo era should be emphasised. The percentage of people using contraception did go up from about 10 per cent in the 1960s to about 50 per cent in the 90s; child mortality was reduced from 24 million a year to about 14 million, and infant mortality was also dramatically reduced. When the focus on numbers became less important what really emerged was the individual: the need to consider the individual as a whole and his or her needs, rather than demographic targets. Cairo emphasised that society accepts that not only men but also women have the right to enjoy sex without the obligation of reproduction and that the principle of equality should underlie the relationship between the sexes. Healthy reproduction and sexuality require care from the early days of life, without sex discrimination by family, parents or health services. After Cairo, the focus shifted to the entire life span, from the girl child or boy child through the maturity.

A tremendous change has also occurred since Cairo in terms of official UN language on population issues. Why has this change come about? Principally because of political work developed throughout the decades prior to the 1990s. A number of actors have played key roles in this shift, among which are women's movements that have been struggling to bring human rights, women's rights and reproductive rights to the fore when discussing population issues. As Jacqueline Pitanguy put it: "I think we are in a time of change. We have not yet had time to measure the concrete effects of this paradigmatic shift. We still don't know yet how to name phenomena in which we are actors and participants, but we do know that what we have to do to understand human rights is to turn to the social history of rights, the social history of education and the social history of health".

In terms of human rights language, reproductive rights occupy a later stage in the discourse together with sexual rights. The first generation of human rights had to do with civil and political rights. The second development focused on social rights. We are only just beginning to talk about reproductive rights. We are at this moment in the process of defining reproductive rights. In this sense, the WHO orientation on health as a human right helps the population field by providing a framework in which to view reproductive health as a right. The concept of health is being detached from the hospital and from the medical field which was its traditional context, and is being given a place also in the field of rights. It has also been possible to identify two main shifts in this human rights language. On the one hand, there is the inclusion of new spheres of life, which need to be protected by appropriate rights, for instance the right to freedom from domestic violence. On the other hand, new categories of people are now recognised as being entitled to the full exercise of rights. These new inclusions have involved major gains in the definition of human and reproductive rights.

The Cultural Context of Population Education

Inevitably, reproductive choices and information available will be conditioned by different cultural contexts, and in particular by different belief systems. The challenge for adult educators world-wide is to come to terms with those systems and find ways to be sensitive to and to respect those cultures on their own terms. In the case of women living under Muslim law, for example, various strategies are being employed that are effective both in achieving the goals of reproductive health education, while remaining sensitive to the prevalent cultural norms. Older women, respected in the community, have been trained to work with young girls and women, in their homes, to teach them about reproductive and sexual health. The notion that reproductive health is a monopoly of Western medicine should be challenged by the exploration of culturally appropriate models.

The example of Nigeria was presented: Nigeria is Africa's most populous nation, and it possesses a rich diversity and a rich mix of cultures. The country has 110 million inhabitants, distributed amongst 350 different peoples which represent different cultures and have distinct characteristics. The reproductive health profile of Nigeria as a nation state also presents numerous challenges to the health care industry and the social sector in general. Pre-natal mortality ranks among the highest in the world, half of which is due to abortions incurred by adolescent girls, who either are uneducated about the dangers or denied access to contraception, information and services as an effective tool. In addition, there is an unacceptably high infant mortality rate, a population growth rate of 3.2 per cent, low contraceptive acceptance rate, and very low levels of female literacy. All this becomes more significant when we realise that in Nigeria, like most African nations, most women are disempowered within the context of the family and cannot make independent choices about their reproductive and sexual health.

In the case of women who live under Muslim law, these women marry very early, some of them as early as ten or eleven years of age. They also enter the child-rearing arena quite early, and they live in a context of almost complete disempowerment. They lack access to information and education about reproductive health and sexual health, and the only information they get is through their husbands. How have these issues been addressed? In Nigeria, for example, elderly Muslim women were employed to go in and teach the women about the basics of reproductive health. They also worked through Muslim leaders and husbands to encourage an increase in the number of years of female education in that region, in the hope that more years of formal education will empower women, expose them to information, delay marriage, and increase awareness and so improve the dignity of all women.

In this issue of culturally sensitive education, it is also vital to stress the interrelationship with pre-testing of educational demands, methods and materials. If adult education is to be culturally sensitive it needs to address issues such as sexuality by working with the community prior to the commencement of programmes to determine what its needs are and how it would like these to be addressed. An emphasis on respect for people, both individuals and larger communities, ensures in turn a positive response. It is important to regard adults as subjects of population education rather than objects. Indeed, educators can learn as much from the adults they are teaching as vice versa, therefore education should be seen as an exchange as well as a process. In addition, the language of sexuality, as distinct from the textbook descriptions of sexuality, and the way in which people express themselves regarding their sexuality and that of others must also be taken into account.

Culturally appropriate materials such as drama and song need to be made use of, too. We should not assume that messages regarding population issues can be communicated through written materials only. Finally, a considerable amount of work needs to be carried out with trainers to help them deal with issues of cultural sensitivity. One example was given of how this training can work.

> "We trained some 20-to 23-year-olds to work in the community in a sexual health project in urban slums of Madras, and in rural parts of Uttar Pradesh, a few miles from Lucknow. After their training these young people went into the community and discussed, after their training, very intimate matters on sex and sexuality with the people in the community. One thing that really shocked me, well surprised me, was that a 23-year-old unmarried Roman Catholic counsellor could sit among 45- and 50-year-old married Hindu gentlemen and talk freely about masturbation, about sex, about intercourse. And if you had told me that a woman, dressed in a sari like me, who is a 23-year-old Roman Catholic, could actually go and talk to married men, I would have been shocked. But it worked, because of the way this lady was trained. She was able to use those skills—bringing out the best from these gentlemen in discussing matters of sex and sexuality".
>
> *Pramilla Senanyake, IPPF*

Sexuality and Adult Learning

Perhaps more than in any other area of adult learning, the subject of sexuality requires to be treated as private and confidential. This particular aspect of population education was something which was emphasised in the workshop. Participants referred to the success of hotline campaigns for young people which protected their anonymity but which nevertheless provided them with much needed information unavailable either through their parents or their schools. These campaigns which ensured confidentiality moreover were often used by parents themselves as a means of finding out information which they could then pass on to their children. They said, "We are parents, and for the first time we have now got ourselves empowered by the information that this programme provided. So we will be better informers and educators for our children. We are expected to provide sex education for our children, but we do not know ourselves, so how can we inform our children? For, strange as it may seem, the bearing and rearing of children does not necessarily mean that parents know how their own bodies function. The non-written media were particularly, important in this respect. In addition to telephone hotlines, the use of the television, particularly through soap operas, as well as popular song and drama, are very effective in combining confidentiality with up-to-date information.

Body knowledge is crucial is sexuality. In general people are aware of how the hands, feet, head, legs and arms work, but in the hidden, there is much ignorance. But mapping of both men's and women's bodies is one educational technique that can be used. Women in particular need to become more aware of their bodies to understand them as part of their personal identity.

Another issue is that of sexuality and language. Language is often used in a different way when referring to sexuality. There is even a definite sub-culture whose manner of expression relates to sexual activity. Adult educators need to be able to understand that language in order to be aware of barriers to understanding and paths to communication.

In general it was stressed that adult educators need to work closely with youth. Often those in charge of programmes did not have direct contact with young people and often had misconceptions about young people's sexuality, believing them to fit the sexually active stereotype. What was needed was to listen to the "voice of youth" and to provide spaces in which they could express their views.

Gender Relations

The relationship between men and women was another theme discussed at the workshop, and crucial in adult learning and population issues. Societies, through social dynamics and hierarchies, often prevent women from having full decision-making responsibilities. Male involvement is therefore necessary for the success and viability of reproductive health programmes. Girls and boys are all part of the human life cycle that needs to be considered in this educational process, too. In turn the issue of inter-generational communication is particularly important. Stress needs to be laid on the wisdom of older people, their acquired experience, and the respect they command in specific societies.

Women's empowerment is crucial. No population plan and no education plan can succeed without it. Empowerment is a concept developed in the Afro-American movement in the U.S. but which has now become commonplace in the women's movement. But what does the concept of empowerment precisely imply? Who is empowering whom?

In social systems where women are always given secondary roles, in life, in society, in family relations, in the education of the children, in decision-making, there is a disempowering aspect to education. Education is part of formal power structures, which impede a women in taking hold of her own life and destiny and exercising power in many different levels of that society. If you have relationships between women, between women and children and between women and men, which are based on hierarchies, you have in the end a disempowering system of social relations. But what is an empowering system?

The women's movement began by creating small groups, called "groups of reflection" which was a way of organising women to talk among themselves, so that they would perceive that they could and that they had something important to say. And in this building of self-esteem there was the sense that this meant being entitled to take decisions regarding their lives. And now, in many countries, there are either governmental bodies or a specific gender public policy perspective in different bodies, that will enable women to be empowered through a number of other mechanisms, education being a key one.

What is the difference between human rights and empowerment? Human rights give us a frame of reference to which we can refer our work, but the tool to have someone exercise their human rights is empowerment. You can have a very good set of laws, but if these laws are not exercised, if men and women do not feel that they are entitled to the exercise of these laws, this frame comes apart. The function of empowerment is to bring laws and the reality of life together.

AIDS Education

AIDS education is closely linked to issues of reproductive rights, women's empowerment, responsible sexuality and adult learning. For many years there was a disempowerment of women in cases of sexually transmitted diseases and HIV/AIDS because AIDS had been projected by the media as a male homosexual or drug-user's condition. So women were disempowered by being led to believe they were not part of a risk group. In other words there was the perception that their was no such a thing as a risk group in itself, but only a population at risk.

AIDS education is only recently adjusting itself to the new reality of sexuality education and women's empowerment. For many years it played on peoples' fears and prejudices even promoting misinformation regarding the transmission of the disease. It has shifted from being perceived as a uniquely homosexual disease to one that affects all groups in society including children.

> The whole concept of education vis-à-vis population issues has a new meaning as defined by the Minister for Women from Chile: "Education no longer means 'classroom'. Education is a permanent process in space and in time. It has a vertical dimension because the life cycle constitutes an educational object. It also has a horizontal dimension as space itself is an opportunity of education...Education on reproductive rights should start at home and in the community and continue through all the channels of formal and non-formal education. A responsible sexuality and the knowledge of each person of her or his reproductive rights require an adequate sexual education which gives both wife and husband the means to take decisions on the basis of ethical criteria corresponding to their culture and religious beliefs".
>
> IPPF brought together a group a young people under the age of 23, and asked them to express what

> they felt were their basic rights in relation to reproduction and health, and the resulting code is now being used around the world. All people, regardless of sex, religion, colour, sexual orientation or mental and physical ability have the following rights as sexual beings: a right to be yourself, a right to protect yourself and be protected from unplanned pregnancy, STDs, HIV and sexual abuse, the right to have health care and the right to be involved in planning programmes. But in order for young people, or indeed for women, to exercise their rights the, providers need to know how to behave and how to provide those rights. This is another area to be developed. In sharing their views with us they let us know how they wanted us to treat them, the importance of confidentiality, their need for information services and in a language or by means that are easily understood, and in a welcoming manner. These points are important for us to realise, because although a woman does have, in most parts of the world, access to her head, to her hair, to her hands, to her arms, to her body, her feet and her legs, in some parts of the world unfortunately, they little bit in between that square does not belong to her. That's guided by certain males of the species. Moralists, politicians, lawyers, all try to tell women how best to use their anatomy, particularly, the reproductive anatomy. So what we are aiming for with empowerment, with education, is to make sure that every part of a women's anatomy belongs to her, that nobody else can take control of it and tell her how she should use it.

Conclusion

NGOs have been extremely active in the field of population education, particularly feminist NGOs focusing on women's rights and on health issues for women. The role of NGOs, however, and their relevance to government policy and adult learning needs to be explained and emphasised. In particular, many innovative approaches initiated by NGOs working with adult educators on population issues could be extended on a larger scale by working with governments. Africa, Asia and Latin America have seen a tremendous growth in NGO activities in that last decade and these NGOs will have to be substantially assisted in terms of growth and in terms of capacity building, so that they can be a vehicle for the development of not only reproductive health and reproductive rights within societies, but of civil society as a whole.

Adult education has a major role to play in communicating the population policy shifts that have taken place since the ICPD Conference in 1994. Programmes are conceived and planned in accordance with culturally appropriate models and take into consideration the new issues of human rights and sexuality, of AIDS prevention and of changing gender relations. Population education is education for life, for a better quality of life for all people.

Part 7

Adult Learning, Media and Culture

21

New Information Technologies: A Key for Adult Learning?

Introduction

The introduction of new technologies into adult education necessitates both a rethinking of traditional relationships and the development of new ones amongst learners, educators, adult education organisations, local and national governments and the many other stakeholders in the field.

Five panellists, representing the key stakeholders, different regions, and levels of technological development, presented their views at the workshop on "New Information Technologies for Adult Learning" at the Fifth International Conference on Adult Learning in July 1997 in Hamburg. The panel consisted of Mamadou Ndoye, Minister of Education, Senegal; Lalita Ramdas, International Council of Adult Education (ICAE), India; Rafael Roncagliolo, World Association of Community Radios, Peru; A.P. Hardhono, Media Research Centre, Indonesia; Eero Pantzar, Department of Education, University of Tampere, Finland. The workshop was chaired by Pauline Marois, Minister of Education, Quebec, Canada.

In preparation for this working group session, three informal meetings were held on the potentials and limits of new information and communication technologies, including an evaluation of the virtual seminar carried out in March, 1977.

The cultural revolution driven by communication and information technologies was seen as an opportunity for the democratisation of education, for enhancing learner-centred flexibility and for reaching out to un-served communities.

But at the same time it was felt necessary to raise questions as to who controls the technology, and why, how and for whom the technologies are being used.

New approaches to the implementation of technologies in adult learning are needed in areas which include access, content, respect for different cultures, languages, copyright and self-learning approaches.

Access to New Information Technologies

Information and communication technology is a powerful tool to increase every citizen's power to have access to information and new forms of education. It can also enrich the learning environment.

At the same time, new technologies reinforce social disparity. The use of the Internet and other information technologies continue to be dominated by persons with higher education and income, because equipment is often unavailable to the others and because there is still wide-spread technological illiteracy.

Many developing countries are nonetheless experimenting with information and communication technologies and evolving new open learning systems.

Questions are also being raised concerning virtual classrooms. Who will produce and deliver the learning materials? Who is to decide on their contents? How can we ensure that people have the possibility of accessing, understanding and becoming familiar with the culture of new technologies from an early age? What conditions could assist in the introduction of information technology in rural and remote areas to help integrate these communities?

Concentration of ownership and a monopoly on information and communication technologies may hinder cultural diversity. Concentration of ownership may upset the fragile balance between holders of intellectual property rights and users of that information.

Access to information content is also threatened. Information programmers and analysts are charging prohibitive prices for software which many countries are unable to afford. The widespread adoption of software is further hindered by legal statues.

> "Why suddenly is there a renewed interest in trying to propagate sudden concern that have-nots who barely have access to a school or to drinking water or to shelter must suddenly have access to information technology...it is important to look at some of these underlying assumptions. Because the market is not necessarily idealistic and innocent. Because over the last three decades we have been at the receiving end of a lot of outdated technology, which the developers of that technology cannot absorb. Can really mere technology and the kind of access to information in itself address the issue of poverty?"
>
> *Lalita Ramdas, ICAE*

Cultural Issues

If the information highway becomes widely accessed without sufficient national input, then it may serve as a one-way channel for disseminating the values, languages and cultural norms of the industrialised nations. Even these countries face tremendous challenges to make sure that the content satisfies the cultural needs and realities of their societies and its minority groups.

If every adult learner is to have adequate access to the required knowledge, then new communication technology and media need to take into account the following factors in the preparation of content and course material for educational programmes:

- indigenous and vernacular knowledge must be valued and used along with relevant exogenous knowledge—acquired beyond the local community;
- international and national strategies for promoting the use of new technologies and media in adult learning must take into account the diversity and integrity of language and culture, and support local and vernacular content;

- international organisations and national agencies—both profit making and non-profit making—must find ways to support the development of learning resources that increase the diversity of learning/teaching materials;
- ways should be found to integrate libraries, museums and cultural centres into learning programmes using the new technologies and media;
- other languages, besides English, must be given public and private space to promote their content and culture.

Distance Education

Millions of adults in all parts of the world take distance education courses each year. One can quote numerous examples of small distance education projects, often based on a virtual classroom model, that use new communication technologies—open secondary schools, open colleges and correspondence programmes. However, only a small minority of adults undertaking distance education courses have access to "new information technologies" such as a PCs with Internet access.

The Indonesian Open Learning University

82 per cent of the persons at the Indonesian Open Learning University are adults of the age 30 years and above.

The Indonesian Open Learning University consists of:

- radio programmes of 25 minutes each at 10 p.m. Indonesian time;
- television programmes four times a month, 25 minutes long, at 11 p.m.;
- 20 computer assisted instructional programmes for students who have access to the Internet;
- communication between learners and the lecturers; counselling through e-mail;
- a network of services with 32 regional offices for learners to register for adult education programmes;

> - 330 supervised examination sites;
> - a communication and information technology infrastructure;
> - satellite educational programmes for the general public.
>
> Many of these programmes have to deal with problems of cost. The other problem is access, only 60,000 adults out of 200 million people have access to the Internet.

There are three broad types of usage of open distance learning systems:

1. for delivery of supplementary study materials to facilitate independent study;
2. as a "stand alone" direct educational intervention;
3. for complementary inter-personal communication and learning support.

Open learning systems address key issues not adequately addressed by conventional systems:

- learner-centred pedagogy, flexible in time and space;
- accessibility in remote areas;
- use of local community services;
- recognition of non-formal and informal learning processes.

The costs of high quality learning materials for distance education programmes (print, audio-visual, CD-ROM kits) can be kept low provided they are reused over several years by large numbers of adults on a given course. However, people involved in course material development and design are not necessarily the educators. The question therefore arises: How can communication technologies be used to bridge this gap between the designers and developers of course material on the one hand and the tutors on the other?

Although teachers and learners in distance education are usually separated in time and space, nearly all distance education programme have an element of face to face contact through para-professionals. Such learner support includes counselling, advice, special registration, flexible tuition, monitoring assessment and accreditation of informal learning.

Distance education is diverse and is usually based on a combination of technologies, making use of whatever is available and accessible to learners. In rural areas of many poorer countries, post, radio, satellite and television are used for transmitting educational programmes. Sometimes non-educational distribution networks for soft drinks are used to deliver print materials.

However, the mere use of technologies does not guarantee that learning will occur. Learning depends on the motivation of learners, on orientation, on the prior acquisition of learning skills, as well as on the competency of professional developers and the quality of local tutors.

In planning and developing study programmes for distance learning many questions have to be addressed: Who is the target? What are the conditions under which he lives? How can he or she study? What kind of media can be used to support learning? How can the participants be helped to become independent learners, taking responsibility for their own learning? How to organise interactive radio or TV instruction?

New Learning environments and the Practice of Adult Education

The change in the learning environment is not just about providing adults with flexible learning opportunities and information services in the work-place and home. It is also about how adults participate in the information and communications technology, how information is used in this environment, how the local cultural infrastructure of museums, science centres and libraries is used, and whether written media are available.

The enrichment of the learning environment through Information and Communication Technology (ICT) depends on several factors:

- political and financial willingness to invest in new technology;

- up-to-date infrastructure, computers, data networks accessible to the public;
- information campaigns (e.g. the BBC campaign);
- suitability of teaching and learning materials for adults;
- more resources for households to spend on the Internet;
- networks providing opportunities for all adults to get familiar with ICT;
- partnership between educational institutions and cultural services.

Non-formal adult and popular educational media are good ways to prepare people for such a scenario. Conventional media, journals, radio and television are an essential part of lifelong learning environment. Researches have shown a greater faith in the information conveyed through radio and television both in formal and informal learning, than in the relatively unreliable knowledge conveyed through the Internet. However, the excessive speed of change tends to isolate individuals and fragment identities. It is therefore all the more necessary to look at technology, communication and information in an integrated way.

New Technologies and Adult Basic Education

While new information technologies might help improvement in the quality of higher education, it has to be underscored that universal literacy and the spread of education, including post-elementary adult education, are a pre-requisite for information technologies to be an effective agent of social transformation.

New information technologies can offer learning opportunities complementary to and/or continuous with mass media, in particular, radio and television. These are being used in several parts of Asia and Africa to promote adult learning, to reduce the cultural barriers to participate in education and to disseminate information on the range of opportunities. The questions of importance here are:

- How can international bodies, governments and private organisations use both new and traditional communication technologies to provide the basic education needed by 900 million illiterate adults so that they can benefit from further opportunities for adult learning?

- How can those organisations ensure that basic education of adults recognises the holistic nature of learning and the advantage of combining health, agriculture, child welfare and social services with adult learning?
- How can literacy, information, skills and knowledge be used and thus sustained through the education system, the working environment, the local economy and the private sector?

Policy Implications

There are four criteria for policy makers for the use of technologies in education systems:

1. the choice of new technologies that are efficient for broadcast media, while at the same time allowing for interaction;
2. their integration into an overall educational strategy;
3. appropriation of these new technologies;
4. mastery of the tools by educational personnel.

The use of new technologies raises many problems that need to be solved in a manner appropriate to each context:

- insufficient attention to the interactive aspect of learning;
- alienation of the people from their everyday social life and local context;
- new technologies relying heavily on written communication; adults not being sufficiently prepared for new technology; technology not yet adapted to mass learning;
- lack of trained local mentors.

Recommendations

The following recommendations were made by the workshop participants.

- Governments should not reduce their support for social and cultural public services such as public libraries and community centres as these are places which the poor use.
- All countries should be not merely consumers but producers of software and programmes.
- Relevant software, programmes and course development should reflect the national and local identities, as well as cultural and linguistic requirements of countries and local communities.
- It should be made easier for learners to choose the information they need for specific purposes.
- New technologies and conventional ones should complement one another and should be integrated.
- The dissemination and uses of information technology should be open to public debate.

Conclusion

It is essential to invest in information technologies because of their great potential for communication and lifelong learning. These technologies can give learners of all ages greater autonomy and wider access to information.

We are in the middle of a true cultural revolution which will inevitably involve integrating technological innovations into education. In a few years, time most university students will have access to the Internet. The rate of growth of Internet users in Lima, for example, is 20 per cent monthly. The new Spanish telephone company and the TV business are prepared to offer cable television services to all cities, including the slum areas.

Though new communication and information technologies are developing globally, they also offer new opportunities for reinforcing local and national communications.

The prime question is therefore not whether new information technologies should be used in education, but rather how to ensure wide access and diversified production and transmission of information.

22

Museums, Libraries and Cultural Heritage: *Demoratising Culture, Creating Knowledge, Building Bridges Between Cultures*

Introduction

Over the past few decades the adult education sector has experienced enormous growth and diversification. Today adult education is being provided not only by educational institutions, both private and official, but also by cultural institutions, such as libraries and museums. Cultural institutions provide both informal individual learning as well as structured learning activities for groups of learners.

The workshop on the role of culture and cultural institutions in adult education at the Fifth International Conference on Adult Education, held in Hamburg in 1997, provided an opportunity to recognise the importance of these institutions for lifelong learning. It synthesised examples of good practice in this field and underlined the importance and the role of cultural education with respect in intercultural understanding, global developments and peace.

The workshop, chaired by Peter Krug from the Federal Ministry of Education, Science and Further Education in Germany, featured the following panel of speakers: Roberto Hernáiz Landáez, Foundación ESARTE Venezuela, Jutta Thinesse-Demel,

Adult Education and Museums in Europe, Arlette Thys, International Library Association; a representative from the Dhaka Asania Mission in Bangladesh, and Brain Martin, Heriot-Watt University, Scotland.

The workshop proposed the development of a comprehensive adult learning concept within and among cultural institutions and the revision of inflexible structures and approaches.

Adult Learning in Museums: An Overview

One might say the collection, conservation and exhibition of artifacts is the museum's primary task. But in fact all museums are first of all learning places. Most museums have pedagogical programmes. School programmes are the most common type of educational service offered by museums, followed by lectures and courses for adults.

Museums offer different types of education/learning opportunities for adults. Most museums have formal services such as gallery talks, lectures, guided tours and publications for distribution, providing structured learning opportunities. At the same time, visitors who go through a collection or an exhibition may experience some individual and informal learning. Many educational institutions use museums as an additional teaching and curriculum resource. In other programmes, the museum is not an adjunct but at the centre of a learning programme. An adult education course can, for example, be structured around an exhibition. Another example is when a museum develops a programme for a specific group of adults. The Museum of the Moving Image in London had a programme for older people to compile oral histories. Such programmes help to make museums more attractive and interactive. Other initiatives try to take the museum out into the community. The aim of such activities is to make museums more accessible to various parts of the population, and more responsive to the visitors' needs and interests. Such initiatives are sometimes developed through a collaborative effort between a museum and an adult education institution.

Learning around museum objects can be an effective way to provide education to people who do not have easy access to the written word or do not speak the dominant language. Museums can also be used for language teaching programmes.

Are Museums in a Crisis?

Despite the many new initiatives by modern museums to make their exhibitions more attractive and no democratise access to the museums, a sense of 'crisis' was reflected in several interventions made during the workshop. It was felt that museums are increasingly being taken over by modern theme parks, television and the Internet, and that the number of visitors to the permanent collections is steadily decreasing.

Museums play a marginal role in current adult education practice. The role of cultural education, and the contribution of museums as sites of cultural learning, is not well organised. The relationship between the museum educators and curators and the adult educators is not always without conflict. Whereas much of adult education is concerned with process-oriented non-formal teaching and pays specific attention to the learning styles and the prior experiences of adults, education programmes offered by museums tend to be structured, using teaching models drawn from the classroom.

Museums often perceive their public as passive recipients who need to be told how a collection has to be interpreted. Collections provide guidance for the individual or the group as to how to "read" an exhibit. Museum collection are often arranged according to someone's interpretation and therefore entail a "programme of learning".

The collaboration between museum educators and adult educators is rendered difficult by the fact that the museums have remained largely separated from the developments in adult education, Museum education has sometimes been criticised by adult educators for not being in touch with the teaching practices and principles of current adult education. Many museums educators, however, see the need for acquainting themselves with new teaching methods and believe that they have much to learn from adult education theory.

New Initiatives

At the same time this "crisis" seems to have actually generated many innovative and creative initiatives. Many museums have successfully restyled their traditional and somewhat out-dated exhibitions. Other museums offer a range of interesting and experimental exhibition projects. Objects are presented in vivid and tangible ways and become integrated in topical relationships and scenarios. Exhibitions are designed to stimulate the imagination and creativity of their viewers.

The Museum Cristobal Rochas in Venezuela

The museum Cristobal Rochas, a museum of visual arts, founded by the *Foundation Estade* in Los Tecques, Venezuela, is not a conventional museum. The founders placed education as a main task alongside the collection and exhibition. Their aim was to use the arts to contribute to the integral, holistic education of the adult. Recognising the fact that the traditional dynamic between museums and the public is not always satisfying, Cristobal Rochas was not conceived as a museum which the public visits, but as one which visits the public. *Foundation Estade* tried to create an active museum which could attract new audiences and make the museum accessible to a wide range of people. It believed that the arts needed to be presented in a way that would bring them closer to people's own experiences. Art needed to be understood not as something exotic, but as part of how everybody experiences and expresses life.

Thus, Cristobal Rochas goes to the schools, the offices and the streets. One of the museum's most innovative projects is an initiative in the local prisons. The prison population is a public which has seldom or never been in a museum. Because of the lack of prior experience with this type of public, the *Foundation Estade* began its work with a very small pilot project in one prison, involving only 9 inmates out of the total prison population of 433. This prison already has a programme of theatre and drawing workshops for its inmates. Awakening an interest in the arts was the main aim the Foundation pursued with this experimental workshop. The project started with a sensitising workshop. The success of this initiative was immediate. The participants had an unusual interest in artistic expression. Even those who were often supposed to have little interest or sensibility for the arts, immediately took hold of this new form of self-expression. Drawing and painting materials were then provided and practical courses in drawing or woodcarving were offered. Participants received a certificate after finishing the course. After 2½ months of work in the prison, the group had expanded to 32 prisoners.

The work in prisons has now developed into one of the most important educational activities of Cristobal Rochas. The project helps inmates to develop their own 'free' personality and to counteract the experience of prison in oppressing mind and soul. Art also helps the prisoners to feel useful in their society. With this project, one of the Foundation's other aims was to convince the community involved with the penitentiary system that activities like these can help improve and reform the situation in prisons.

New partnerships between adult educators and museums can emerge from this search for new ideas and concepts in museum work. Adult education with its specific approach to learning can help make the museum a more accessible and attractive place. Museums and museum education have the potential for reform and innovation allowing them to extend their traditional functions and to take on new roles as learning institutions. The example here from Venezuela is a particularly interesting case; it demonstrates that museums can reach beyond the confines of other own buildings and their traditional public.

Partnerships Between Museums and Adult Educators

Museums have a unique contribution to make in partnership with adult education, namely by providing the resources and methods for learning from objects. Museums and their staff have considerable experience in this field. While in schools and adult education classrooms teaching mainly works around 'second hand' sources, in museums the objects of learning can be seen and possibly even touched. In this sense, the museum can be a place for autonomous learning, can encourage enquiry and critical analysis and thus be empowering. Informal learning takes place while visitors have the pleasure and amusement of looking at an exhibit. After all, such pleasure may be the main reason why people go to a museum.

The Munich Adult Education Centre's "Museums-werkstatt", a Programme of Experimental Activities in Museums

This programme, starting as a pilot initiatives in 1984, was aimed at migrant workers and their families who attend language and professional skills training classes at the Munich Adult Education Centre (*Volkshochschule*). After the end of its experimental phase, in 1988, the project was extended. Since then it has also opened for Germans and includes a programme for disabled people. The project aims to reach people who do not normally visit museums or art gallerias. It tries to help them discover and enjoy the world of art and science.

A course for teaching German has been developed which includes working with the foreign students in a museum. Language is seen as a form of cultural expression and so language teaching in the museums has the advantage of providing an environment which reflects culture, in this case German culture. Students can explore language and culture in a different way and they are encouraged to develop their own impressions. The overall aim of the project is to develop new models of language learning.

Many adult and museum educators see the need for more research, documentation and dissemination in this area, and the possibility of replicating such approaches in other contexts. One example of how the demand for more collaboration and exchange of information at the international levels can be responded to is the project "Adult Education and Museums" (AEM). The project, funded by the European Union under the Socrates programme, promotes the role of museums in adult education. It identifies and analyses innovative projects with museums and adult education institutions in the 15 member states of the European community. The main features of these initiatives, along with the obstacles and difficulties faced, are identified and analysed and a case study produced. The projects show a great variety of approach and involve a range of different people. Examples include:

- early retirement programmes with senior adults;
- reintegration programmes for unemployed adults;
- activities with disabled people;
- language learning in museums;
- occupational training for younger people;
- apprenticeship qualification courses;
- projects with prisoners.

These examples demonstrate that learning programmes for children and lecture presentations for adults are no longer the only type of activities museums have to offer. Adult education, with its informal and non-formal learning practice, can contribute significantly to museum learning. The final report of the project highlighted the need for new forms of advocacy and training opportunities for museum personnel.

The Place of Libraries in Adult Learning

Libraries are a natural resource of formal and non-formal learning for all those who seek information and knowledge or come for the pleasure of reading.

Education has always been accepted by public libraries as one of their most important tasks. In recent years, many libraries have extended their education services and become involved in open learning schemes. They are acquiring new forms of learning materials, such as multi-media learning materials, and are developing into resource centres. The increasing pressure on many adults to keep up with technological developments, to keep themselves informed and to explore new fields of activity and knowledge are leading to libraries becoming important sites for informal and self-guided learning.

In the present policy context, libraries are receiving renewed attention from governments. Public libraries are regarded as essential partners in many governments' efforts to increase educational standards in the country. However, such policies are not without ambiguity, as many neighbourhood libraries are being closed down because of local budget constraints.

Libraries play an important role in individual and community lives. Comparative figures on the attendance at museums and art galleries and libraries in the UK show libraries to be the most popular form of public cultural provision. Figures also show that libraries are used by a wider section of the public than other cultural institutions; visitors include people from all social classes and all generations.

Broadening Access to Information through Libraries

The role of libraries in the promotion of reading was given particular attention by the workshop. A main concern was to find ways to broaden the accessibility of libraries and to consider how to adopt them to the new demands of the information society.

The project "The Library and the Public" started in November 1996, when the Florentine public library Isolotto brought together a group of public libraries from Catalonia, Flanders, Denmark and Italy. These libraries shared one characteristic: they all made considerable efforts to break out of the confines of the library building and its traditional public and to reach those adults who normally do not visit libraries. The librarians who attended the meeting in Florence developed a joint project on the promotion of reading through the work of libraries. This project, which received a grant from the European Commission's Socrates programme, tries to improve cooperation between libraries among European countries. It was later tutored by a team from the University of Florence. The overriding aim is to enhance to exchange of experiences and provide a forum for the comparison of new methods. In facilitates links between libraries and provides support with the introduction of new approaches including training for library staff.

The focus is on new ways to promote reading and to disseminate information beyond the library buildings. Particular emphasis was placed by the librarians in this project on promoting the role of libraries with respect to new information technologies. The development of the information society and the increasing use of new media in communication and business creates new forms of exclusion. The ability to participate in these new communicative practices depends not only on access to technical means but also on having access to the required skills. It was felt that those who already experience difficulties with traditional literacy are the most disadvantaged with regard to computer literacy.

The project highlighted the urgent need for public institutions to develop new policies in order to address these inequalities. Governments need to take into account the demands of its population for information and skills acquisition. Access to new skills needs to be guaranteed. Increasing the number of training courses alone would not resolve the problem: training and information services need to be adapted to the interests and reading abilities, skills level and language.

Libraries can be important partners in such new strategies, provided their functions are revised and adapted to meet the new demands. They can help provide access to the new communicative media, in much the same way as they have always disseminated the traditional print media. In order to fulfil their new roles, libraries should join forces with other educational and cultural institutions, in particular with adult education centres. The Socrates Project has demonstrated that libraries can be effective in ventures, even without additional financial means being granted.

The Role of Village Libraries

Village libraries are one of the more common forms of post-literacy provision in many literacy programmes in developing countries where learning opportunities are extremely scarce and there are hardly any reading materials. Their main goal is to help learners retain their literacy skills and to provide opportunities for further reading and studying in other areas of interest for themselves and their communities. Post-literacy does not take place in structured courses, but learning is self-directed and autonomous. Improving learners' self-learning skills is an important aim of the village libraries.

The Asania Mission in Bangladesh has set up village libraries in about 55 communities throughout the country. Approximately 5500 learners are involved in the Mission's continuing education programme. This is particularly relevant for a country such as Bangladesh with a very low literacy rate, and where only 25 per cent of the women are literate.

Post-literacy education through libraries consists of a 12 months continuing education programme. In addition to further literacy learning, participants receive training in other skill areas. They can form development groups and receive micro credits in order to set up small enterprises. The neo-literates achieve autonomy of learning and improve their skills.

The village libraries are linked to a mobile library which in turn is connected to the central library. The mobile library provides new books and materials to the village library once or twice every month. At the central level, the Mission's Material Development Division produces new materials which are then circulated through the mobile library system. In this way a very large number of materials can be distributed without the need to produce large quantities of each booklet or text and so production costs can be kept relatively low. A large variety of materials are produced by the Asania Mission, including easy-to-read magazines, newsletters, wall magazines, posters, books and guides, on topics such as health, nutrition, law and environment.

The Kerala Village Libraries

The Kerala Village Libraries in India is part of a library movement that started in the 19th century. This movement grew out of the Kerala Library Association, formed in 1943, and which with the support of the state government set up village libraries throughout the state. In the 1970s, the Kerala Library Association launched a functional literacy campaign.

> Although the village libraries are mostly used by those who are comparatively well educated, it is believed that the village libraries and the reading rooms have contributed to the high literacy rate in Kerala (above 90 per cent in 1990). The fact that so many people can read and write generates in turn a demand for these libraries.

Like the example from Bangladesh, many countries have set up local libraries as a component of an education programme and to function as learning centres which have a facilitator role and a set curriculum. In many cases the library in managed by a local person or facilitator with little or no specific training. In some cases, participants have to pay for the use of materials in the library.

Although several countries are now trying to develop the local libraries into 'local learning centres' with trained staff, as in Namibia, or into 'continuing education centres' as in India, in many other contexts these libraries remain underdeveloped. They often consist of little more than a box with a few books and documents.

Many practitioners and planners involved in post-literacy activities regard the local libraries as a failure. In practice the libraries have encountered a range of problems and they have often not led to the development of sustainable regarding programmes. Distribution is a serious problem. Even if the materials reach the local centres, they are not distributed to the learners. In some cases the materials are rarely used because they are not relevant to local concerns, culturally inappropriate, written in the wrong language or just uninteresting. Many adults with low literacy skills are also uncomfortable with self-learning. Access is a further problem. Materials may not reach those they were meant for, as local libraries can be dominated by users from the more educated population or by school children.

Environmental and Cultural Heritage

Places of cultural heritage provide the viewer with an almost direct access to historical events. Critical interaction with such objects can help to develop awareness of one's own culture and historical background. This can foster an understanding of the complex web of national and international relations and circumstances which shape local developments and events.

Environmental heritage can be regarded as an extension of cultural heritage. It can mean a variety of things, from a person's knowledge of her natural environment to the development of a critical awareness of the links between man and nature.

For the purpose of educational activities, however, environmental and cultural heritage need not be treated separately. Cultural and educational tourism programmes can include both learning about the culture and about the natural environment of the region in question. Such an approach allows for a better understanding of the interrelationship between developments in human society and changes in the natural environment. Places of cultural heritage as well as natural sites can be used as objects for such kinds of learning. By exploring the significance of such sites, learners can also develop their own sense of belonging to and being part of the history of their communities.

Environmental and cultural learning can be part of an education project which examines current social and political issues as well as future-oriented ones. At the University of Naples, such education projects have been developed. They focus on the immediate environment of the participants. The Region of Tuscany is involved in a similar project together with the Greek ministry of education and the generality of Catalan. This joint initiative is entitled "Mediterranean routes for the environmental and cultural education of the European citizen".

The Relevance of Cultural Learning in the Context of Current Challenges

In view of the many challenges contemporary societies are facing, in terms of poverty, unemployment, racism, migration and civil war, cultural education may seem to have little relevance or be a luxury for the minority of well-off and well-educated citizens. Frequently, people argue that culture, in the form of art or literature, has few links with the problems and experiences of individual people and the challenges of everybody life. But experiences such as those presented during the workshop, demonstrate the significant contribution cultural learning can make and its relevance with regard to contemporary societal issues.

Cultural learning is crucial for both personal and social development. Consequently, there must be a right to cultural education for each citizen. Adult education through cultural institutions can contribute to the development of personal and collective identity, while at the same time fostering an understanding of different cultures.

Museums, libraries and other cultural institutions can address inter-cultural issues because they have audiences from different cultural backgrounds. The scientific, cultural and technical collections of museums and libraries are able to make world-wide developments and structural relations visible, showing the connections between local events and global conditions. Museums can allow the visitor to compare different times and different cultures, and thus to discover both the diversity and the uniqueness of humanity as it is found in different cultures and populations. Similarly, libraries with their books, magazines, videos, tapes and Internet facilities can help promote knowledge and understanding of different cultures and situations.

The workshop underlined the social and political significance of cultural education. Participants shared a view on cultural which goes beyond the conventional elitist notions of high culture. Fostering the knowledge and understanding of the languages and cultures of other populations, of political systems and economic developments in other countries is an essential component of all future-oriented and socially engaged adult education. The aim is to improve the international dimension of adult education and to encourage it to see its responsibility to contribute to more tolerance and peace. However, the question raised was what kind of educational facilities museums and cultural institutions should offer in order to be able to address these issues.

Conclusion

Museums are more than auxiliaries to teaching. Libraries are more than places to borrow books from and cultural heritage can mean more than visiting war monuments or touring through wildlife parks. All are special sites of learning and offer 'open-ended' learning situations which can provide a range of meaningful experiences for adults.

These new experiences in adult education activities with and by museums, libraries and other cultural institutions, some of which have been illustrated on the previous pages, demonstrate the particular and unique contribution cultural institutions can make. Yet, this contribution is not always recognised. Cultural education is not a priority in the new adult education policies in many countries.

But there are positive developments. The importance of informal learning, its contribution to success in formal education and its part in the well-being of individuals and societies is now increasingly being recognised. This trend has a positive impact on the cultural sector as more attention will be paid to the contribution of museums, public libraries and other cultural institutions to such informal learning.

That cultural education has a significant and unique contribution to make in the overall field of adult education and with respect to lifelong learning is without question. However, as one speaker said, what this contribution of museums, libraries and other cultural institutions consists of needs to be made much more explicit. It is the task of the educators in this field to make their contribution more transparent and to convince policy-makers of the importance of cultural education.

In order for cultural education to make its contribution to adult education, the workshop endorsed two further recommendations:

1. As cultural institutions are an essential part of adult learning libraries, museums, theatres, ecological parks and other such institutions need to be strengthened and appropriate funds should be allocated in order to develop these as adult learning resources.

2. The conservation and use of cultural heritage as a lifelong learning resource needs to be promoted and methods and techniques for strengthening heritage and cultural learning be developed.

Part 8
Adult Learning and Groups with Special Needs

23

Adult Learning and Ageing Populations

Introduction

Everywhere in the world, in both developed and developing countries, population patterns are changing and people can now expect to live much longer than they did 50 years ago. Consequently, there is a growing demand for adult education as well as other social services as it is realised that education can play a vital role in enabling older people to remain independent, to keep up with changes in society and to make their lives more fulfilling.

This chapter highlights the main issues raised at the workshop "Adult Learning and Ageing Populations" held during the Fifth International Conference on Adult Education in Hamburg in July 1997. The purpose of this workshop was to discuss issues relating to the educational needs and demands of older people, to examine current education policies for older people in various countries and regions, and to plan future approaches and activities at the regional and international levels. The workshop—the first on this issue ever run at the conference—also focused on special education projects for older people and on the broader question of how to increase governments awareness of older people's educational needs.

Prior to the conference, a discussion guide on "Learning and ageing populations" had been drawn up at a meeting organised by the European Association for Adult Education (EAEA). The workshop itself was chaired by Lesley Hart, Senior Studies

Institute, University of Strathclyde, Scotland; Huib Hinnekint, Centrum voor Andragogisch Onderzoek, Belgium and Alex Withnall, University of Keele. The panel of speakers consisted of Nelly Schwarz, Adult Education Council of Latin America (CEAAL-ANOS, Chile); Alistair Crombie, Australian Association for Adult and Community Education; David Lance, Bilan University, Israel; Yosep Rochera, International Federation of Senior Citizens Associations (FIAPA), Rosa Maria Falgas (ICAE-EAEA), Spain; Theresa Lodetti, European Federation of Pensioners and Older People, Italy; Noel Ray, International Federation of Third Age Associations (FIAPA, France).

A commitment to older people's education is only starting to gain momentum and much remains to be done both in the area of advocacy and in the development of appropriate learning possibilities towards giving older people the attention they deserve.

The workshop on "Adult Learning and Ageing Populations" was part of this growing movement. Another major step forward which will provide important opportunities to bring older people's concerns to the forefront is the fact that the United Nations has declared the year 1999 "The Year of Older People".

The Context: An Ageing World

More than 25 per cent of the adult population are aged 60 years of older. In some regions this proportion is expected to rise to about 40 per cent due to better conditions of health, wealth and education.

It is estimated that between 1990 and the year 2030 the number of people aged 60 and over will have tripled world-wide. Persons aged 65 or older will increase from 155 to 325 million in developing countries, and from 131 to 188 million in the developed countries. While the rates of increase are lower in the South, this is compensated by the higher overall population growth in these countries.

During 1995, the world's population of over 60s increased by more than 12 million with nearly 80 per cent of these occurring in less-developed countries.

In Latin America, the number of people older than 60 was 20 million in 1975. It is estimated that in 2050 there will be 95 million people aged 60 and over. This growth is the result of increased life expectancy.

Life expectancy rates are also different between the sexes with the result that among older adults women outnumber men. At the age of 60, the male/female ratio is 99 males to 100 females. At the age of 80 and over, there are only 69 males for every 100 females.

The increase in the proportion of older people to the general population everywhere in the world is a clear indicator of the changing age structure of our populations.

The Situation of Older People in Contemporary Society

Older people should not be considered a homogenous group. Indeed, this section of society can be characterised by its heterogeneity. Many are fit and active, but a large proportion of older adults, mainly those living in poor conditions, are threatened by isolation, poverty social exclusion and loss of human dignity. In both developed and developing countries many older people live in poverty and are denied access to proper health care and other basic services. They are marginalised within their own families, by their communities and by the larger society.

For many older people in the world earning a living after officially retiring from work is a necessity rather than just a desire to remain active and productive in the later part of life: State pensions are often too small to allow for a decent living and many order citizens depend on their families and friends for support. However, the type of employment open to older citizens is often marginal and characterised by low pay and little or no job security.

In some countries, older people are more respected by their families and communities but severe poverty combined with ill health may nevertheless prevent them from taking a more active role in the community or in social life. These elderly people may be home-bound and unable to travel long distances in order to see a doctor or a nurse. Many people have no pension and have to find other ways to ensure economic security. Ensuring their survival is the biggest concern of these older people.

Compared to the younger generations, the majority of older citizens have lower levels of formal education. This is even more true of older women. The level of functional illiteracy among older people is relatively high compared to illiteracy levels among the younger generations. The lack of reading and writing skills makes it difficult for older people to gain access to information and services. It often makes them more dependent on others for help. They might, for example, need to be helped with understanding a drug prescription.

A Limited View of their Situation and Lack of Information

Younger generations have rather limited views about older people and their way of life. Older citizens are often portrayed as passive dependent. They are considered a social and economic burden to society. Not many seem to be aware of the difficult conditions of life older people often have to face. Their contributions to their families, their communities and to society at large often go unrecognised.

Despite the more positive view of the physical and cognitive abilities in old age now being advocated by medical science and gerontology, many people still believe that old age means pathological biological decay and loss of intellectual capacity. Even social science disciplines have looked at older citizens as being dependent and lacking the capacity to be self-supporting. Such deficit notions still dominate public option and policy-making.

In the field of education, older people are often assumed to be a difficult clientele. They are believed to be slow and passive learners, and lacking memory in their learning process.

Education Project for Older Citizens in Chile

This programme provides basic education, health education and organisational skills training for older men and women in the capital Santiago and in the southern rural areas of the country.

- The participants organise themselves in groups.
- The main aim is to improve social participation of older people.

> The groups are given training for one year, after which they will continue to work together on their own.

A major difficulty when trying to lobby for older people's concerns is the lack of information about their situation. Research results from the few studies that are available show that older people have a variety of livelihood strategies.

> **Help Age International, UK**
>
> Is a network of independent organisations in developed and developing countries working with older people. It has initiated a research project on the contributions older people make to development in Africa. Focuses on:
>
> - the livelihood strategies of disadvantaged older people;
> - the perceptions of well-being;
> - the contributions of older people to family and community;
> - the issue of the lack of information on older people, including their educational needs;
> - influencing social policy discussion and policy-making on ageing in Africa and other developing countries.
>
> It is planned that in a second phase, similar research will be carried out in Latin America and the Caribbean.

Making people aware of the situation of older people through research and information campaigns is an urgent task which needs to be addressed by both governments and the public. Although the demographic changes are now being recognised, the implications of these changes are still a matter of much debate. Among policy-makers, the discussion has been dominated by concerns about the financial costs to society. The main question being raised, especially in industrialised countries, is how publicly funded pensions, welfare and health care can be secured.

Governments, are emphasising the need for reforms in the pension system. Such reforms often mean a reduction of state support for older people. At the same time, governments are openly encouraging younger citizens to invest in private pensions schemes.

Towards a More Positive View on Ageing

Many older people in both developed and developing countries are actively involved in productive life far beyond the official age of retirement, in various types of voluntary and non-remunerated work. Others contribute to easing the workload of their families by taking care of daily housework. It is also very common for older people to take on an important role in the education of their grandchildren.

The notion of retirement does not make much sense in many economies where the boundaries between formal employment and informal sector activity are more fluid, with many people at all ages out of formal employment for long periods of their lives, or self-employed.

Older generations make significant contributions to the subsistence of their families. A survey among older people in a township in Durban, South Africa, has revealed that almost all of those participating in the survey who received a state pension shared this income with their families. Since unemployment rates are high in the township, the pension is often the only income for a family with several children and grandchildren. This forces elderly people to use their pensions to help their families survive. (OPL, Participatory, Needs Assessment, MUSA, Durban, South Africa, 1996).

The amount of work older family members are responsible for can be significant. In countries with a high rate of labour migration and urbanisation, migrants to urban areas can put additional pressure on the older people who remain in the rural areas. Where HIV and AIDS are a major problem, older people are particularly affected as they often have to take over as carers and economic providers for their adult children and orphaned grandchildren.

Older people also play an active role in communal and societal affairs. They engage in a variety of tasks and new activities, playing a crucial role in local decision-making processes and holding important responsibilities as members of local committees which address development issues. A more positive view of the Third Age is thus highly appropriate and urgently needs to be promoted.

Within adult education, it is important to build on the positive aspects of ageing, on older people's involvement and experience and their potential for development and a fulfilling life in old age. Adult education has a lot to contribute to supporting active and successful ageing.

When older adults are involved in education programmes, the experience has been positive. Older people possess a range of learning skills from prior experience, and they are no less active and motivated learners than younger people. Studies on learning capacity have shown no major decline in learning capacity before the age of 75. Most older adults can achieve high levels of intellectual capacity. Their ability to learn does not decrease, nor does it necessarily remain statics. In some cases, learning abilities can even increase. Illness may sometimes be an obstacle to learning, but this need not always be the case. Most older people today are relatively healthy and some difficulties, such as sight problems for older literacy learners, can be overcome quite easily. Literacy programmes for older people are, in fact, an interesting way to illustrate the often wrong assumptions about older people's learning abilities for they have shown that the older participants are as persistent in their learning as their younger co-learners and equally successful.

New notions of active and successful ageing and the positive view of older people and their contributions to society need to be applied in the design and implementation of programmes. It is necessary to recognise the creative potential of older citizens, their capacity to learn and to engage in new activities, their enthusiasm and their willingness to contribute to improving their quality of life. They are a positive force in the community.

Education and Welfare Policies

Growing Demand for Education

There is a growing demand by men and women aged 60 and over for a more active life and the fact that education has a major role to play is being increasingly recognised. Organisations of older people, such as Age Concern in the UK, provide services for older people, develop their own local initiatives and network with similar groups. Such local initiatives create a demand for various forms of training and education, including training in organisational issues for members of local groups or skills training for income-generation and supporting local carers.

> *The Australian Association of Adult and Community Education* received a grant from the government in 1995 to undertake policy research into third age learning in Australia. The research report contained the demographic facts of life among older people in Australia; an extensive national and international literature review of the research available on older adults and learning; and policy recommendations.
>
> The research was initiated as part of a response to the growing recognition in Australian society of the demographic changes which started to become obvious in the 70s and 80s. In the beginning, financial issues, such as the growing problems of pension provision and of meeting health needs of older people were in the forefront. But lately there has been growing interest from the Education Ministry in the contribution of Third Age learning to successful ageing. There are strong indicators that sustained cognitive inquiry and intellectual activity is correlated with greater self-esteem and self-reliance.
>
> In 1997, the Association formulated its own policy for Third Age learning. The fundamental axiom of this policy is that this learning should be under the control of Third Age people. In an attempt to put this policy into practice, a Third Age person has

> been nominated to the executive of the Association and is responsible for the learning programme. At the regional level, the Association, which is an active member of the Asia-South Pacific Bureau of Adult Education (ASPBAE), has offered to become the lead agency to develop a network among organisations working with older people throughout the Asia-Pacific region.

Many organisations such as Help Age International also devote a lot of their efforts to advocacy and lobbying activities for they are aware of the importance of getting the support of the general public and the politicians, and making the needs and contributions of older people more widely known.

Education for older people should no longer be confined to the margins and, indeed, there are many interesting and innovative activities going on in this field. In Australia, for example, the situation of older people is now receiving the increasing attention by the government: Australia is one of the few countries which has a law to protect older people from discrimination. Policy-makers are also beginning to see the link between an intellectually and psychologically fulfilled life in old age and sustained good health.

Similar surveys to the one just described are being conducted in other countries. There is increasing co-operation between non-governmental organisations, universities and governments in developing joint activities.

New Experiences with Education Programmes for Older Persons

Merely providing access is insufficient. Older people need specific learning programmes, different from the education opportunities open to younger citizens. Education should not only be for, but also with and by older participants.

The fact that older people are often seen as dependent and lacking initiative and determination may lead to education programmes being conceived in a top-down, patronising manner which give learners no opportunity to set their own priorities or make their own decisions. It is not unusual for older people to hold such views themselves. Many have little faith in their own ability to learn and feel that they need to be taught in a very structured way.

Despite such difficulties, older people are more often than not motivated to learn. They have very clear ideas about what and how they want to learn and often express their demands. Some even take the initiative and set up their own learning structures.

"Learning in Later Life Programme" University of Strathclyde, Glasgow

In 1987, the University of Strathclyde in Glasgow, initiated a pilot programme with daytime classes for older adults. The founders of the initiative "older people only" were aware of the fact that very few older adults participated in the regular programme of adult evening classes. The new programme was entitled Learning in Later Life and aimed at the 50+ age group. In 1987 it started with only 200 learners. This year there are about 2000 participants. The biggest increase in participants is among the age group of 50 to 59, reflecting the trend for early retirement in Scotland.

In 1988, the Learning in Later Life Students Association was set up following an initiative by the older learners themselves. Because they enjoyed the classes so much, they wanted to continue meeting over the summer period when the university classes stopped. As a result, the older learners founded their own association. It now has about 750 members and organises a range of cultural and social activities, study trips and outings. The Students Association runs 14 different learning clubs, which are self-organised and independent from the more formal Learning in Later Life programme. Creative writing or urban walking are two examples of learning clubs.

The Older People's Literacy Project in Durban, South Africa

The literacy programme for older citizens in a township of Durban was set up in 1997 by the Muthande Society for the Aged (MUSA), an organisation which works with disadvantaged older people in the Durban area of South Africa. MUSA's aim is to help older people remain independent by providing services such as a home-based health care programme. The Literacy Programme for Older People (OPL) was developed in response to a demand by the older people with whom MUSA works. At a participatory needs assessment, the older citizens decided that they needed to learn how to read and write. Literacy in KwaZulu, their mother tongue, and English would help them to handle tasks such as paying bills or using public transport, meeting with the officials at the pension office on a more equal footing and organising social and income-generating activities. For the older learners, literacy is one of the skills they need in order to gain more control over their lives. A literacy course, which now runs in two townships, has been designed and a curriculum has been developed by the older people. The course focuses on the literacy-related tasks and the literacy uses in daily life including aspects such as filling in forms or understanding a prescription. Teaching is in Kwagulu and English, acknowledging the demand from the older people for both languages. Facilitators are older people from the community who have been trained to teach their peers. Not only has participation in this project enabled members to learn to read and write, but it has also conferred less obvious benefits of literacy: status, greater access to their rights with regards to government pensions, greater security and personal fulfilment. The project is being supported by Help Age International and the Department for International Development in the UK.

The above examples from South Africa and Scotland are very different. However, some of the issues raised, as the next example will also reveal, are similar despite the differences in social context and cultural environment. One important consideration is how to set up learning opportunities for older people which are simultaneously empowering, supportive of their own initiatives, and which let them a share in decision-making within the project.

One area of great interest today to older learners is computers and computer literacy. Bilan University Programme in Applied Gerontology has a programme for Third Age learning where over 3000 senior citizens have learned how to work with computers. The university is also compiling a bibliography on older learners and computers.

The University runs a research programme on the problems of ageing in society. However, rather than use younger researchers, who might not be the supreme experts in the study of ageing, it is the older people in this programme who are not just the subjects of the research but also those involved in carrying it out. Another programme, called Contact, sends students from the university to visit isolated and house-bound older people. The emphasis in this programme is not on formal education, but on the informal encounter between different generations.

The Senior Community Leadership Programme offers training and retraining for senior members of community organisations who wish to be involved in developing new kinds of social programmes in areas such as education or health.

Recognition of Various Forms of Learning

Learning not only takes place in classrooms or other formal settings but in many and varied situations. The amount of informal, self-organised, unstructured and individual learning most people are involved in is much greater than any provided by formal education.

Older people in particular have accumulated unaccountable hours of informal learning. Whether and how such prior learning can be recognised and accounted for once people enrol in more formal programmes, is an important question. Recognising prior learning also means acknowledging the richness and wisdom of older people's life experiences. It is not enough to give older people access to existing services: it is equally important to create educational environments which recognise and support all forms of learning and all forms of prior experience.

Intergenerational Learning

Older citizens have great potential for contributing to the education of the younger generations. However, given the still prevailing negative views of older people we can foresee problems with younger people accepting tuition from their elders. Older people's wisdom and experience is often seen as irrelevant to modern day issues, particularly in the field of technology and communication involving computers and internet. However, as the above example from Bilan University in Israel shows, such as assessment may not always be true.

The Senior Studies Institute, University of Strathclyde

The success of the Learning in Later Life Programme at the University of Strathclyde led, in 1991, to the setting up of the Senior Studies Institute, the first of its type of Scotland. The Institute has a range of activities and learning programmes for older citizens. Learning starts at beginners level and goes up to first year undergraduate university level. Students can then, if they wish, pursue formal undergraduate studies.

Collaborative research, skills training workshops, intergenerational activities and voluntary projects are essential parts of the above Institute's work. Its founders strongly believe in the benefits of linking the older people to the younger generations. One voluntary project exemplifies the possible contributions of older adults to helping younger people cope with specific difficult circumstances in their lives. This project is located in Scotland's spinal injury unit in the Glasgow hospital. Many patients stay here for periods of 6 months or even a year. Very often the patients and young people who have had serious accidents and who must now adjust to a life very different from their previous, often sports oriented and very active one. A group of volunteers was trained by the Senior Studies Institute to work with the patients towards the end of their rehabilitation programme, trying to help them get over this traumatic time and adapt to their new life. The older volunteers particularly support the patients in their attempts to get on with, and find new meanings in, their lives.

Based on the concept of collaboration and partnership with older people, programmes such as the examples from Scotland and Israel show that it is possible to develop projects that involve both younger and older persons. Such initiatives can be beneficial to both generations. The Senior Studies Institute not only profits the older learners, it is also been positive for the younger students at the University who now accept their older colleagues as an integral part of the college.

Conclusion

Towards a Society of All Ages is the official subtitle of the 1999 UN Year of Older People. As the workshop emphasised, such a motto is indeed highly appropriate and urgently needed.

Older people have a lot to say and should be enabled to have a continuing voice in society. It is time the older generations were no longer marginalised, and their experience and knowledge were valued. Education has a major part to play in this process, enabling older people not only to pursue their own learning aspirations, but also to share their experience with others and to contribute their skills to their communities.

We need to direct our efforts towards overcoming an image of the elderly as distinct and different from the rest of society. Older people are a part of society, a part from which the younger generations have much to learn.

It is crucial to affirm that the right to education is a human right for all. Education for older people needs commitment from the State and all institutions; the State has a responsibility to provide education for older citizens.

Governments should make adult education for the elderly population a priority.

Their commitment to the goal of "Education for All by the Year 2000" must mean policies to include older persons. The adult education sector must receive more support from the government. Governments should not retreat from their responsibility towards providing education for their older citizens. Available resources must be invested in learning opportunities for older people, in addition to primary education and vocational training. State-sponsored literacy education should include older people in addition to those of working age. People should not be made redundant on account of age. Access to vocational retraining programmes should not be denied to older people. Companies should not argue that it is inefficient to train workers who are close to their retirement age.

Older people need to be given the right to make decisions about their own learning. Education which is aimed at empowering older people to remain creative and independent, cannot be one which simply assumes in can supply older people's needs and denies them the right to choose what and how they want to learn. Such programmes need to build on the resources, the creativity and the experience of older people.

Learning between and about different cultures and population groups and between and among different generations needs to be encouraged.

We need to be aware of the ever prevailing tendency to exclude older people from educational opportunities.

24

Adult Learning for Prisoners

Introduction

A prison sentence is intended as a deprivation of library. But, all over the world, it usually means a violation and deprivation of many other human rights as well, including the right to adult education. Access to adult learning is not only a basic human right. It is a crucial step towards the reintegration and the rehabilitation of prisoners.

These and other issues were discussed at the Workshop "Adult Learning for Prisoners" at the UNESCO Fifth International Conference on Adult Education held in Hamburg in July 1997. Former inmates spoke about their experiences. Their presentations revealed that adult learning in prisons should go beyond just training. The demand for learning opportunities in prisons was widely expressed. At the same time it was felt that this demand was not being met by appropriate provisions. The discussions looked into initiatives for improving learning possibilities in prisons. Future strategies and the issue of the right to adult education for inmates were raised. Most importantly, the workshop explored ways to continue and improve co-operation and networking ambng those involved in prison education.

The chair of the session was Robert Badinter, former Minister of Justice in the French Government and former President of France's Constitutional Council. Speakers included Bernard Bolze, Observatoire International des Prisons; Jean-Claude Delcorps, Ex-Inmate, Belgium; Postora Ortega, Secretarioado Paz, Justicia, y no

Violencia, Nicaragua; Zoongo Marie-Lea, Union Inter-Africaine des Droits de I'Homme, Burkina Faso.

It was stressed that in many countries, including industrialised ones, human rights abuses in prisons are still common. Prisoners are denied access to the most basic services such as personal hygiene, health and nutrition. Advocacy for the education of prisoners is therefore difficult, but vitally necessary.

The Right of Prison Inmates

The International Legal Framework

Most countries have signed and ratified the international and regional human rights legal instruments which ensure better detention conditions for prisoners. These include, the Universal Declaration of Human Rights (1948), the International Convenant on Civil and Political Rights (1966), the African Charter on Human and Populations Rights, the Convention against Torture and other Degrading Treatments, the Standard Minimum Rules for the Treatment of Prisoners (1955).

Rules and Basic Principles for the Treatment of Prisoners Adopted by the United Nations

1. Provision shall be made for the further education of all prisoners capable of profiting thereby, including religious instruction in the countries where this is possible. The education of illiterates and young prisoners shall be compulsory and special attention shall be paid to it by the administratioEEn.
2. So far as practicable, the education of prisoners shall be integrated with the educational system of the country so that after their release they may continue their education without difficulty.

Article 77 *Standard Rules for the Treatment of Prisoners.*

Adopted by the first United Nations Congress on the Prevention of Crime and the Treatment of Offenders, held at Geneva in 1955.

> Conditions shall be created enabling prisoners to undertake meaningful remunerated employment which will facilitate their reintegration into the country's labour market and permit them to contribute to their own financial support and to that of their families.
>
> Article 8 *Basic Principles for the Treatment of Prisoners*
>
> Adopted and proclaimed by General Assembly on 14 December, 1990.

In spite of the existence of international and regional frameworks, there is a lack of an international body to ensure the enforcement of international laws. In many countries national laws have not been adapted to the international rules and principles concerning the treatment of prisoners. Nor are national policies designed to implement the provisions of ratified covenants and treaties. In many countries there are no laws on the administration of penitentiary services. In others, numerous bills and amendments lie unapproved, gathering dust. In particular, there is a widespread lack of provision for the education of adult prison inmates.

The Situation: Detention Conditions in Prisons

Hardships endured by prisoners are numerous. Inadequate infrastructure and the lack of space are major concerns. Children are separated from adults and detained in separate wings. Hygiene is precarious, and basic sanitation services are scarce.

In many countries detention centres exist that were built during the colonial period. These centres are old and badly maintained. Prisons are overcrowded, and the separation of women from men is often not enforced. Equipment and furniture and minimal. Health care for inmates is not provided on a regular basis owing to lack of personnel and medicines. Prisoners very often lack basic sanitary necessities including soap. Even food is a problem and relatives often have to bring it from outside. Given this situation, it is not difficult to understand why governments do not view the right to education for prisoners as a priority.

Education for Adult Prison Inmates

The Declaration of Kampala recommendations that: "The prisoners must have access to education and to a vocational training providing them a chance to a better reintegration into the society after their release". The basic objectives of education for prisoners are:

- to teach them new skills;
- to help them retain previous vocational skills, necessary for their later social reintegration.

Yet, even where such programmes exist, they often have severe short-comings. Many prison training programmes are not linked with the regular educational system outside the prisons. As a result, the transition from one to the other is hard to make. Adult education programmes in prison seldom give information on the rights of individuals. Little or no attempt is made to promote creativity. Little attention is paid to the personal biographies of prison inmates.

A serious problem is the lack of a national curriculum. Consequently, when prisoners change prisons, they are confronted with an adult learning system which is completely different from the one they have previously been exposed to.

There is nevertheless a general consensus that adult education for prisoners is a fundamental step towards their social reintegration. The following are some of the important considerations for the development of successful policies in this area.

- Education practices that stress personal development should be advocated for prison inmates.
- Adult vocational education must take into account other dimensions of the educational process such as personal development and attitudinal change.
- The education process should begin as soon as the inmate is sentenced. It is also crucial to offer adult educational opportunities after the release of prison inmates. This would maximise the possibility of social reintegration.

- The issue of motivation to study is also fundamental in adult learning for prison inmates. The problem is not only an individual motivational one but also a social problem. The involvement of many other actors needs to taken into account, including the attitudes of guardians and of other inmates. Other issues relate to the choice between studying and working and of creating a learning environment in prisons.
- All adult education projects must try to link adult learning with the social context of the learner. It is necessary to take into account the variety of social contexts of prison inmates when designing adult learning projects:
  - the social context of delinquency;
  - the social context in prisons;
  - the social context after prison life.

More research is needed on these contexts as well as on illustrating/demonstrating the relationship between adult education in prisons and the process of rehabilitation.

Education should be seen not only as the imparting of skills and knowledge. Most importantly it should be viewed as inculcating values and attitudes enabling the individual to take control of his own life. At the same time it is important to start a debate on the issue of what education should mean to prison inmates. The inmates themselves should be an integral part of this debate. They should air their views on society, on the way it is organised and on the issue of law and order.

The Experiences of Adult Education for Prisoners

Provisions for adult education in prisons in many countries are minimal or non-existent. Where education facilities do exist, these are subject to governmental constraints with regard to teaching materials and equipment. Access is also restricted on grounds of financial cuts.

Yet, in many countries, including those where resources are scarce, there are examples of good practice. An example from

Nicaragua showed how social reintegration of inmates was facilitated by providing them with the possibility to follow a package programme such as Baccalaureate or a course on peace, non-violence and human rights; such courses promoted self-esteem, solidarity, tolerance and conflict resolution—all of which are crucial to prisoners for their later reintegration into society. The approach adopted is one that encourages programmes to be open to inmates as well as to their relatives and to prison staff. The success of this project can be attributed to the participatory, methodology, which used dynamic and creative educational techniques. A set of educational handbooks has been published on this project. In fact the project has been so successful that the NGO implementing it has been asked to train local and religious leaders as well as teachers and peasants.

In many countries programmes exist for imparting skills for personal and group development. They focus on promoting dialogue between prisoners in solving problems of conflict or violence. They encourage attitudes of friendliness and respect for human rights. The overriding aim is to promote a culture of peace and social reintegration.

Several adult learning projects that use alternative methodologies are being tried out in many other countries. In Burkina Faso prisoners can choose to take general education or vocational training courses. Literacy courses are offered in the national language in three prisons of the country. In others French is offered. Prisoners are able to enrol for high school education. They can also choose between different vocational trades such as carpentry, weaving knitting, tailoring or other handicrafts.

There are also agricultural and farming projects in prisons in which prisoners grow rice and raise sheep, cows, pigs and poultry. This contributes to the subsistence needs to prisoners.

Unfortunately such examples do not reflect the situation of prisons the world over. In many countries, such as Vietnam for example, prisoners are prohibited from enrolling for a training course, learning foreign languages or reading books on foreign cultures. Dictionaries are often confiscated and prisons are still compelled to read books on Marxism. All prison inmates, including the old and disabled, and forced to work.

The Educational Staff

A top priority in adult learning for prisoners should be designing programmes for the educational staff, who need to understand the value of such education. The staff could include trained prison inmates. Another option could be the training of volunteers. NGO support could concentrate on the design or purchase of educational and didactic materials.

It is important to develop short-term courses that are well tailored to prisoners needs and conditions. The best method of recruiting new adults to learning programmes is to use prisoners' own motivation to promote their own education. Care should be taken to treat these trainers as having the same rights as other trainers outside of prisons.

Problems of Adult Education for Prison Inmates

There are many financial, social and political problems in designing programmes of adult education for prison inmates:

Funding

The lack of funds for adult education of prison inmates in developing and developed countries is well known. Budgets granted to the administration of prisons are minimal. Often there is greater urgency in providing prisoners with food, health care and decent housing than adult education.

NGOs and associations have, however, developed initiatives with the support of financial partners. Their aim is to:

- improve the detention conditions of prisoners;
- help them in their social reintegration;
- provide education to prisoners;
- organise information and sensitisation campaigns on human rights among the prisoners and the prison staff.

Social Context

The development of education is also hampered by the little public interest in prison education. There is often a negative reaction to the notion of education for prison inmates, particularly in countries where provision and access to education for the general population is limited to a few. In such cases the attitudes of the general population are often biased against providing funding to improve the basic life conditions of prison inmates.

Political Reasons

In many countries governments have no national laws relating to education for prisoners. In some countries policies state that education for prison inmates should be restricted to political training. Professional reintegration or rehabilitation is not the aim of such training. In fact reading or other creative activities are often prohibited. This is a clear violation of the right to education. Governments should introduce laws to correspond with international declarations to which they are signatories. They should establish policies for adult education in prisons.

The progressive democratisation in many countries in different parts of the world could serve as a crucial context for making prisons more humane. However, true participative democracy can only be achieved when the development of human beings is made the centre of all political decision-making. Prisons should be treated not only as penitentiaries but as places where the prison inmates can learn to understand themselves and the world. Adult education of prison inmates must be seen as a priority by political decision-makers. It is a necessary for successful social reintegration of prison inmates. It can contribute to a real and sustainable development of these countries.

Conclusion

Participants to the CONFINTEA workshop on Adult Learning for Prisoners reiterated the fact that the right to education is a universal right of all people. It was imperative to recognise the right to learn for all prison inmates by:

- providing prison inmates with information on and access to different levels of education and training;
- building a basic national curriculum that can be followed in different prisons;
- developing and implementing comprehensive education programmes in prisons, with the participation of inmates, to meet their educational needs and learning aspirations;

- facilitating the work in prison of non-governmental organisations, teachers and other providers of educational activities;
- providing prisoners with access to educational institutions;
- encouraging initiatives that link courses inside and outside prisons;
- strengthening international co-operation;
- organising a global survey for a better understanding of the situation concerning education in prisons throughout the world;
- revalorising the role of all people working in prisons, informing them of the benefits of adult education in prisons.

25

Making Education Accessible and Available to all Persons with Disabilities

Introduction

The workshop "Adult learning for disabled people" held during the Fifth International Conference on Adult Education (CONFINTEA), in Hamburg in July 1997, examined educational provision for adult learners with special needs. The term "special needs" is often used interchangeably with "special educational needs", "people with disabilities", "people with learning difficulties" or "disabled people". Because the term disabled people is preferred by the disability movement, this is used throughout this booklet.

The workshop was chaired by Lucy Wong Hernandez, Executive Director, Disabled Peoples International. The panel consisted of the following speakers: Khalfan Khalfan, DPI, Tanzania; Nawaf Kabbara, National Association for the Rights of Disabled People, NARD, Lebanon; Jahda Abu Khalik, Director, NARD-Women and Disability, Lebanon; Bill Langner, International Centre for Lifelong Learning, USA.

Perceptions and definitions of disability change over time and between cultures and this creates difficulties in obtaining precise world-wide statistics. However it is estimated that there is a higher percentage of disabled people in developed countries than in developing countries. This variation has to do with the fact that disabled people in the developed world have a higher life expectancy and that there is a correspondingly high proportion of disabled people in the older age range.

> In 1994, to reaffirm the rights of disabled people, the United Nations produced a set or rules or guidelines in an attempt to influence international policy and practice. Many of the ideals embodied in this document reflect the changes in thinking about disability that have occurred over the last ten years. There has been a theoretical shift, though not generally concomitant shifts in practice:
>
> - from movements for disabled people to movements of disabled people;
> - from the dependencies model to one where disabled people have the same rights and responsibilities as all citizens;
> - from disabled people having to fit into regular society to society changing to include everybody;
> - from following a path on leaving school that is determined by others to one which they determine for themselves;
> - from being seen as a perpetual child to bring accorded full adult status.
>
> Lasley Dee and Elisabeth Maudslay.
>
> *Adult Learning and People with Special Needs,*
>
> Paper produced for the UNESCO/CONFINTEA Hamburg, Germany, July 1997.

One of the objectives of the workshop was to discuss the implications of these trends for the adult education service and for disabled people as adult learners. It began by exploring the changing perceptions and definitions of disability.

The Changing Concept of Disability

Before we can examine adult learning for disabled people, it is necessary to investigate people's perceptions of disability and how they have shifted in the course of time.

The eighteenth and nineteenth centuries regarded disability from a purely medical standpoint. The disabled individual was seen as necessarily dependent on others, there was a growth of charitable organisations established to care for disabled people, and as a result education was not considered purposeful or necessary. While this viewpoint is still prevalent today, the latter half of the twentieth century has nevertheless seen a growth in movements of disabled people prepared to voice their options and a change in attitude towards their education. The social significance of education, the disabled learners' needs, the content of educational programmes and the training of teachers all now have to be considered.

Society's attitude to disabled people has been unfair in the past, even preventing them from doing what they can do well. While it is true that some disabilities do bar certain activities, most disabled people can perform as well as the non-disabled.

As a consequence of this, disabled groups have begun to point out that barriers facing disabled people are not considered to be inherent in the individual impairment of the disabled person but are socially created by environmental restrictions and social attitudes. Some even stress differences rather than attempting to measure abilities against what is considered "normal", and rather than accepting an imposed ideal of normality towards which disabled people are supposed to aspire, they advocate differentiated assimilation for the disabled.

In the disability debate, individual and social factors are currently opposed. While some maintain that disability is entirely socially created, others stress the need to maintain a balance between factors pertaining to the individual and those pertaining to the environment. However, in practice the legacy of earlier models is still strong.

Because of the dominant voice of the developed world, it is easy to assume that disability is perceived in the same way in all countries and that programmes for disabled people can be automatically transferred from one culture to another, which is far from true. Although this is an under-investigated area, the research there has been shows how different cultures have very different views on what constitutes a disability, what causes it and what programmes are required (Disability Awareness in Action,

1995). The difference is particularly marked when one compares egocentric societies where individual autonomy is seen as paramount with sociocentric ones, where people are primarily considered in relation to others. Many Western programmes for disabled people focus very strongly on developing individual independence, a concept which may be far less important in a strongly sociocentric society.

International and National Contexts

These changing perceptions of disability need to be set within a broader socio-economic context. It is necessary to remember that both the United Nations and the European Union have produced policy statements on the rights of disabled people which incorporate many of the theoretical ideas on disability described above. The United Nations Standard Rules on the Equalisation of Opportunities for Persons with Disabilities (1994) and the Salamanca Statement and Framework for Action on Special Needs Education (1994) reaffirm the rights of disabled people to equal opportunities, full participation in society, and equal partnership in the planning and implementation of those policies which affects their lives.

The United Nations statement is an attempt to improve the status of disabled people by influencing the custom and practice of nation states. However, it is not legally binding and must be seen in the context of the effects of the global economy. As social policy tries to adjust to the demands of the global market, it is increasingly difficult in this context for individual countries to maintain social justice and equity, even where there has been a strong tradition for this.

International bodies have sought to safeguard the rights of disabled people, one of them is the Declaration on the Rights of Disabled Persons:

> Disabled persons have the right to medical, psychological and functional treatment, including prosthetic and orthetic appliances, to medical and social rehabilitation, education, vocational training and rehabilitation, aid, counselling, placement

> services and other services which will enable them to develop their capabilities and skills to the maximum and will hasten the processes of their social integration or reintegration.
>
> *Article 6* **Declaration on the Rights of Disabled Persons.** *Proclaimed by General Assembly resolution 3447 (XXX) of 9 December 1975.*

In most Western countries recent social policy has been characterised by centralised policy formation with decentralised implementation. The changing view of disability has led to corresponding changes in thinking on adult education provision for disabled people as well as on policy and practice issues including the role of disabled people in formulating policies and practice, equal opportunities, inclusion, transition and adult status.

Adult Learning

Adult learning takes place, both formally and non-formally, in many different context which themselves vary from country to country. Learning is not necessarily limited by age or setting, but can occur at any stage in a person's life and in the work-place, in the community or in formal educational institutions. Adult education may include vocational training as well as opportunities for personal, social and cultural development and it therefore has the potential to empower disabled people, to increase their autonomy and economic self-sufficiency and to reduce their dependency on others. However, there is also a need to provide special support learning services such as libraries for the blind, special clubs for the deaf and centres where people with special needs could receive food, clothing and other forms of help.

A Need for Policies for Adult Learning for People with Disabilities

The second part of this century has been a shift from movements for to movements of disabled people. There is an increasing demand for people with disabilities to be seen as equal partners in the formulation of policies and in determining provision. Policies must give birth to new laws for disabled people.

The lobbying by the disability movement has certainly had some effect in influencing legislation. However, legislation which specifically pertains to adult education for disabled people is still rate. A 1996 UNESCO survey shows how only a quarter of countries surveyed had any policies for vocational education for young disabled adults beyond school leaving age. However, even in countries where laws for disabled people exist, they are not always applied. Despite the growing world-wide movements of disabled people, their involvement in policy formulation still appears to be rare.

Many projects have succeeded in empowering disabled people. One project in Mexico, for example, almost entirely staffed by disabled people, functions as a source of advice to neighbouring states and offers training courses throughout Mexico and South America. Such a project serves as a model for all.

Many disabled young people leave school with few or no qualifications and have limited access to improve their situation. As provision for disabled people is now generally being discussed in terms of equal opportunities based on the belief that all people should have equal rights, even if they may have different needs, this means that the disabled should have equal access to information and equal opportunities for participation, opportunities which are often denied to disabled people, particularly women (UNESCO 1994). Recent developments in new technologies as well as accessible buildings, re-designed materials and adapted curricula can be especially beneficial in this respect to certain disabled people.

Existing legislation supporting the participation of disabled people in adult education is based on a variety of models. In some countries, the law still considers the disabled person as a socially disadvantaged person who requires special measures. In contrast, there are other instances where the law supports a social concept of disability based on the notion that all people have equal rights to access mainstream provision and that it is not a person's impairment but the physical environment and social attitudes which create barriers.

In terms of organisational practice, provision varies between countries and also within individual countries. In some countries, disabled people have full access to adult education provision and every attempt is made to eliminate environmental and social barriers. But, in some other places, disabled people, particularly those with more complex disabilities, are either excluded from adult education altogether or are only allowed to participate in certain designated programmes. Irrespective of legislation, the actual quality of adult education for disabled people is ad hoc with the best provision dependent on committed individuals rather than a matter of right. Adult education for disabled people must be seen within a context of equal opportunities as it is exposed in article 2 of the above mentioned declaration.

Placing disability within an equal opportunities context moves it away from a dependency model, as disabled people are seen as people who have both equal rights and equal obligations.

Inclusion of People with Disabilities in the Community and Adult Learning

Adult learning is one of several complementary services working with disabled people and its role is to support their full participation in the community by offering education and training. Inclusion means making fundamental changes in society so that all disabled people become equal participants. It is necessary, however, to make a difference between the inclusion of disabled persons and their integration. Integration is generally accepted as a process enabling people with disabilities to live and work alongside others without disabilities in mainstream settings. Inclusion is regarded as a wider concept and focuses on the changes needed within society to end the exclusion of certain groups so that all citizens are accorded full human rights and equal status. For education, inclusion implies the need for changes in every aspect of the education system to create environments where all who wish to do so can learn.

The UNESCO's 1995 survey of special needs education for school age pupils reported that 92 per cent of countries had policies on integration, although not necessarily legislation. A subsequent study (1996) on integration legislation distinguishes between pedagogic and socio-economic integration, the latter being likely to have more relevance for adult education. Twenty countries have objectives related to integration into the labour market, health, leisure and cultural activities as well as education.

But, although there is widespread international commitment to the integration ideal, variations exist in how integration is interpreted in practice and the extent to which policies and practice are becoming more inclusive. In spite of national commitments, evidence suggests that in reality, much local practice continues to target support at individuals rather than at changing the general education system. For example, there appears to be a need for an holistic approach to curriculum for young disabled persons in which vocational training and basic skills can be emphasised. The OECD/CERI (1986) project report on the transition of disabled adolescents from school to adult life identified the failure of many countries to manage this transition effectively and made a number of far-reaching proposals. Transition is defined as both a phase and a process. It is the phase between childhood and adulthood which is marked administratively by the end of secondary schooling, a period of vocational or academic study and the start of employment. It is also a psycho-social process during which a young person develops from a department child to an independent young adult. The research recommended that if transition is to be managed effectively, states require a nationally agreed concept of transition, a legal framework, co-ordinated and coherent services and an accessible system of post school education and training.

At the moment, however, there is no uniform cross-cultural agreement on the characteristics of adulthood since each society has its own 'markers' although the OECD proposed in 1987 the following indicators of adult status:

- employment, useful work or valued activity;
- personal autonomy and independent living;
- social interaction and community participation;
- adult roles within the family.

It should be noted that these indicators are influenced by Western values, for in many societies adult status is not always accorded to disabled people, who may be kept in a state of perpetual dependency. In recent years, though, more emphasis has been placed on employment and in many countries, various kinds of sheltered workshop or schemes to support disabled people in regular employment have been established. For successful inclusion into the workforce, however, the workplace itself must undergo change.

While inter-agency collaboration has not been the subject of extensive research, inter-agency project, or other forms of partnership, may be a good way of responding to the holistic needs of disabled people.

A project was developed in the late 1970s by the World Health Organisation (WHO). It was a response to the growing number of disabled people living in the community due to the closure of long stay institutions. WHO formulated the concept of Community Based Rehabilitation (CBR), whereby the families of disabled people and community personnel could be trained to deliver basic care. Despite enormous variations in the actual delivery of programmes and many problems in their implementation, the ideals of CBR present both a commitment to furthering the rights of disabled people and a belief that this must occur through involvement of, and changes within, the community. The success of this community-based project is now raising world-wide interest.

Conclusion

From the discussions at this workshop it was clear that educational opportunities for people with disabilities and integration into society can only be promoted by:

- making all forms of learning and training accessible to them and ensuring that the learning and training matches their educational needs and goals;
- fostering institutional policies that ensure equal access, services and vocational and employment opportunities, with appropriate learning technology;

- involving agencies who are supporting the handicapped including pharmaceutical firms, car manufacturers as well as policy makers.

It was also suggested that international co-operation should be enhanced to avoid people becoming disabled, through education for peace programmes and by working to change public opinion. The main consensus of the workshop was that disabled people have the same right to adult learning as other people, do not need special education, except in special circumstances, and should have the same right of access as the non-disabled.

Part 9
The Economics of Adult Learning

26

The Economics of Adult Learning: *The Role of Government*

Introduction

This chapter highlights issues that were raised at the workshop. "The Economics of Adult Learning" held during UNESCO's International Conference on Adult Education in 1997 in Hamburg. It discusses the importance of a proper evaluation of the social and economic benefits of adult education, examines the different mechanisms of its financing, and reflects on the sharing of private and social benefits in relation to how costs are shared.

The focus of the workshop was to propose a new vision of the economics of adult learning, looking at adult learning not as an expense, but as an investment to be analysed and managed as such.

The workshop chaired by Ylva Johansson, Ministry of Education and Science, Sweden, featured the following panel of speakers: Toshiko Nomura, Nomura Centre for Lifelong Integrated Learning, Japan; Ronald Pugsley, Department of Education, United States; Jan Van Ravens, Ministry of Education, Culture and Science, Netherlands; Roy Carr Hill, United Kingdom; Qutub Khan, UNESCO Regional Office, Bangkok; David Atchoarena, International Institute for Educational Planning, UNESCO, Paris; Bhaskar Chatterjee, National Literacy Mission, New Delhi; Abrar Hasan, OECD; and Dirk van Damme, Ministry of Education, Flemish Community, Belgium.

Changing Goals of Adult Learning

It has been argued in the past that the benefits of investment in adult learning were less certain and more long-term than for investment in children's education. Most importantly it was held that money was best spent outside the adult education sector.

Today, however, there seems a shift in thinking and more resources are being allocated to adult learning. This is largely due to outside forces. For instance, global competition in creating a need for adults to remain competitive. Also, increasing geographical and occupational mobility is creating a corresponding demand for language and upgrading courses for immigrants. At the same time there is broad consensus emerging in many countries that government has an important role to allocate more resources for providing disadvantaged populations equal access to lifelong education.

All these issues are having a profound impact on the goals, aims and the nature of adult learning. The major goals of adult learning now include promoting employment and social inclusion. It is characterised by a shift from supply-driven to demand-driven organisations and economies. There is a shift from education to learning.

There is also a shift in thinking regarding the distribution of responsibilities for adult learning over various actors: the state, the education sector, the firm, the learner and the NGOs. Governments in many countries are adopting a steering role and giving more direct responsibilities to institutions at the local level in promoting effective and efficient use of adult learning resources.

Costs and Benefits of Adult Learning

In order to assess the direct/indirect costs and individual/social benefits it is important to distinguish different types of adult learning. These have been described in the literature on the economics of adult learning as remedial, popular and professional.

1. Remedial or palliative second-chance education does not require large-scale investment in infrastructure and equipment since it relies on formal initial education structures. The unit and opportunity costs tend to be low because of the link

between education and employment. However, there are often quite high costs involved in identifying the adults in need of remedial education.

2. Popular community education also involves low costs because of its voluntary character. While indirect costs, such as family or work absences on account of this voluntary commitment, are mostly measurable, the major problem is one of measuring changes, which is its main objective.

3. Though vocational or professional education is supposed to be cost beneficial and cost-effective from the point of view of individual earnings, the social rate of return of vocational education depends also on the number of over-qualified adults in the formal system.

Individual and Social Benefits from Adult Learning

In recent years studies are emerging which confirm the economic, social and individual benefits from adult learning. It has been found that:

- New thinking skills such as problem-solving and team-work as well as personal skills such as responsibility and honesty can make individuals more efficient and more competitive in a global economy.
- Language courses funded by adult education programmes can promote economic independence among immigrants and an ability to exercise their rights and responsibilities as citizens. It has been shown that literacy, especially communication skills, can reduce costs in many other social sectors such as health, family and child care services. Immigrants, for example, who cannot communicate in the official language may increase the cost of health care (need for translation, lack of health awareness), of child-rearing (remedial costs of deficient child-rearing practices) and family services (cost of domestic violence). The assumption behind these costs is that education promotes greater awareness of health and of preventive understanding.

- Studies in America on family literacy programmes which help parents and children learn together, and impart such skills as parenting education and parent-child interaction, confirm that children also learn more and are better prepared for school when parents are involved in their education. So that return on investment is high for parental education, encouraging children to go to school, as well as promoting family planning. Inter-generational approaches increase the economic benefit of literacy programmes.
- A number of family literacy programmes, for example, have successfully targated people on welfare. The savings rapid the total direct cost of the family literacy programmes.
- Improving literacy skills of prison inmates is expected to improve self-sufficiency and rehabilitation, as well as contributing to employment opportunities.

The benefits of adult learning need to be measured more objectively in future. A major problem has been in establishing a causal link between literacy and social benefit. The samples on which many of the conclusions are based are not scientifically established. The link between education and health has been difficult to prove in the past. Nor have there been definite conclusions on the effectiveness of rehabilitation programmes.

Financing Formal Vocational Training in Educational Institutions

Many adult learning systems focus purely on formal educational institutions, especially on covering their cost. Input costs for financing inputs of formal institutions for work-oriented adult learning and high because:

- the learner's productivity is almost zero during time off work for learning;
- teachers and trainers have to be paid;
- infrastructure costs such as classrooms have to be financed;

- the returns on the investment in formal education is demonstrably low;
- formal education is financed regardless of whether learning takes place;
- firms use the opportunity to shift their learning costs on to government by delegating learning to the formal education system. One implication is pedagogical quality, another is that people opt for formal education rather than on-the-job training for reasons of status.

Work-related Training

The distribution of financial responsibilities between the government, the learner and the market has a lot to do with national culture of the country concerned. In some cases it encourages explicit national policies for adult learning involving stakeholders such as the industrial sector. In other cases national policies leave it to the market or the firm as main co-ordinating mechanisms for financing adult training. In the latter case, labour markets are said to be more flexible. Furthermore, it is alleged that in workplace-oriented training systems, the low quality of school leavers' competencies is eventually compensated for by higher quality workplace learning.

Financing Work-related Learning Environments in OECD Countries

In Germany and the Netherlands, the business sectors themselves play an important role in co-ordinating education and private training. Firms play an active role in providing training and education. Various business sectors maintain a fund for training to which each firm contributes regularly. However, the current trend is that firms within each sector are increasingly distancing themselves from others to become competitive. Company-specific training is becoming more and more common.

In the UK as in the USA, companies have the freedom to organise training in institutes or workplace. But economies of scale can only be realised in the larger enterprises. Governments, too, tend to leave work-related learning to market forces. In the United States, for instance, learners' own financial contributions are alleged to cause under-investment in regular vocational education.

In France the Law of 16 July 1971 obliges firms to contribute financially to adult learning, as well as meeting training targets. Though the government in France has a larger role in work-related adult training than in other OECD countries, the business sector and the market also play an important role in vocational training.

An important characteristic of the Japanese system of vocational training is firm-based training. This is in line with the Japanese culture of lifetime employment in large enterprises. The advantages are a low rate of labour turnover and high investment in personnel for the benefit of the firm. However, it must be noted that this practice is confined mainly to large enterprises and requires a situation of full employment. Small firms have problems in financing high quality training and serve mainly as a buffer in times of economic decline among large firms.

The Dynamics of the Knowledge Society

The economics of formal education has until now been focused on the cost side because inputs in the formal system have been easy to measure. Even in workplace training models, the focus has been on formal learning only. Formal learning, leading to certification, is based on criteria of selection and exclusion. These approaches are unlikely to survive unchanged in a knowledge society.

The cost of financing work-related adult learning will have to be re-evaluated because of a diversity of learning styles and non-traditional learning environments that has been neglected by formal educational policies.

New factors are calling for a shift in the vision of adult learning, with greater emphasis on:

- experientiall and contextual learning that relates to work, the home, and community;
- use of technology, especially in the area of distance learning;
- support for continued research and development in effective work-related adult learning practices;
- professional development and training;
- outcome-based measurement of adult learning, in addition to inputs;
- widening the recognition of competencies to all areas of learning.

All these are expected to promote more cost-effective learning. The recognition of non-formal competencies is beneficial to the applicant in that it increases the opportunities for employment. It also promotes social recognition and inclusion, and increases competency as a citizen, family member, etc.

The variety of instruments to increase competencies and focus on learning outcomes will be the hallmark of the knowledge society in both developed and developing countries.

The expansion of knowledge and explosion of information are causing new competencies to be acquired throughout life. Diplomas provide less and less accurate data on an individual's capabilities and potential and are no longer a guarantee for mastery of a craft or trade for a lifetime, as they used to be. New techniques for recognising competencies are being created for their information function rather than for their screening function.

Alternative Accreditation

1. In many countries, the recognition of prior learning has become an integral part of basic and vocational adult education.
2. In the US ISO-9000 is being applied to assess the quality of services. Competencies are deleted from personal records unless reassessed within a certain period of time.

3.	In British higher education a system for accrediting prior experiential learning (APEL) has been introduced.

Many governments have also been moving in the direction of formulating policies towards the better management of competencies. Some of these policies are clearly based on the changing demands of economy and society.

Adult Learning is an Investment

The increased recognition of adult learning as an investment is supported by three current tendencies:

- a growing focus on intangible assets such as knowledge, attitudes, behavioural patterns. Firms and finding these crucial to their performance;
- government attitudes to expenditure on education as investment. Education was treated in the past as a consumer item—one reason why the education sector is subject to budget cuts. This will change if governments treat education as a potentially fruitful investment, whereby expenditure on education and other learning pays back;
- a recognition of the hidden cost of not investing in adult environmental and health education.

Sharing Financing Responsibility for Adult Learning

Financing of adult learning cannot rely solely on the budgets of governments. All the same, leaving the law to the different areas of the market may increase the overall cost of training. Businesses, regional communities, non-governmental organisations and individuals are therefore all called upon to contribute to this investment, as well as the government.

The financing of adult learning raises 3 central questions: Why should one invest in the competency of people in this sector? What are the available sources? How can they be mobilised?

Emerging from the practice of countries, financial and regulator partnership structures are an effective instrument in developing adult learning. The sharing of costs is closely related to the sharing of responsibilities..

The diversifications of public sources of finance, which could include taxes on business, is a critical issue. The establishment of an "embryo partnership" with business may give the necessary impetus to defining principles and methods of joint funding of training. Important examples to consider include the experience of France in this domain, the new Swedish special training fund and the Danish policy of job rotation.

Adult Learning in the United States: Growing Public Support

The federal government's role is to provide funds that leverage state investment in education opportunities for persons who are educationally disadvantaged and most in need of services. The small federal share of expenditures is allotted to state educational agencies based on the population eligible for services in each state. The states allocate federal and other funds to local organisations who actually provide services to educationally disadvantaged adults.

In 1996 the adult literacy education delivery system in the U.S. served some four million adult learners—under-educated adults with limited basic skills, or with limited English proficiency. These adults were served at over 24,000 learning sites attended to by over 184,000 teachers, volunteers, and administrators.

Special focuses in state programmes—such as opportunities to obtain a high school credential or to learn at the workplace—have been put in place in response to changes in the federal adult education statue over time.

Local providers offer services designed for adults in diverse locations and on flexible schedules so that adults can work and learn around their responsibilities as parents and employees. Local providers may be local school districts, community colleges, community-based organisations or alliances of eligible organisations and private enterprises.

> There are many factors that are shaping adult education in the United States. Welfare reform in the United States is an important force shaping adult education. A new law requires that welfare recipients engage in work in order to receive benefits. Therefore it is becoming imperative that welfare recipients have good basic skills. A number of states are changing curriculum to include more job readiness training and work-related contexts for basic skills.
>
> Learning basic skills is done in real-life contexts of work, parenting and citizenship and is aided by technology that provides access to learning even at home.
>
> As a result of the 1991 National Literacy Act, states are required to develop indicators of programme quality and to use them in measuring local effectiveness. The indicators, which govern the direction of programme improvement, are also steered by a variety stakeholders.
>
> The level of adult education services is directly related to demand—such as the demand to be more competitive, demand for language courses for immigrants, demand for education among prisoners and welfare recipients.
>
> Changes in the Adult Education Act require that states spend at least 10 per cent of their federal adult education funds on programmes for institutionalised persons, including not only prisoners, but participants in transitional programmes. This has been a response to the National Adult Literacy Survey (IALS) in which about half of the prisoners reported not having a high school diploma.

Conclusion

Adult learning needs to be reassessed as a productive investment. The benefits—to the individual, the community and society as a whole—can be far-reaching. Formal, non-formal and informal learning styles and environments must be taken into account in the financing of adult education. New formulae must be found to address wider aims such as the promotion of citizenship, democratisation, cohesion and cultural development.

Investment in adult education can pay dividends, not only in terms of economic growth, earnings and employment, but also in health and demographic behaviour. There are social benefits in improved quality of life and the overall development of society.

Beneficial effects extend beyond the actual learners—the direct consumers of education—to affect children, families, and communities as well. There are also hidden social costs involved in not investing in people's competencies.

In order to have a better understanding of the costs-benefit relationship, there is need for more research on indicators of how to measure, quantify and isolate certain factors. New monitoring is required to assess the level of participation and the processes involved, keeping in mind the need for social and regional equity. The experiences of various countries must be compared and discussed in order to arrive at an optimal financing model.

To support the shift from education to learning, and from supply-driven to demand-driven approaches, policies will be needed to stimulate the education and training demands which have not been and cannot be met by formal educational systems.

Only when adult learning is seen, assessed and evaluated as an economic and social investment, will appropriate financing policies be possible.

Part 10
Enhancing International Co-operation and Solidarity

27

Enhancing International Cooperation and Solidarity

Introduction

What should be the purpose of international cooperation in the field of adult learning? What should be its meaning in today's global context? What are the mechanisms which make international cooperation effective in accomplishing its objectives? These and many related issues were discussed at the workshop "Enhancing International Cooperation and Solidarity" held at the 1997 Fifth International Conference on Adult Education (CONFINTEA V), in Hamburg. The workshop was chaired by Kasama Varavarn, Ministry of Education, Thailand. The panel of speakers featured Paul Fordham, University of Warwick, International Centre for Education in Development; John Oxenham, Economic Development Institute, World Bank; Rajesh Tandon (ASPBAE); Clinton Robinson, Collective Consultation of NGOs for Literacy and Education for All; Peter Inkei, Ministry of Culture and Education, Hungry; Joe Samuel, Lecturer, Centre for Adult and Continuing Education, University of Western Cape, South Africa; Barry Wilson; and Ingemar Gustavson, Department of Democracy and Social Development, SIDA Stockholm.

A major thrust of the conference was to shift the emphasis in international cooperation from assistance to one of the partnership, participation, networking and mutuality. The participants in the workshop stressed that these concepts, which are central to adult learning, need to be taken all the more seriously at a time of increasing economic globalisation and accelerating development in the field of information and communications.

Like many other conferences, CONFINTEA V proposed the strengthening of international cooperation in adult learning. However, unlike previous conferences, it ensured that international cooperation did not mean simply cooperation between governments, nor the dominance of the North over the South. Care was taken to include NGOs in the process and to maintain a balance of regional interests through a series of preliminary regional meetings.

International Cooperation in the Past

In its earlier phase, international cooperation essentially took the form of a one-way assistance from the richer North to the poorer South. This assistance also tended to be linked to unilateral conditionalities. Preconditions still imposed by some donors inhibit openness in awarding contracts and make it difficult to involve NGO's participation in the implementation of programmes.

Most governments in industrialised countries have created a ministry or agency for international cooperation. At times these bodies are forced to adapt to criteria set by ministries of economy and finance. Under such circumstances adult education and community participation do not always receive the attention they deserve in development programmes.

The Issues

In the field of international cooperation there are now many changes taking place. First, globalisation is creating the perception that major problems in the world today are shared by everyone on the planet. Secondly, after the end of the Cold War and the breakdown of the Eastern Block, the old geo-political divisions have lost their meaning. Increasingly there is a realisation that human societies rest on shared fundamental values and their it is in their interest to cooperate. This also applies to the area of development. Sustainability demands that the objectives, values and goals of development of the programmes be shared by both partners and donor agencies and defined in an atmosphere of mutual trust.

The New Paradigm of International Cooperation in Adult Education

International cooperation should not mean merely the transfer of resources and technical know-how but rather mutual learning and sharing of experiences. It should also involve institutional and organisational development, reciprocal communication and all parties learning from the process of international cooperation.

International cooperation needs to be viewed as a mutually beneficial exercise between partners, for the purpose of enhancing their capacities to pursue their educational goals. It should be a mutually empowering experience and include a wide variety of actors from the grassroots to the national and international level. Only this plurality of activities and plurality of partners can give the right kind of thrust and momentum that is necessary for accomplishing the goals of international cooperation in adult education.

New Vision in Adult Learning

Adult learning is based on cooperation. National as well as international cooperation should follow the principles of adult learning, i.e. mutuality, participation and partnership. Mutual learning is one of the approaches characteristic of this vision. Other essential features of the new approach to adult learning are:

1. It is increasingly world-wide, corresponding to common concerns that connect people across the world.
2. Much of it takes place outside the fold of formal education, in informal settings.
3. Adult learners are treated as autonomous and responsible beings and not as passive consumers.
4. Adult learning is not longer confined to the traditional education sector but encompasses virtually all areas of life from health and population to multiculturalism and the economy.
5. The focus is on local groups wanting to learn as well as on a holistic education where job-related adult education and capacity building in civil society are brought

together. It seeks to create active and inclusive citizenship by encouraging individuals to learn to transform themselves from within. Creativity, imagination and promotion of an active citizenship are seen as important parts of learning to change.

6. Learners are encouraged to be active participation in all programmes from the planning stage onwards.

Only by viewing learning as capacity building of the whole civil society is there hope that disparities between people will diminish and an inclusive, more democratic society be created.

International cooperation also needs to take into account some of the risks that go with these new developments in adult education, for example:

- Many social movements and networks are finding wider economic and political events beyond their control.
- There are risks in moving away from the old discourse of education to the new one of "learning". It is easier for public figures to make pronouncements about the right to learn, but fail to act when it comes to provision. Furthermore, the notion of adult "learning" could be used as an excuse for leaving adults to struggle on their own.
- High participation figures do not necessarily mean democratic involvement, greater accessibility for the 'have-nots' or genuine social mobilisation.
- Although the new extended vision of adult education cuts across all sectors, many educators of adults, such as health workers, do not see themselves as part of the adult learning enterprise.

Mechanisms for Effective International Cooperation

Participation is the key word in international cooperation. New partnerships are being created. Government agencies, a multiplicity of development NGOs, women's organisations, trade unions, business corporations, human rights and environmental groups—all of these are now becoming engaged in the work of international advocacy for adult learning. All these partners should agree on joint objectives of programme planning, implementation, monitoring and evaluation. They need to see themselves as actors in adult education in a holistic sense, where learning includes as aspects of life and all sectors of development.

The role of NGOs in adult education must be sufficiently appreciated. In the context of international cooperation, NGOs are becoming increasingly involved in adult learning programmes. A collective consultation mechanism has been specially negotiated by UNESCO in order to ensure a strong representation of NGOs in the adult learning sector. NGOs should be adequately acknowledged in government policies, and their diversity and autonomy sufficiently recognised. It is necessary to use their potential to the fullest, enhancing cooperation between government and NGOs as well as among NGOs themselves and other players in development. There is a need for NGOs to be present in international forums to receive information which they can then disseminate to other organisations in the field.

Creating an environment conductive to international cooperation also entails providing greater opportunities for grassroots workers and learners to meet and interact with one another on both a South-South and a North-South basis.

Job-related training and education for active citizenship are complementary and should not be treated as separate entities. Training networks across regions should serve as mechanisms for upgrading adult education and making it more holistic.

A critical task at the macro level is to avoid negative impacts of structural adjustment programmes and other policies (fiscal, trade, work, health, industry) affecting the allocation of resources to the education sector.

Public policy frameworks need urgent review in many countries. The extended networks in the field of adult learning can become active only if there is a suitable public policy environment. There should be greater commitment by both member states and donor agencies to adult education as an integral part of learning throughout life.

To make adult education an integral part of development projects depends to a great extent on the policies of the partner countries and on breaking down the division of planning projects according to sectors. To make projects sustainable certain standards for adult education should be established, such as respect for human rights, protection of the environment, empowerment of women and participation of learners in planning and evaluation to secure ownership.

Sensitive monitoring and evaluation of adult learning programmes and project should be done in cooperation with all actors involved, and built on regular dialogue and discussions, so that they can become a continuous and common learning process. Monitoring is also important in order to take steps to avoid the negative impacts of structural adjustment programmes and other policies on the allocation of resources to the education sector, with special reference to adult education. Different actors and social partners should be given to mandate to carry out evaluation and monitoring.

Multilateral financial institutions should be:

- involved in the debate on adult learning in relation to the negative impact of structural adjustment programmes on education;
- encouraged to contribute financially to networks for local, regional and global cooperation between adult educators;
- involved in a transfer of resources where all partners play an active role;
- encouraged to respect the visions of their partners;
- encouraged to influence the policies of member states in favour of adult learning, rather than simply acquiesce in policies and projects promoted by borrowing members. In this regard, however, multilateral financial institutions need to be provided with the information with which they can advocate policies and projects, for example data on the state of adult learning, the theories of effective adult learning, the social and individual costs and

benefits of adult learning programmes, the conditions for successful implementation of programmes and the effects of literacy and adult learning on abilities to absorb, organise and transmit information.

In a period of rapid change it is necessary to have regular exchange of experience and expertise between sectors and between regions and countries facing similar problems. An important way of disseminating information is by preparing national and regional reports and disseminating them among public and private agencies, trade unions and social partners involved in adult learning.

Mutual learning requires networking at all levels because the actors involved in adult learning are increasing and because new bridges are being built between formal and non-formal education. Mutual learning is the test whether partnership as a principle of cooperation and solidarity has been put in practice.

Conclusion

Following CONFINTEA V, UNESCO will be playing a leading role in international cooperation in the field of adult learning and in mobilising support of all partners, not only within the United Nations and multilateral systems, but also among non-governmental and other organisations in civil society.

For reasons of economy and efficiency, international cooperation will be based on existing institutions, structures and networks. The aim is to make the existing machinery for action, coordination and monitoring more effective, rather than duplicating it.

The challenge of a global economy must be met through global cooperation by:

- promoting lifelong learning, taking into account advantages in terms of flexibility, diversity and availability at different times and in different places;
- enhancing the new vision of adult learning which is both holistic, embracing all aspects of life, and cross-sectoral, including all sectors of cultural, social and economic activity;

- expanding the capacities of government, NGOs and the private sector to develop alliances to promote "learning societies";
- promoting an understanding of international human rights as the framework for the global society;
- governments acting on the consensus developed among multilateral organisations that each industrialised country should devote 0.7 per cent of gross national product to international cooperation and that each development project should include an adult learning component.

Part 11
The Hamburg Declaration and the Agenda for the Future

28

The Hamburg Declaration on Adult Learning

1. We, the participants in the Fifth International Conference on Adult Education, meeting in the Free and Hanseatic City of Hamburg, reaffirm that only human-centred development and a participatory society based on the full respect of human rights will lead to sustainable and equitable development. The informed and effective participation of men and women in every sphere of life is needed if humanity is to survive and to meet the challenges of the future.

2. Adult education thus becomes more than a right; it is a key to the twenty-first century. It is both a consequence of active citizenship and a condition for full participation in society. It is a powerful concept for fostering ecologically sustainable development, for promoting democracy, justice, gender equity, and scientific, social and economic development, and for building a world in which violent conflict is replaced by dialogue and a culture of peace based on justice. Adult learning can shape identity and give meaning to life. Learning throughout life implies a rethinking of content to reflect such factors as age, gender equality, disability, language, culture and economic disparities.

3. Adult education denotes the entire body of ongoing learning processes, formal or otherwise, whereby people regarded as adults by the society to which they belong develop their abilities, enrich their knowledge, and improve their technical

or professional qualifications or turn them in a new direction to meet their own needs and those of their society. Adult learning encompasses both formal and continuing education, non-formal learning and the spectrum of informal and incidental learning available in a multicultural learning society, where theory- and practiced-based approaches are recognised.

4. Though the content of adult learning and of education for children and adolescents will vary according to the economic, social, environmental and cultural context, and the needs of the people in the societies in which they take place, both are necessary elements of a new vision of education in which learning becomes truly lifelong. The perspective of learning throughout life commands such complementarity and continuity. The potential contribution of adult and continuing education to the creation of an informed and tolerant citizenry, economic and social development, the promotion of literacy, the alleviation of poverty and the preservation of the environment is enormous and should, therefore, be built upon.

5. The objectives of youth and adult education, viewed as a lifelong process, and to develop the autonomy and the sense of responsibility of people and communities, to reinforce the capacity to deal with the transformations taking place in the economy, in culture and in society as a whole, and to promote co-existence, tolerance and the informed and creative participation of citizens in their communities, in short to enable people and communities to take control of their destiny and society in order to face the challenges ahead. It is essential that approaches to adult learning be based on people's own heritage, culture, values and prior experiences and that the diverse ways in which these approaches are implemented enable and encourage every citizen to be actively involved and to have a voice.

6. This Conference recognises the diversity of political, economic and social systems and governmental structures among Member States. In accordance with that diversity and to ensure full respect for human rights and fundamental

freedoms, this Conference acknowledges that the particular circumstances of Member States will determine the measures governments may introduce to further the spirit of our objectives.

7. The representatives of governments and organisations participating in the Fifth International Conference on Adult Education have decided to explore together the potential and the future of adult learning, broadly and dynamically conceived within a framework of lifelong learning.

8. During the present decade, adult learning has undergone substantial changes and experienced enormous growth in scope and scale. In the knowledge-based societies that are emerging around the world, adult and continuing education have become an imperative in the community and at the workplace. New demands from society and working life raise expectations requiring each and every individual to continue renewing knowledge and skills throughout the whole of his or her life. At the heart of this transformation is a new role for the state and the emergence of expanded partnerships devoted to adult learning within civil society. The state remains the essential vehicle for ensuring the right to education for all, particularly for the most vulnerable groups of society, such as minorities and indigenous peoples, and for providing an overall policy framework. Within the new partnership emerging between the public, the private and the community sectors, the role of the state is shifting. It is not only a provider of adult education services but also an adviser, a fonder, and a monitoring and evaluation agency. Governments and social partners must take the necessary measures to support individuals in expressing their educational needs and aspirations, and in gaining access to educational opportunities throughout their lives. Within governments, adult education is not confined to ministries of education; all ministries are engaged in promoting adult learning, and interministerial co-operation is essential. Moreover, employers, unions, non-governmental and community organisations, and indigenous people's and women's groups are involved and have a responsibility to interact and create opportunities for lifelong learning, with provision for recognition and accreditation.

9. Basic education for all means that people, whatever their age, have an opportunity, individually and collectively, to realize their potential. It is not only a right, it is also a duty and a responsibility both to others and to society as a whole. It is essential that the recognition of the right to education throughout life should be accompanied by measures to create the conditions required to exercise this right. The challenges of the twenty-first century cannot be met by governments, organisations or institutions alone; the energy, imagination and genius of people and their full, free and vigorous participation in every aspect of life are also needed. Youth and adult learning is one of the principal means of significantly increasing creativity and productivity, in the widest sense of those terms, and these in turn are indispensable to meeting the complex and interrelated problems of a world beset by accelerating change and growing complexity and risk.

10. The new concept of youth and adult education presents a challenge to existing practices because it calls for effective networking within the formal and non-formal systems, and for innovation and more creativity and flexibility. Such challenges should be met by new approaches to adult education within the concept of learning throughout life. Promoting learning, using mass media and local publicity, and offering impartial guidance are responsibilities for governments, social partners and providers. The ultimate goal should be the creation of a learning society committed to social justice and general well-being.

11. *Adult literacy.* Literacy, broadly conceived as the basic knowledge and skills needed by all in a rapidly changing world, is a fundamental human right. In every society literacy is a necessary skill in itself and one of the foundations of other like skills. There are millions, the majority of whom are women, who lack opportunities to learn or who have insufficient skills to be able to assert this right. The challenge is to enable them to do so. This will often imply the creation of preconditions for learning through awareness-raising and empowerment. Literacy is also a catalyst for participation in

social, cultural, political and economic activities, and for learning throughout life. We therefore commit ourselves to ensuring opportunities for all to acquire and maintain literacy skills, and to create in all Member States a literate environment to support oral culture. The provision of learning opportunities for all, including the unreached and the excluded, is the most urgent concern. The Conference welcomes the initiative for a literacy decade in honour of Paulo Freire, to begin in 1998.

12. *Recognition of the right to education and the right to learn* throughout life is more than ever a necessity; it is the right to read and write, the right to question and analyse, the right to have access to resources, and to develop and practise individual and collective skills and competences.

13. *Women's integration and empowerment.* Women have a right to equal opportunities; society, in turn, depends on their full contribution in all fields of work and aspect of life. Youth and adult learning policies should be responsive to local cultures and give priority to expanding educational opportunities for all women, while respecting their diversity and eliminating prejudices and stereotypes that both limit their access to youth and adult education and restrict the benefits they derive from them. Any attempts to restrict women's right to literacy, education and training must be considered unacceptable. Practices and measures should be taken to counter them.

14. *Culture of peace and education for citizenship and democracy.* One of the foremost challenges of our age is to eliminate the culture of violence and to construct a culture of peace based on justice and tolerance within which dialogue, mutual recognition and negotiation will replace violence, in homes and communities, within nations and between countries.

15. *Diversity and equality.* Adult learning should reflect the richness of cultural diversity and respect traditional and indigenous peoples' knowledge and systems of learning; the right to learn in the mother tongue should be respected and implemented. Adult education faces an acute challenge in preserving and documenting the oral wisdom of minority groups, indigenous

peoples and nomadic peoples. In turn, intercultural education should encourage learning between and about different cultures in support of peace, human rights and fundamental freedoms, democracy, justice, liberty, co-existence and diversity.

16. *Health.* Health is a basic human right. Investments in education are investments in health. Lifelong learning can contribute substantially to the promotion of health and the prevention of disease. Adult education offers significant opportunities to provide relevant, equitable and sustainable access to health knowledge.

17. *Environmental sustainability.* Education for environmental sustainability should be a lifelong learning process which recognizes that ecological problems exist within a socio-economic, political and cultural context. A sustainable future cannot be achieved without addressing the relationship between environmental problems and current development paradigms. Adult environmental education can play an important role in sensitizing and mobilizing communities and decision-makers towards sustained environmental action.

18. *Indigenous education and culture.* Indigenous peoples and nomadic peoples have the right of access to all levels and forms of education provided by the state. However, they are not to be denied the right to enjoy their own culture, or to use their own languages. Education for indigenous peoples and nomadic peoples should be linguistically and culturally appropriate to their needs and should facilitate access to further education and training.

19. *Transformation of the economy.* Globalization, changes in production patterns, rising unemployment and the difficulty of ensuring secure livelihoods call for more active labour policies and increased investment in developing the necessary skills to enable men and women to participate in the labour market and income-generating activities.

20. *Access to information.* The development of the new information and communication technologies brings with it new risks of social and occupational exclusion for groups of individuals

and even businesses which are unable to adapt to this context. One of the roles of adult education in the future should therefore be to limit these risks of exclusion so that the information society does not lose sight of the human dimension.

21. *The ageing population.* There are now more older people in the world in relation to the total population than even before, and the proportion is still rising. These older adults have much to contribute to the development of society. Therefore, it is important that they have the opportunity to learn on equal terms and in appropriate ways. Their skills and abilities should be recognized, valued and made use of.

22. In line with the Salamanca Statement, integration and access for people with disabilities should be promoted. Disabled persons have the right to equitable learning opportunities which recognise and respond to their educational needs and goals, and in which appropriate learning technology matches their special learning needs.

23. We must act with the utmost urgency to increase and guarantee national and international investment in youth and adult learning, and the commitment of private and community resources to them. The Agenda for the Future which we have adopted here is designed to achieve this end.

24. We call upon UNESCO as the United Nations lead agency in the field of education to play the leading role in promoting adult education as an integral part of the system of learning and to mobilize the support of all partners, particularly those within the United Nations system, in order to give priority to implementing the Agenda for the Future and to facilitating provision of the services needed for reinforcing international co-ordination and co-operation.

25. We urge UNESCO to encourage Member States to adopt policies and legislation that are favourable to and accommodate people with disabilities in educational programmes, as well as being sensitive to cultural, linguistic, gender and economic diversity.

26. We solemnly declare that all parties will closely follow up the implementation of this Declaration and the Agenda for the Future, clearly distinguishing their respective responsibilities and complementing and co-operating with one another. We are determined to ensure that lifelong learning will become a more significant reality in the early twenty-first century. To that end, we commit ourselves to promoting the culture of learning through the "one hour a day for learning" movement and the development of a United Nations Week of Adult Learning.

27. We, gathered together in Hamburg, convinced of the necessity of adult learning, pledge that all men and women shall be provided with the opportunity to learn throughout their lives. To that end, we will forge extended alliances to mobilize and share resources in order to make adult learning a joy, a tool, a right and a shared responsibility.

29

The Agenda for the Future

1. This *Agenda for the Future* sets out in detail the new commitment to the development of adult learning called for by the Hamburg Declaration on Adult Learning.

2. The *Agenda* focuses on common concerns facing humanity on the eve of the twenty-first century and on the vital role that adult learning has to play in enabling women and men of all ages to face these most urgent challenges with knowledge, courage and creativity.

3. The development of adult learning requires partnership between government departments, intergovernmental and non-governmental organisations, employers and trade unions, universities and research centres, the media, civil and community-level associations, facilitators of adult learning and the adult learners themselves.

4. Profound changes are taking place both globally and locally. They can be seen in a globalisation of economic systems, in the rapid development of science and technology, in the age structure and mobility of populations, and in the emergence of an information-based and knowledge-based society. The world is also experiencing major changes in patterns of work and unemployment, a growing ecological crisis, and tensions between social groups based on culture, ethnicity, gender roles, religion and income. These trends are reflected in education, where those responsible for complex education systems are struggling to cope with new opportunities and demands, often with declining resources at their disposal.

5. In the course of the present decade, a series of conferences has focused world attention on key international problems. Beginning with the World Conference on Education for All: Meeting Basic Learning Needs (Jomtien, Thailand, 1990), they have included the United Nations Conference on Environment and Development (Rio de Janeiro, 1992), the World Conference on Human Rights (Vienna, 1993), the International Conference on Population and Development (Cairo, 1994), the World Summit for Social Development (Copenhagen, 1995), the Fourth World Conference on Women (Beijing, 1995), the United Nations Conference on Human Settlements (Habitat II, Istanbul, 1996) and the most recent, the World Food Summit (Rome, 1996). At all these conferences world leaders looked to education to release the competence and creativity of citizens. Education was seen as a vital element in a strategy to nurture the sustainable development processes.

6. There have been parallel changes in education as well. Since its foundation, UNESCO has played a pioneering role in the conception of adult education as an essential part of any education system and of human-centred development. There are now numerous agencies active in the field, many of which have taken part in the Hamburg conference.

7. The first International Conference on Adult Education (Elsinore, Denmark, 1949) was followed by conferences in Montreal (1960), Tokyo (1972) and Paris (1985). Other important milestones include the 1972 Report of the International Commission on the Development of Education chaired by Edgar Faure, *Learning to Be: The World of Education Today and Tomorrow*, and the influential 1976 UNESCO Recommendation on the Development of Adult Education which set out the vital role of adult education 'as forming part of lifelong education and learning'.

8. During the twelve years that have elapsed since the Paris Declaration, humanity has been affected by profound changes resulting from the processes of globalisation and technological advance, together with a new international order, all of which have led to far-reaching transformations in the political, cultural and economic fields.

9. A quarter of a century after *Learning to Be*, the International Commission on Education for the Twenty-first Century, chaired by Jacques Delors, said that, 'The concept of learning throughout life is the key that gives access to the twenty-first century. It goes beyond the traditional distinctions between initial and continuing education. It links up with another concept, that of the learning society, in which everything affords an opportunity for learning and fulfilling one's potential'. The Commission's report, *Learning: The Treasure Within*, emphasised the importance of the four pillars of education: learning to know, learning to do, learning to live together and learning to be. As indicated in the Hamburg Declaration, adult learning has grown in depth and scale, and has become an imperative at the workplace, in the home and in the community, as men and women struggle to create new realities at every stage of life. Adult education plays an essential and distinct role in equipping women and men to respond productivity to the constantly changing world and in providing learning which acknowledges the rights and responsibilities of the adult and the community.

10. In Hamburg the broad and complex spectrum of adult learning was considered under ten thematic headings:
    - *Adult learning and democracy: the challenges of the twenty-first century*
    - *Improving the conditions and quality of adult learning*
    - *Ensuring the universal right to literacy and basic education*
    - *Adult learning, gender equality and equity, and the empowerment of women*
    - *Adult learning and the changing world of work*
    - *Adult learning in relation to environment, health and population*
    - *Adult learning, culture, media and new information technologies*
    - *Adult learning for all: the rights and aspirations of different groups*
    - *The economics of adult learning*
    - *Enhancing international co-operation and solidarity*

Theme 1: Adult Learning and Democracy: The Challenge of the Twenty-first Century

11. *The challenges of the twenty-first century require the creativity and competence of citizens of all ages in alleviating poverty, consolidating democratic processes, strengthening and protecting human rights, promoting a culture of peace, encouraging active citizenship, strengthening the role of civil society, ensuring gender equality and equity, enhancing the empowerment of women, recognising cultural diversity (including the use of language, and promoting justice and equality for minorities and indigenous peoples) and a new partnership between state and civil society. Indeed, to reinforce democracy, it is essential to strengthen learning environments, to reinforce the participation of citizens, and to create contexts where the productivity of people will be enhanced and where a culture of equity and peace can take root.*

    We commit ourselves to:

12. Creating greater community participation:

    (a) by promoting active citizenship and improving participatory democracy in order to create learning communities;

    (b) by encouraging and developing leadership capabilities among the adult population and especially among women, enabling them to participate in institutions of the state, the market and civil society.

13. Raising awareness about prejudice and discrimination in society:

    (a) by ensuring the legitimate right of people to self-determination and to the free exercise of their way of life;

    (b) by taking measures to eliminate discrimination in education at all levels based on gender, race, language, religion, national or ethnic origin, disability, or any other form of discrimination;

    (c) by developing education programmes that enable men and women to understand gender relations and human sexuality in all their dimensions;

(d) by recognising and affirming the rights to education of women, of indigenous peoples and nomadic peoples, and of minorities by ensuring equitable representation in decision-making processes and provision, and by supporting the publication of local and indigenous learning materials;

(e) by recognising that all indigenous peoples and nomadic peoples have the right of access to all levels and forms of state education, and the right to enjoy their own cultures and to use their own languages. Their education should be linguistically and culturally appropriate to their needs and should facilitate access to further education and training by working together, and learning to respect and appreciate each other's differences in order to ensure a shared future for all members of society.

14. Encouraging greater recognition, participation and accountability of non-governmental organisations and local community groups:

(a) by recognising the role non-governmental organisations play in awareness-raising and empowerment of people, which are of vital importance of democracy, peace and development;

(b) by recognising and appropriately funding the growing role of non-governmental organisations and local community groups in providing educational opportunities for adults in all sectors, in reaching the most needy and in contributing to an active civil society.

15. Promoting a culture of peace, intercultural dialogue and human rights:

(a) be enabling citizens to approach conflicts in an empathic, non-violent and creative manner, with peace education for all, peace journalism and peace culture as important components;

(b) by strengthening the educational dimensions of human rights activities in formal and non-formal adult learning provisions at community, national, regional and global levels.

Theme 2: Improving the conditions and quality of adult learning

16. *While there is a growing demand for adult education and an explosion of information, the disparities between those who have access and those who do not are also growing. There is therefore a need to counter this polarity, which reinforces existing inequalities, by creating adult learning structures and lifelong learning environments that can help to correct the prevalent trend. How can the conditions of adult learning be improved? How can we overcome inadequacies in its provision? What kind of measures and reforms should be undertaken in order to achieve greater accessibility, relevance, quality, respect for diversity and recognition of prior learning?*

We commit ourselves to:

17. Creating conditions for the expression of people's demand for learning:

    (a) by adopting legislation and other appropriate means recognising the right to learn of all adults, proposing an enlarged vision of adult learning and facilitating co-ordination between agencies;

    (b) by facilitating the expression of the learning demand of people within their own culture and language;

    (c) by creating public information and counselling services and developing methods for the recognition of experimental and prior learning;

    (d) by developing strategies to extend the benefits of adult learning to those currently excluded and to help adults make informed choices concerning the learning routes best suited to their aspirations;

    (e) by promoting a culture of learning through the 'one hour a day for learning' movement;

    (f) by underlining thew importance of observing International Women's Day (8 March) and International Literacy day (8 December) and of using the International Literacy Prizes for the promotion of adult learning, and by developing a United Nations Week of Adult Learning.

18. Ensuring accessibility and quality:

    (a) by adopting legislation, policies and co-operation mechanisms with all partners to make access easier, to facilitate the participation of adults in formal education and education at the workplace and in the community, and to support and extend programmes for rural and isolated areas;

    (b) by developing a comprehensive policy, taking into account the critical role of the learning environment;

    (c) by improving the quality and ensuring the relevance of adult education through the participation of learners in designing programmes;

    (d) by facilitating co-operation among adult learning initiatives related to different institutions and sectors of activity.

19. Opening schools, colleges and universities to adult learners:

    (a) by requiring institutions of formal education from primary level onwards.

Part 12

Fifth International Conference on Adult Education Hamburg, Germany

30

Final Report of the Fifth International Conference on Adult Education

PART I

Summary of the Plenary Discussions

A. Introduction

1. The 5th International Conference on Adult Education (CONFINTEA V) was convinced by the Director-General of UNESCO in pursuance of resolutions 1.1 (para 2 A.g) and 1.4 (para 3) adopted by the General Conference at its twenty-eighth session of the General Conference of UNESCO and in accordance with the work plan of the Approved Programme and Budget for 1996-1997 (28C/5 Approved, para 01507). At the invitation of the Government of the Federal Republic of Germany, the Conference was held at the Congress Centrum Hamburg from 14 to 18 July, 1997. The Conference was organised with the following partners: FAO; ILO; UNAIDS; UNICEF; UNDP; UNFPA; UNHCR; UNIDO; World Bank; WHO; Council of Europe; European Union, OECD.

2. The Conference was attended by a total of 1507 participants including 41 Ministries 15 Vice-Ministers and 3 Sub-Ministers: 729 representatives from 130 Member States; 2 Associate Members; 2 Non-Member States; 1 Palestine; 14 representatives of Organisations of the UN System, and 21 representatives from Intergovernmental Organisations, 478 NGO representatives; and 237 foundation representatives.

3. The CONFINTEA V was held on the eve of the new millennium and followed the four previous Conferences (Elsinore, 1949; Montreal, 1960; Tokyo, 1972; Paris 1985). A wide range of preparatory activities—five regional consultations, (Barcelona, Cairo, Dakar, Jometien, Brasilia), a questionnaire sent to all Member States and 12 international NGOs and various meetings with different themaic groups—have been carried out in the course of preparing the Conference.

B. Opening of the Conference

4. The Plenary Session opened with the presentation of speakers by Ms. Kasama Varavarn, Chairperson of the Governing Board of the UNESCO Institute for Education and by dance performance groups from Thailand, Brazil and Germany.

5. Mr. Henning Voscherau, First Mayor of the Free and Hanseatic City of Hamburg, welcoming all participants to the City of Hamburg, stressed that education and adult education are instruments which foster competence, values and behaviours to meet the challenges of tomorrow and to enable the nations of the world to live peacefully together.

6. Her Excellency Ms. Sheikh Hasina, Prime Minister of the Peoples' Republic of Bangladesh, in her keynote address, spoke on the importance of adult literacy, the close linkage between education and economic productivity and the need to ensure high quality adult learning in the perspective of lifelong learning. She stressed that "international co-operation will bring forth a prosperous world community—one in which even the poorer developing nations can begin to share in the new growth possibilities opened up by recent technological advances".

7. The President of the Federal Republic of Germany, Mr. Roman Herzog, referred to his country's 46 years' commitment to UNESCO and pointed to the fact that "the UNESCO Institute was the first institution of the international community to be established in this country". Referring to CONFINTEA V, he, moreover, underlined the importance of a new form of growth supported by knowledge, lifelong learning and the role of adult education to promote peace.

8. Mr. Federico Mayor, the Director-General of UNESCO, welcomed all participants to CONFINTEA V and expressed the hope that the Conference would "define the new roles of adult education to meet the aspirations of women and men in all countries within the new world that is taking shape about us". He then requested participants to observe a one minute silence in remembrance of Paulo Freire who "revolutionarized" the whole concept of education by linking literacy and liberation. Mr. Mayor posed a question "How will the Hamburg Conference be remembered fifty years hence? He answered that it "depends on our vision and commitments, now and hereafter". He also reminded participants that CONFINTEA V is different from the previous one in so far as it aims at reaching the outcome of the Conference through a close dialogue and partnership with NGOs. Finally, Mr. Mayor interrupted his speech for a few minutes to give the floor to Ms. Nonkosinathi Hathuku from Hanover in the Northern Cape Province of South Africa, a former adult illiterate, who has become literate through her participation in the Masakhane Literacy Project to present her personal experience and opinions on how useful and important it is to be a literate person.

C. Work of the Conference

9. At the end of the Opening Ceremony, the Plenary meeting moved on to item 2 of the provisional agenda and elected Ms. Rita Süssmuth, President of the German Parliament, as the President of the Conference. Stressing that "continuing education is an investment for the future", she asserted: "adult education must involve people as actors who decide for themselves in the societal process of change, and give them the knowledge they require for this purpose, together with the skill to apply this knowledge responsibility". She spoke on the opportunity and challenge of lifelong learning, the importance of open lifelong learning without frontiers and also the new alliances between the state, civil society, NGOs and private organisations.

10. Upon adoption of the Rules of Procedure, the Conference elected the following Members of the Bureau of the Conference:

President:	Ms. Rita Süssmuth	President of the German Parliament
Vice-President:	Mr. Ashk Sadeque	Minister of Education, Bangladesh
	Mr. Emil Gheorghe Moroianu	Director-General of International Relations Ministry of Education, Romania
	Ms. Pauline Morois	Minister of Education, Quebec, Canada
	Mr. Abdul-Jabbar Tawfik Muhamad	Minister of Education, Iraq
	Ms. Aissata Moumouni	Minister of Education, Niger
	Mr. Jaime Nino Diez	Minister of Education, Colombia
	Mr Fenton Ferguson	Parliamentary Secretary Ministry of Education, Youth and Culture, Jamaica
Chairperson of Commission I	Mr. Luis Benavides	Director, Centro Internaciónal Prospectiva y Altos Estudios, México
Chairperson of	Dato Haji Annuar Bin	Minister of Rural Development, Malaysia
Commission II	Haji Musa	
Rapporteur-General	Ms Esi Sutherland-Addy, Gnana	

The drafting committee, composed of persons from different regions, was created and worked closely with the Bureau of the Conference in order to examine and incorporate draft amendments into the draft *Declaration* and the draft *Agenda for the Future*. The drafting committee consisted of the following members:

Mr. J. Ellis (Chairman, Namabia); Mr. A Manouaun (Ivory Coast); Ms. S. Correa (Brazil); Mr. L.E. Lopez (Peru); Ms M.L. Doronila (Philippines); Ms T. Marja (Estonia); Mr. S. Poulsen-Hansen (Denmark); Ms Al-Doy (Behrain); Mr. Daswani (India); Mr. T. Geer (Australia).

11. The Plenary of the Conference, after adopting the Organisation of Work and of the Agenda, welcomed Mr. Kim Howells, Minister of Lifelong Learning, Department for Education and Employment, United Kingdom. He declared: "Today is part of this new beginning for the UK-our first opportunity since we were elected to contribute to a major UNESCO conference as a Member". Expressing his Government's pledge to work with UNESCO closely, he concluded: "We have put education at the heart of our national agenda. I am proud that we are once again part of UNESCO because UNESCO too has education at the centre of its priorities.

12. The Plenary meeting then dealt with oral reports on the results of the regional consultation meetings. In addition, one or two ministers from the regions were invited to address the Plenary, as well as representatives from regional organisations.

The following delegates addressed the Plenary on behalf of their regions:

Asia and Pacific Region:	Ms. Kasama, Varavarn, Director of Non formal Education, Ministry of Education, Thailand; Ms. Maria Lourdes A Khan, Secretary General, ASPBAE; Mr S R Bommai, Minister of Human Resource Development, India.
European Region:	Mr Jürgen Rüttgers, Minister of Education, Science, Research and Technology, Germany; Mr Ole Vig Jensen, Minister of Education, Denmark; Mr. Antoni Comas, Minister of Social Welfare of the Catalan Region of Spain; Mr. Paolo Federighi, European Association of the Education of Adults; Mr. Mait Klaassen, Minister of Education, Estonia.

African Region:	Mr. Mammadou Ndoye, Minister of Education, Senegal; Mr. Albert Mberio, Minister of Education, Central African Republic; Mr. Arnaldo Valente Nhavoto, Minister of Education, Mozambique.
Latin American and Caribbean Region:	Mr. Jaime Nino Diez, Minister of Education, Colombia; Ms Celita Eccher, NGO representative of CEAAL; Mr. Renford Shirley, President, Caribbean Regional Council for Adult Education (CARCAE); Ms Josefina Bilbao, Minister for Women, Chile.
Arab Region:	Mr. Hamed Ammar, Ain Shams University, Egypt; Ms. Nadia Gamal El Din Yousef, Director, National Centre of Educational Research and Development, Egypt; Mr. Ibrahim Alsheddi, Assistant Deputy Minister of Education for Culture, Saudi Arabia.

13. Along with the presentations of the Regional Reports, the following representatives of Organisations of the United Nations System, Intergovernmental Organisations and NGOs delivered speeches:

OECD:	Mr. Thomas Alexander, Director of Education, Employment, Labour and Social Affairs
UNDP:	Mr. Richard Jolly, Special Advisor to the Administrator
ICAE:	Ms. Lalita Ramdas, President
UNFPA:	Mr. O J Sikes, Chief, Education, Communication and Youth Branch
UNICEF:	Ms. Mary Joy Pigozzi, Senior Advisor Education
World Bank:	Mr. John Oxenham, Senior Training Officer
European Commission:	Mr. Tom O'Dwyer, Director-General of the Directorate-General XXII.

14. Included in the Plenary of the Conference was a Dialogue session with multilateral agencies and delegates on the theme "The future of co-operation in lifelong learning", in which the following persons participated.

Chair: Mr. Boutros Boutros Ghali, former UN Secretary General

Moderator: Mr. Wadi Haddad

Panelists:

1. Ms. Higuette Labelle, President CIDA
2. Mr. Ingemar Gustafsson, Director, SIDA
3. Mr. John Lawrence, Education-for-All, UNDP
4. Mr. Richard Sack, Secretary-General, Association for the Development of Education in Africa
5. Mr. Mohammad Ahmed Rasheed, Minister of Education, Saudi Arabia
6. Mr. Soedijarto, Director-General, Out-of-School Education, Youth and Sports, Ministry of Education, Indonesia
7. Mr. Johann Galtung, Professor of Peace Studies, Norway
8. Mr Rafael Roncagliolo, World Association of Community Radios, Peru

15. At the Closing session of the Conference, Mr. Süssmuth, President of the Conference, declared that the Hamburg, Conference was a success in terms of the richness of the ideas and of the strong commitment manifested by participants. At the same time, the Conference addressed a range of problems which lie ahead of us. The Report of the Conference presented by the Rapporteur-General, Ms Esi Sutherland-Addy, the *Declaration* and the *Agenda for the Future* were adopted. There were short interventions by a ministerial representative from each of the four groups: Ms. Gufu Ndbele, (Director of Adult Education and Training Department, South Africa); Mr. Abdulazi Alsunbul.

Deputy Director-General of ALECSO; Mr. Abdellatif Fetni (Director-General of the National Office of Literacy and Adult Education, Algeria); Mr. Devi Prasad Ojha (Minister of Education, Nepal); Mr. Sumuel Lichtensztejn (Minister of Education, Uruguay). A representative of the International Council for Adult Education also made an intervention, underlying the new co-operation between governments and civil society.

Mr. Mayor, speaking for all the participants, thanked the Federal Government of Germany, the Free Hanseatic City of Hamburg, the University of Hamburg, and NGOs. He concluded, "It is our moment to seize this momentum, recover the basis for practice, and get to work. Rather the building a wall to keep out the wind, we must build a windmill and generate the tremendous human power that adult education and lifelong learning can bring.

PART II

A. Commissions

16. The simultaneous Commission sessions were held with all participants and observers. Commission I dealt with the *Declaration* and Chapters I and X plus follow-up to the *Agenda for the Future*. Commission II dealt with the Chapters II to IX (incl.) of the Agenda for the Future. Commission I elected Mr. Umaru Aji (Nigeria) and Ms. Nora Rameka (New Zealand) as Vice Chairpersons and Mr. Dominique Schalchli (France) as a Rapporteur. Commission II elected Mr. Hussein Al Wad (Tunisia) as Vice Chairperson and Ms. Vida A Mohorcia Spolar (Slovania) as a Rapporteur.

B. Thematic Working Groups

17. Following the Plenary Session, the following half-day mixed thematic working groups (Annex VIII) were organised and attended by specialists from governments, IGOs, UN bodies, NGOs, research centres and universities, etc. to discuss together the various concepts, issues, and prospects on the following themes centring around adult learning:

- *Literacy in the world and its major regions;*
- *Learning and learning strategies;*
- *Women's Education: The contending discourses and possibilities for changes;*
- *Changes in the world of work and their impact on adult education and training;*
- *University-community partnerships: Links with the adult education movement;*
- *Monitoring of adult learning for knowledge-based policy-making;*
- *Enhancing international co-operation and solidarity;*
- *The multiplicity of research on "Learning for all, a key for the 21st Century";*
- *Health promotion an health education for adults;*
- *Cultural citizenship in the 21st century; adult education and indigenous peoples;*
- *Literacy, education and social development;*
- *Literacy research, evaluation and statistics;*
- *Literacy and technology;*
- *Literacy in multilingual/intercultural settings;*
- *Raising gender issues in different educational settings;*
- *Adult education and population issues in the post-Cairo context;*
- *Museums, libraries and cultural heritage: democratizing culture, creating knowledge and building bridges;*
- *The changing world of work: Implications for adult education programmes;*
- *Global community of adult education through information and documentation: developing a network of networks;*
- *Adult environmental education: awareness for environmental action;*
- *Adult learning for prisoners;*

- *Making education accessible and available for all persons with disabilities;*
- *The politics and policies of the education of adults in a globally transforming society;*
- *Literacy and basic skills for community development in industrialised countries;*
- *Literacy for tomorrow;*
- *Adult education and co-operation among majority and minority communities;*
- *New information technologies: a key for adult learning;*
- *Adult environmental education;*
- *Policy and social implications of the chancing world of work;*
- *Migrant education;*
- *Adult learning; democracy and peace;*
- *Adult learning and ageing populations;*
- *Universities and the future of adult education in the 21st Century: the demise of the ivory tower;*
- *The economics of adult learning: the role of government.*

C. Public Round Tables

18. Three self-financed public round tables were held during the conference on the following themes:

- Learning gender sensitivity—practising gender justice;
- Cities of learning;
- Consequences of literacy: adult learning and human-centred development.

PART III

Documents Issued by the Conference

A. Report of the Conference by the Rapporteur-General

Madame Chair,

Members of the Conference Bureau,

Distinguished Delegates,

Distinguished Participants,

It is my very great honour to present to you the oral report of the Fifth International Conference on Adult Education.

What I have tried to do in this report with the help of a wonderful team from the Secretariat is to synthesize the main trends of our discussions, and to capture the general atmosphere of the Conference, I, however, take full responsibility for this presentation.

I will also be taking the liberty afforded me by this great opportunity to make a few, very brief, personal reflections on matters which have struck me profoundly during the Conference.

Oral Report Part I

The Free and Hanseatic city of Hamburg, with its tradition of openness, dialogue, creativity and hospitality, provided an exciting and dynamic scene for a wide and multiform exchange on adult learning for the twenty-first century.

One ambition of this Conference, which has brought together about one thousand five-hundred representatives of governments, NGOs and international agencies, was to capture, reflect and promote the multi-layered concept of adult learning to which different actors, the state, the civil society and the private sector and social partners are contributing within a concerted and negotiated framework.

The motto of the Conference, *Adult Learning as a right, a tool, a joy and shared responsibility,* truly reflected the atmosphere which prevailed. CONFINTEA V created the learning environment and practised the learning culture which has always characterized the adult education movements. Inter-learning, co-operation and exchange have taken place, not only in the formal sessions, but also during the multi-varied gatherings, the media events which culminated in the teleconferencing dialogue with India. A moment of learning took place also through the dialogue on the rebuilding and revitalization of two former industrialised cities, Detroit and Windsor. More importantly, a wide range and thorough exchange of experiences in building sustainable gender justice in education and development, formed part of the learning process.

On-going women caucuses, regional and subregional consultations, informal gatherings of all kinds, exhibits of colourful and symbolic art objects, freshly produced books, etc. played a constructive role in the Conference.

A moving homage to two eminent adult educators and world citizens, Dame Nita Barrow and Paulo Freire, provided an inspiring testament to the refreshing and lasting validity of the goals, methods and spirit of adult education.

1. We saw the emergence of a New Vision of Adult Learning: A Call for a Shift

Drawing attention to a politically, economically and socially transformed world, dramatically different from the realities of the Fourth International Conference on Adult Education held in 1985 the key speakers of the Conference called on the gathering to define the new roles of adult education which would take into account changes taking place.

The indicated that the challenges resulting from the ongoing process of globalization, the tension and risk of marginalization that characterize our present time that is pregnant of the hopes and fear of the nascent century, call for new and imaginative solutions. Therefore, the Conference was viewed and lived by many participants as a sounding board to construct a new vision, looking at adult learning as an integral part of a lifelong and life-wide learning process, promoting family and community learning as well as dialogue between cultures, respecting differences and diversity and thereby contributing to a culture of peace. Acknowledging the learners not as objects, but as subjects of their learning processes, adult education should more specifically contribute to:

- the struggle for social and economic development, justice, equality, respect for traditional cultures, and recognition of dignity of every human being through individual empowerment and social transformation;

— addressing human sufferings in all contexts—oppression, poverty, child labour, genocide, denial of learning opportunities based on class, gender, race or ethnicity;

— individual empowerment and social transformation.

A special call was made to the effect that adult education should target the educated powerful elites in society as much as those who are the so-called marginalized and illiterates, since the macro-policies such as globalization and structure adjustment which have affected the human condition so severely, are created today by the educated, the rich and powerful. This new vision of adult education calls for the creation of inclusive learning societies building on all the potential and resources of all the people and the environment.

2. Travelling from CONFINTEA IV to CONFINTEA V

The reports of the various regional consultations showed that while some progress has been made in adult education, the process since CONFINTEA IV (1985) has not been able to stimulate a major shift towards integrating adult education in the overall basic education country policies. The short accounts made, pointed to some trends and more specifically the regions reported in the following manner:

(a) The African Region

Since 1985 an increasing number of adult illiterates have benefited from literacy programmes and numerous local initiatives; however, due to rapid population growth the absolute number of illiterates is still increasing.

Africa gives notice of the need to see adult education as a tool for development and indicates the need for politics of inclusion in the global management of information technology and world economies, particularly the debt burden, since the need for rapid modernization is as notable as they might be elsewhere in the world.

However, illiteracy is particularly high and human and financial resources for learning are difficult to mobilize due to civil wars, poverty and structural adjustment programmes. The mobilization of local communities and their commitment to the search for collective solutions to individual problems as well as their demand for more participation and responsibility in fostering sustainable development gives a ray of hope for the future.

The engine of this transformation is to be found in the emergence of an active civil society through associations, NGOs and other socio-professional and culture movements. In response, African governments have undertaken reforms that seek to emphasize decentraization and grassroots empowerment for more significant participation in the national development.

(b) The Asia and Pacific Region

— increasingly, policies and corresponding investments recognize adult education as a means to reach and empower the disadvantaged, to ensure equitable and sustainable development, to harness potentials for national competitiveness and to enhance lifelong learning opportunities;

— the vision and scope of adult education has expanded and created strategies developed as a result of partnership among educational institutions, NGOs people's organisations, the media and the private sector as a whole;

— innovative models for mobilizing support for mass literacy campaigns and to provide alternative education for the out-of-school children were highlighted;

— greater concern for gender sensitivity, local responsiveness and quality are evident in many functional literacy programmes;

— closer linkages have been forged between education and sustainable development;

— new forms of vocational, technical and workplace education have been initiated.

(c) The Latin American and Caribbean Region

There is pervasive evidence of NGO-government partnership in adult education which has led, for example, to innovations in curriculum development. In several countries women are increasingly seen as a priority group in education. However, educational policies do not yet respond to local realities and do not always go beyond conventional models of classroom teaching; building the largely desired multi-sectoral and inter-institutional co-operation has proven to be slow in taking the required foundation.

The region reports a notable increase in the role of the media and the involvement of civil society; a stronger involvement of the government in the field of adult education and the need for revising national educational policies from the perspective of lifelong learning.

One of the strongest recommendations of the region is that adult educators pay attention to the young adults as a key strategy. Latin America and the Caribbean strongly echoed the need for a creative management of the debt burden in favour of crucial programmes such as the programme of adult learning.

(d) The European Region

Residual functional illiteracy is also a reality in this region and efforts are being made to monitor and control the circumstances that have brought it about. However, the concern for Europe is to move towards an expanded vision of adult education as an integral part of lifelong learning. There is recognition of the implications for education with regard to the diverse patterns of development in the region. The report put a new emphasis on lifelong learning with the Declaration of 1996 as European Year of Lifelong Learning.

One of the defining features of adult education is the growth outside the formal systems, initiated by a variety of popular movements ranging from trade unions to rural development organisations to temporary movements. Experience in Europe sharpened awareness of the rich diversity which exists not only of structures, but also of content and even of understanding.

The report emphasized the role of education in promoting the concept of active citizenship which comprises the ability to interpret experience, to make individual decisions, to participate in political processes and the fulfilment of individual dignity.

Europe calls for a racial change of attitude on the part of education institutions and organisations, including the school system, universities, enterprises and all the social partners. An extended form of dialogue between institutions is therefore necessary to allow for mobility between different learning environments and to promote new kinds of learning for the acquisition of new knowledge. A dynamic lifelong learning environment cannot be directed from the top down, but presupposes a high degree of participation from adult citizens.

The region shared the following proposals for action:

— an hour a day of learning to create a culture of a learning society;

— the announcement of a world day of Adult Education.

(e) The Arab Region

During the last 12 years the number of literate adults has increased significantly. Today, two third of the adult population of the region are literate. Beyond this general achievement, the literacy rate of women remains still significantly lower than that of men. To continue to correct this imbalance and to intensify the effort is a challenge for the years to come.

In the Arab region, a new trend is taking place where the priority of adult literacy is increasingly seen as an integrated part of the larger objective of education throughout the adult life. The first priority of 3 Rs. for all is redefined in the larger version of the 3 Ls (lifelong learning for all).

Oral Report Part II

THEMATIC GROUPS

Let me now attempt the ambitious task of sharing with you the gist of the 33 working sessions of the thematic groups.

The richness of the panel discussions cannot be captured in a series of brief notes and I am sure all of us will be awaiting the publication on the proceedings and messages of this Conference as early as possible. We say in Ghana that when you want to speak to God you speak to the wind.

Governments were urged to give more recognition and support with regard to the following points raised in the different Working groups:

The Conference managed to stimulate a process of redefining literacy stressing the need to move away from the deficit approach. Literacy acquisition is concerned with the making of and participation in a literate culture at individual, local, national and regional levels. Apart from being considered a condition for economic development, literacy does contribute greatly to the facilitation of the lifelong learning process of adults and children, but at the same time, it can only be sustained, if embedded in a literate culture. Literacy has many faces and the diversity of literacies today has to be acknowledged and built upon. Literacy as a social practice has to build upon the existing capitals of local languages, cultures and knowledge—thus serving, inspiring and strengthening civil society and social justice.

The intricate relation between literacy and mother tongue was greatly emphasized; consequently in multilingual societies the broad and rapid promotion of literacy and education cannot be channelled through one official and foreign language; the participatory approach which is a key to adult education also means taking into consideration mother tongues. What then emerges is that multilingualism is not an obstacle, but a potential for literacy.

Literacy has recently become an issue also in the industrialized countries. They have come to acknowledge the fact that in spite of a range of experiences with alternative and successful literacy and basic skills programmes, exclusion from learning opportunities based on race, gender, social background is still rampant. The need for participatory approaches, recognition of cultural diversity, networking, partnership and flexibility were key issues raised. A young Canadian Inuit told us: "Everyone in Canada and everyone in the world has a part to play in ensuring that I keep my culture and my language".

Much has been said about the significant gap that often persists between what is claimed to be a literacy success and the actual result from the perspective of the grassroots. The quality and transparency of information has to be greatly improved. A better information base with better knowledge of what works, with whom and in what context, is the prerequisite for developing sustainable literacy policies and may result in increased financing. Monitoring adult learning is of essential importance provided that this does not limit creativity; a standardized module for adult education data collection, covering qualitative and quantitative elements, could be a precious tool for the community of adult educators and researchers. It is my sense that the Conference would like this to be further explored.

It was emphasized that in a dramatically changing world context the need for qualitative research is more important than ever. However, state policies are slow to change and most funding goes still to quantitative research.

There is a strong need for a networks of documentation and information services. In spite of the explosion of knowledge and new media, equitable access to information and knowledge on adult learning today remains a dream for many individuals and groups.

Adult education has always been confronted with the world of work, which is today rapidly changing. We need to redefine the concept of work, which has to go beyond the idea of paid work and pay tribute to every area in which productive and reproductive responsibilities are taken; this notably concerns women's activities. The new paradigm of work should inform adult and continuing education policies and inspire lifelong learning programmes in the work place. Those countries which do not have integrated adult education in their lifelong learning policies are urged to do so applying a participatory approach.

Furthermore, the 21st century will witness increasing migration which is likely to be linked with oppressive working and living conditions. There is a need for collaborative and sustained efforts to promote migrant education from the perspective of empowerment. This can be best achieved through a participatory learning approach integrating social and life skills, education for citizenship, human rights, consciousness-raising, as well as multi cultural and anti-racist education.

So-called minorities are often discriminated against, institutionally or in a subtle manner and hence are often deprived of many rights including the right to education. Feelings of deprivation create tensions that can easily escalate in armed conflicts. The uniqueness of minorities has to be respected and valued; actually it is the majority who has to unlearn discriminatory concepts, acquire knowledge and develop empathy and compassion in order to respect the diversity of cultures; it is the obligation of the educational authorities to see that teaching methods, learning approaches and curricula for adult non-adult education reflects and enhance all these elements.

There is a positive trend of change of Government directives and policies towards indigenous people. The four "pillars of learning" from the Delors commission can be referred to indigenous people as follows:

— learning to be or the right to identity

— learning to know or the right to self-knowledge

— learning to do or the right to self-development

— learning to live together or the right to self-determination

The reality of an ageing population was brought home to the Conference. More than 25 per cent of the world population is over 60; this proportion in the population will rise constantly while societies are still ill prepared to face those historically new demographic conditions. Adult education can make a difference by promoting a new vision of older adults as autonomous, responsible persons and a productive force in society, given them access to new knowledge and new learning. 1999, the international year of the older people; is a strong symbol of our changing world, and demography.

Women and youth have been brought back to the centre of population issues from a human rights and a development perspective; this requires listening to their point of views and respecting them as active subjects, finding appropriate creative imaginative methodologies to educate a whole range of diverse groups in different situations.

In a plea for gender-sensitive lifelong learning, the need to recognize women's knowledge and potential was emphasized, particularly in an environment in which women's work tends to be devaluated. Although there are many excellent policy documents in place, the implementation is lacking. As women, including those of us who have achieved influential positions, we have the responsibility to use our power and competence to advance the education of girls and women.

While formal schooling in certain contexts has contributed to the implementation of women, it is also true that it has resulted in the reproduction and reinforcement of gender inequalities and stereotype gender roles. Some non-formal education programmes have successfully addressed the issue of women's empowerment by building on their family and community experiences, but much remains to be done to implement programmes geared towards making both men and women gender-sensitive, thereby narrowing the existing social and economic gender gaps.

One of the hottest topics at the eve of an era of a world wide high tach web is new technology, and while it is true that technologies bear great potential for an can contribute to adult learning, given that there is the political will and support for the active appropriation of these tools, it is however important to remain critical about why how and for whom the technologies are being used.

Additional Reading

Bhaskara Rao, Digumarti (1994). *Scientific Aptitude,* New Delhi: Ashish Publishing House. ISBN 81-7024-658-X.

Bhaskara Rao, Digumarti (1995). *Animal Kingdom.* New Delhi: Discovery Publishing House. ISBN 81-7141-274-2.

Bhaskara Rao, Digumarti (1995). *Batracology.* New Delhi: Discovery Publishing House. ISBN 81-7141-279-3.

Bhaskara Rao, Digumarti (1997), *Scientific Attitude.* New Delhi: Discovery Publishing House. ISBN 81-7141-308-0.

Bhaskara Rao, Digumarti (1996). *Scientific Attitude vis-à-vis Scientific Aptitude.* New Delhi: Discovery Publishing House. ISBN 81-7141-308-0.

Bhaskara Rao, Digumarti, Editor (1996). *Encyclopaedia of Education for All,* 5 Volumes. New Delhi: APH Publishing Corporation. ISBN 81-7024-759-4 (set).

Vol. I *Education for All: The World Conference.* ISBN 81-7024-760-8.

Vol. II *Education for All: The EPA-9 Summit.* ISBN 81-7024-761-6.

Vol. III *Education for All: Quality Education for All.* ISBN 81-7024-762-6.

Vol. IV *Education for All: Planning and Monitoring.* ISBN 81-7024-763-4.

Vol. V *Education for All: The Indian Scenario.* ISBN 81-7024-764-0.

Bhaskara Rao, Digumarti, Editor (1996). *Global Perceptions on Peace Education*, 3 Volumes. New Delhi: Discovery Publishing House. ISBN 81-7141-319-6.

Bhaskara Rao, Digumarti, Editor (1996). *National Policy on Education*. 2 Volumes. New Delhi: Anmol Publications Pvt. Ltd. ISBN 81-7488-323-1.

Bhaskara Rao, Digumarti, Editor (1997). *Care the Child*, 2 Volumes. New Delhi: Discovery Publishing House. ISBN 81-7141-394-3.

Bhaskara Rao, Digumarti, Editor (1997). *Education for the 21st Century*. New Delhi: Discovery Publishing House. ISBN 81-7141-389-7.

Bhaskara Rao, Digumarti, Editor (1997). *Reflections on Scientific Attitude*. New Delhi: Discovery Publishing House, ISBN 81-7141-319-6.

Bhaskara Rao, Digumarti, Editor (1997). *Success Story of a Primary Education Project*. New Delhi: APH Publishing Corporation. ISBN 81-7024-850-7.

Bhaskara Rao, Digumarti, Editor (1997). *World Food Summit*. New Delhi: Discovery Publishing House. ISBN 81-7141-386-2.

Bhaskara Rao, Digumarti, Editor (1998). *Adolescence Education*. New Delhi: Discovery Publishing House. ISBN 81-7141-432-X.

Bhaskara Rao, Digumarti, Editor (1998). *Community and School Nutrition Education*. New Delhi: Discovery Publishing House. ISBN 81-7141-435-4.

Bhaskara Rao, Digumarti, Editor (1998). *District Primary Education Programme*. New Delhi: Discovery Publishing House. ISBN 81-7141-396-X.

Bhaskara Rao, Digumarti, Editor (1998). *Earth Summit*, 2 Volumes. New Delhi: Discovery Publishing House. ISBN 81-7141-435-4.

Bhaskara Rao, Digumarti, Editor (1998). *National Policy on Education: Towards an Enlightened and Humane Society*, New Delhi: Discovery Publishing House. ISBN 81-7141-426-5.

Additional Reading

Bhaskara Rao, Digumarti, Editor (1998). *Reforming Schoo*
New Delhi: Discovery Publishing House. ISBN 81-
6.

Bhaskara Rao, Digumarti, Editor (1998). *Teacher Education*
New Delhi: Discovery Publishing House. ISBN 81-71
0.

Bhaskara Rao, Digumarti, Editor (1998). *World Summit for S Development*. New Delhi: Discovery Publishing House. IS 81-7141-420-6.

Bhaskara Rao, Digumarti, Editor (2000). *Education for All: Achievi the Goal*, 3 Volumes, New Delhi: APH Publishing Corporatio ISBN 81-7648-152-1.

Vol. I *The Global Consensus*. ISBN 81-7648-155-6.

Vol. II *Mid-Decade Review Reports of Regional Seminars*. ISBN 81-7648-154-8.

Vol. III *Issues and Trends*. ISBN 81-7648-155-6.

Bhaskara Rao, Digumarti, Editor (2000), *International Encyclopaedia of AIDS*, 11 Volumes in 13 Parts. New Delhi: Discovery Publishing House. ISBN 81-7141-6 (Set).

Vol. 1 *Introduction to HIV/AIDS*. ISBN 81-7141-523-7.

Vol. 2 *HIV/AIDS—Issues and Challenges*, 2 Parts. ISBN 81-7141-524-5.

Vol. 3 *HIV/AIDS—Socio Economic Realities*. ISBN 81-7141-524-3.

Vol. 4 *HIV/AIDS—Law Ethics and Human Rights*, 2 Parts. ISBN 81-7141-526-1.

Vol. 5 *AIDS and NGOs*. ISBN 81-7141-527-X.

Vol. 6 *AIDS and Home Care*. ISBN 81-7141-528-8.

Vol. 7 *STD Case Management*. ISBN 81-7141-529-6.

Vol. 8 *HIV/AIDS Prevention and Care—Teaching Modules for Nurses and Midwives*. ISBN 81-7141-530-X.

Vol. 9 *HIV Prevention Education for Education for Educational Institutions*. ISBN 81-7141-531-8.

Vol. 10 *Instructional Modules for AIDS Education*. ISBN 81-7141-532-6.

Vol. 11 *School Health Education to Prevent AIDS and STD—A Package for Curriculum Planners*. ISBN 81-7141-5338-4.

Bhaskara Rao, Digumarti, Editor (2000). *International Encyclopaedia of Science and Technology Education*, 11 Volumes. New Delhi: Discovery Publishing House. ISBN 81-7141-548-2 (Set).

Vol. 1 *Science and Technology Education*. ISBN 81-7141-568-7.

Vol. 2 *Science Education in Developing Countries*. ISBN 81-7141-570-9.

Vol. 3 *Organisational Structure of Science*. ISBN 81-7141-570-9.

Vol. 4 *Science Education in Asia and the Pacific*. ISBN 81-7141-571-7.

Vol. 5 *Science and Technology Education for All*. ISBN 81-7141-572-5.

Vol. 6 *Values, Ethics, Talent and Girls in Science and Technology Education*. ISBN 81-7141-573-3.

Vol. 7 *Popularization of Science and Technology Education*. ISBN 81-7141-574-1.

Vol. 8 *Science, Power and Society*. ISBN 81-7141-575-X.

Vol. 9 *Information Technology*. ISBN 81-7141-576-8.

Vol. 10 *Teacher Training in Science and Technology Education*. ISBN 81-7141-577-6.

Vol. 11 *Teacher Training in Science and Technology: A Curriculum Framework*. ISBN 81-7141-578-4.

Bhaskara Rao, Digumarti, Editor (2001). *Distance Education in Different Countries*. New Delhi: APH Publishing Corporation. ISBN 81-7648-229-3.

Bhaskara Rao, Digumarti, Editor (2001). *Decentralised Management of Education (Management of Education in Panchayati Raj and Municipal Bodies)*. New Delhi: Discovery Publishing House. ISBN 81-7141-617-9.

Bhaskara Rao, Digumarti, Editor (2001). *Electrochemistry for Environmental Protection*. New Delhi: Discovery Publishing House. ISBN 81-7141-619-5.

Bhaskara Rao, Digumarti, Editor (2001). *Global Educational Studies*. New Delhi: Discovery Publishing House. ISBN 81-7141-616-0.

Bhaskara Rao, Digumarti, Editor (2001). *Global Synthesis of Educational Assessment*. New Delhi: Discovery Publishing House. ISBN 81-7141-613-6.

Bhaskara Rao, Digumarti, Editor (2000). *International Encyclopaedia of Human Rights*. 7 Volumes in 13 Parts. New Delhi: Discovery Publishing House. (Royal Size). ISBN 81-7141-567-9 (Set).

Vol. 1 *International Instruments of Human Rights*, 2 Parts. ISBN 81-7141-595-4.

Vol. 2 *Regional Instruments of Human Rights*. ISBN 81-7141-604-7.

Vol. 3 *Human Rights and the United Nations*, 2 Parts. ISBN 81-7141-605-5.

Vol. 4 *Fact Files of Human Rights*, 3 Parts. ISBN 81-7141-605-3.

Vol. 5 *Study Stories of Human Rights*, 3 Parts. ISBN 81-7141-607-3.

Vol. 6 *International Meetings on Human Rights*, 2 Parts. ISBN 81-7141-608-X.

Vol. 7 *Professional Training in Human Rights*. ISBN 81-7141-609-8.

Bhaskara Rao, Digumarti, Editor (2001). *Jomtein Decade of Education*. New Delhi: Discovery Publishing House. ISBN 81-7141-618-7.

Bhaskara Rao, Digumarti, Editor (2001). *Nuclear Materials: Issues and Concerns*, 2 Volumes. New Delhi: Discovery Publishing House. ISBN 81-7141-611-X.

Bhaskara Rao, Digumarti, Editor (2001). *World Conference on Education for All*. New Delhi: APH Publishing Corporation. ISBN 81-7141-274-9.

Bhaskara Rao, Digumarti, Editor (2001). *World Conference on Higher Education*, New Delhi: Discovery Publishing House. ISBN 81-7141-610-1.

Bhaskara Rao, Digumarti, Editor (2001). *World Conference on Science*. New Delhi: Discovery Publishing House. ISBN 81-7141-612-8.

Bhaskara Rao, Digumarti, Editor (2003). *Inspiring Experience in Teacher Education*. New Delhi: Discovery Publishing House. ISBN 81-7141-656-X.

Bhaskara Rao, Digumarti, Editor (2003). *International Studies in Education*, 3 Volumes, New Delhi: Discovery Publishing House. ISBN 81-7141-647-0.

Bhaskara Rao, Digumarti, Editor (2003). *Military Conversion: Impact on Science and Technology*, New Delhi: Discovery Publishing House. ISBN 81-7141-578-4.

Bhaskara Rao, Digumarti, Editor (2003). *United Nations Millennium Summit*. New Delhi: Discovery Publishing House. ISBN 81-7141-632-2.

Bhaskara Rao, Digumarti, Editor (2003). *World Assembly on Aging*. New Delhi: Discovery Publishing House. ISBN 81-7141-637-3.

Bhaskara Rao, Digumarti, Editor (2004). *World Conference on Human Rights*. New Delhi: Discovery Publishing House. ISBN 81-7141-661-6.

Bhaskara Rao, Digumarti, Editor (2003). *World Education Forum*. New Delhi: Discovery Publishing House. ISBN 81-7141-639-X.

Bhaskara Rao, Digumarti, Editor (2004). *Education Employment and Human Resource Development*. New Delhi: Discovery Publishing House. ISBN 81-7141-681-0.

Bhaskara Rao, Digumarti, Editor (2004). *Successfully Schooling*. New Delhi: Discovery Publishing House. ISBN 81-7141-677-2.

Bhaskara Rao, Digumarti, Editor (2004). *European Education and Teachers*. New Delhi: Discovery Publishing House. ISBN 81-7141-702-7.

Bhaskara Rao, Digumarti, Editor (2004). *Teachers in a Changing World*. New Delhi: Discovery Publishing House. ISBN 81-7141-694-2.

Bhaskara Rao, Digumarti, Editor (2004). *Learning to Live Together*, 4 Volumes. New Delhi: Discovery Publishing House.

Vol. 1 *International Conference on Learning to Live Together.*

Vol. 2 *Globalisation and Living Together.*

Vol. 3 *Curriculum for Learning to Live Together.*

Vol. 4 *Science Education for the Contemporary Society.*

Bhaskara Rao, Digumarti (2004). *International Guidelines on Open and Distance Education*, New Delhi: Discovery Publishing House.

Bhaskara Rao, Digumarti, Editor (2004). *Adult Learning in the 21st Century*. New Delhi: Discovery Publishing House.

Bhaskara Rao, Digumarti, Editor (2004). *Educational Practices: Research and Recommendations*. New Delhi: Discovery Publishing House.

Bhaskara Rao, Digumarti, Editor (2004). *Chernobyl: Never Again*. New Delhi: APH Publishing Corporation.

Bhaskara Rao, Digumarti, Editor (2004). *Virology and Immunology*. New Delhi: APH Publishing Corporation.

Bhaskara Rao, Digumarti, C.A.P. Swami and B.S.V. Dutt (1997). *Self-Evaluation in Student Teaching*. New Delhi: Discovery Publishing House. ISBN 81-7141-374-9.

Bhaskara Rao, Digumarti and B.S.V. Dutt, Editors (2003). *Education: Programmes and Policies*. New Delhi: APH Publishing Corporation. ISBN 81-7648-470-9.

Bhaskara Rao, Digumarti and D. Naresh Kumar (2004). *School Teacher Effectiveness*. New Delhi: Discovery Publishing House.

Bhaskara Rao, Digumarti and D. Sridhar (2002). *Job Satisfaction of School Teachers*. New Delhi: Discovery Publishing House. ISBN 81-7141-652-7.

Bhaskara Rao, Digumarti and Digumarti Pushpa Latha (1994). *Achievement in Biology*. New Delhi: Discovery Publishing House. ISBN 81-7141-264-5.

Bhaskara Rao, Digumarti, C. Sridevi and K. Vijaya (1995). *Achievement in Social Studies*. New Delhi: Discovery Publishing House. ISBN 81-7141-281-5.

Bhaskara Rao, Digumarti and Digumarti Pushpa Latha (1995). *Achievement in English*. New Delhi: Discovery Publishing House. ISBN 81-7141-283-1.

Bhaskara Rao, Digumarti and Digumarti Pushpa Latha (1994). *Achievement in Science*. New Delhi: Discovery Publishing House. ISBN 81-7141-280-70.

Bhaskara Rao, Digumarti and Digumarti Pushpa Latha (1995). *Achievement in Mathematics*. New Delhi: Discovery Publishing House. ISBN 81-7141-278-5.

Bhaskara Rao, Digumarti and Digumarti Pushpa Latha, Editors (1998). *International Encyclopaedia of Women*. 5 Volumes. New Delhi: Discovery Publishing House. ISBN 81-7141-410-9.

Vol. 1 *Status of World's Women*. ISBN 81-7141-494-X.

Vol. 2 *Women, Education and Empowerment*. ISBN 81-7141-498-1.

Vol. 3 *Women Challenges and Advancement*. ISBN 81-7141-497-4.

Vol. 4 *Women and Family Health*. ISBN 81-7141-497-4.

Vol. 5 *Women and International Action*. ISBN 81-7141-498-2.

Bhaskara Rao, Digumarti, Digumarti Pushpa Latha and Digumarti Harshitha, Editors (2001). *Biological Warfare*. New Delhi: Discovery Publishing House. ISBN 81-7141-597-0.

Bhaskara Rao, Digumarti, Digumarti Pushpa Latha and Digumarti Harshitha, Editors (2001). *Women as Educators*. New Delhi: Discovery Publishing House. ISBN 81-7141-602-0.

Bhaskara Rao, Digumarti and Digumarti Harshitha, Editors (2001). *Education in India*. New Delhi: APH Publishing Corporation. ISBN 81-7141-207-2.

Bhaskara Rao, Digumarti, Digumarti Pushpa Latha and Digumarti Harshitha, Editors (2001). *Assessing Learning Achievement*. New Delhi: Discovery Publishing House. ISBN 81-7141-601-2.

Bhaskara Rao, Digumarti, Digumarti Pushpa Latha and Digumarti Harshitha, Editors (2001). *Energy Security*. New Delhi: Discovery Publishing House. ISBN 81-7141-598-9.

Bhaskara Rao, Digumarti, Digumarti Harshitha and K.R.S.S. Rao, Editors (1999). *Advanced Biotechnology*. New Delhi: Discovery Publishing House. ISBN 81-7141-516-4.

Bhaskara Rao, Digumarti and K.R.S. Sambhasiva Rao, Editors (1996). *Current Trends in Indian Education*. New Delhi: Discovery Publishing House. ISBN 81-7141-311-0.

Bhaskara Rao, Digumarti and K. Vijaya (1995). *A Text Book of Evaluation*. Ambala Cantt: The Associated Publishers.

Bhaskara Rao, Digumarti and N.V.M. Mohana Rao (2002). *Problems of Mentally Handicapped Children*. New Delhi: Discovery Publishing House. ISBN 81-7141-645-4.

Bhaskara Rao, Digumarti and S. Chandra Mohan (2002). *Sports Management*. New Delhi: APH Publishing Corporation. ISBN 81-7648-467-9.

Bhaskara Rao, Digumarti and Sk. Johni Basha (2004). *Teachers' Population Education Awareness*. New Delhi: APH Publishing Corporation.

Bhaskara Rao, Digumarti, V.V. Rao, V.V. Lakshmi and V.V. Krishna, Editors (1999). *Status and Advancement of Women*. New Delhi: APH Publishing Corporation. ISBN 81-7648-169-6.

Babu, P.C., Author and Digumarti Bhaskara Rao, Editor (2004). *Flowers of Wisdom*. New Delhi: Discovery Publishing House. ISBN 81-7141-695-0.

Bhagya Lakshmi, Lingineni, Author and Digumarti Bhaskara Rao, Editor (2000). *Reading and Comprehension*. New Delhi: Discovery Publishing House. ISBN 81-7141-543-1.

Bhuvaneswara Lakshmi, Gadde, Author and Digumarti Bhaskara Rao, Editor (2000). *Attitude Towards Science*. New Delhi: Discovery Publishing House. ISBN 81-7141-541-6.

Devraj, T.A.S., Author and Digumarti Bhaskara Rao, Editor (1997). *Trace Analysis of Uranium and Thorium*. New Delhi: Discovery Publishing House. ISBN 81-7141-375-7.

Durga Rani, K., Author and Digumarti Bhaskara Rao, Editor (2000). *Educational Aspirations and Scientific Attitudes*. New Delhi: Discovery Publishing House. ISBN 81-7141-555-55.

Dutt, B.S.V. and Digumarti Bhaskara Rao (2001). *Empowering Primary Teachers*. New Delhi: Discovery Publishing House. ISBN 81-7141-615.2.

Ediger, Marlow and Digumarti Bhaskara Rao (1996). *Science Curriculum*. New Delhi: Discovery Publishing House. ISBN 81-7141-321-8.

Ediger, Marlow and Digumarti Bhaskara Rao (2000). *Teaching Mathematics Successfully*. New Delhi: Discovery Publishing House. ISBN 81-7141-552-0.

Ediger, Marlow and Digumarti Bhaskara Rao (2001). *Teaching Science Successfully*. New Delhi: Discovery Publishing House. ISBN 81-7141-600-4.

Ediger, Marlow and Digumarti Bhaskara Rao (2001). *Teaching Social Studies Successfully*. New Delhi: Discovery Publishing House. ISBN 81-7141-596-2.

Ediger, Marlow and Digumarti Bhaskara Rao (2002). *Philosophy and Curriculum*. New Delhi: Discovery Publishing House. ISBN 81-7141-631-4.

Ediger, Marlow and Digumarti Bhaskara Rao (2002). *Improving School Administration*. New Delhi: Discovery Publishing House. ISBN 81-7141-633-0.

Ediger, Marlow and Digumarti Bhaskara Rao (2002). *Elementary Curriculum*. New Delhi: Discovery Publishing House. ISBN 81-7141-658-6.

Ediger, Marlow and Digumarti Bhaskara Rao (2003). *Language Arts Curriculum*. New Delhi: Discovery Publishing House. ISBN 81-7141-657-8.

Ediger, Marlow and Digumarti Bhaskara Rao (2004). *Teaching Language Arts Successfully*. New Delhi: Discovery Publishing House. ISBN 81-7141-678-0.

Ediger, Marlow and Digumarti Bhaskara Rao (2004). *Teaching Mathematics in Elementary Schools*. New Delhi: Discovery Publishing House. ISBN 81-7141-687-X.

Ediger, Marlow and Digumarti Bhaskara Rao (2004). *Teaching Science in Elementary Schools.* New Delhi: Discovery Publishing House. ISBN 81-7141-709-4.

Ediger, Marlow and Digumarti Bhaskara Rao (2004). *School Curriculum and Administration.* New Delhi: Discovery Publishing House. ISBN 81-7141-709-4.

Ediger, Marlow and Digumarti Bhaskara Rao (2004). *Modern Elementary School.* New Delhi: Discovery Publishing House.

Ediger, Marlow and Digumarti Bhaskara Rao (2004): *Relevancy in Elementary Curriculum.* New Delhi: Discovery Publishing House. ISBN 81-7141-751-5.

Ediger, Marlow and Digumarti Bhaskara Rao, (2004). *Teaching Social Studies in Elementary Schools.* New Delhi: Discovery Publishing House.

Ediger Marlow, B.S.V. Dutt and Digumarti Bhaskara Rao (2004). *Teaching English Successfully.* New Delhi: Discovery Publishing House. ISBN 81-7141-707-8.

Harshitha, Digumarti and Digumarti Bhaskara Rao, Editors (2004). *Educational Innovations.* New Delhi: Discovery Publishing House.

Indira Devi, Author and J. Prasanth Kumar and Digumarti Bhaskara Rao, Editors (2004). *Values in Language Text Books.* New Delhi: Discovery Publishing House.

Jayasree, Kandi, Author and Digumarti Bhaskara Rao, Editor (1999). *Correlates of Socialisation.* New Delhi: Discovery Publishing House. ISBN 81-7141-517-2.

John Babu, Chikati, Author and T.J.R. Prasad, G.M. Madhukar and Digumarti Bhaskara Rao, Editors (1996). *Problem Solving in Mathematics.* New Delhi: APH Publishing Corporation. ISBN 81-7648-273-0.

Lalitha, T., Author and K.S. Prabhakaram, D.S.N. Sastry and Digumarti Bhaskara Rao, Editors (2004). *Educational Philosophic Beliefs.* New Delhi: Discovery Publishing House. ISBN 81-7141-765-5.

Madhu Bala, Jampala, Author and Digumarti Bhaskara Rao, Editor (2004). *Adjustment Problems of Hearing Impaired*. New Delhi: Discovery Publishing House.

Marja, Talvi and Digumarti Bhaskara Rao, Editors (1996). *Educational Leadership and Social Changes*. New Delhi: Discovery Publishing House. ISBN 81-7141-320-X.

Nirmala Jyothi, M., Author and Digumarti Bhaskara Rao, Editor (2003). *Non-detention Systems in School Education*. New Delhi: Discovery Publishing House. ISBN 81-7141-654-3.

Prabhakaram, K.S., Author and Digumarti Bhaskara Rao, Editor (1998). *Concept Attainment Model in Mathematics Teaching*. New Delhi: Discovery Publishing House. ISBN 81-7141-424-9.

Prasanth Kumar, J., Author and Digumarti Bhaskara Rao, Editor (1998). *Effectiveness of Distance Education System*. New Delhi: Discovery Publishing House. ISBN 81-7141-437-0.

Prasanth Kumar, J., Author and G. Sundara Rao and Digumarti Bhaskara Rao, Editors (2000). *Open University Student Support Services*. New Delhi: Discovery Publishing House. ISBN 81-7141-550-4.

Ramatulasamma, K., Author and Digumarti Bhaskara Rao, Editor (2002). *Job Satisfaction of Teacher Educators*, New Delhi: Discovery Publishing House. ISBN 81-7141-655-1.

Rama Krishnaiah, D., Author and Digumarti Bhaskara Rao, Editor (1998). *Job Satisfaction of College Teachers*, New Delhi: Discovery Publishing House. ISBN 81-7141-438-9.

Rama Kumar Ratnam, M., Author and Digumarti Bhaskara Rao, Editor (1998). *Dukka: Suffering in Early Buddhism*. New Delhi: Discovery Publishing House. ISBN 81-7141-653-5.

Rathaiah, Lavu and Digumarti Bhaskara Rao, Editors (1996). *International Innovations in Education*. New Delhi: Discovery Publishing House. ISBN 81-7141-359-5.

Ramesh, Ganta and Digumarti Bhaskara Rao, Editors (1998). *Environmental Education: Problems and Prospects*. New Delhi: Discovery Publishing House. ISBN 81-7141-423-0.

Rathaiah, Lavu and Digumarti Bhaskara Rao (1997). *Achievement Correlates*. New Delhi: Discovery Publishing House. ISBN 81-7141-385-4.

Reddy, Sudhakar Y., Author, and Digumarti Bhaskara Rao, Editor (2003). *Creativity in Adolescents*. New Delhi: Discovery Publishing House. ISBN 81-7141-659-4.

Reddy, M.S., Author and Digumarti Bhaskara Rao, Editor (2004). *Creativity in College Students*. New Delhi: Discovery Publishing House. ISBN 81-7141-697-7.

Radramamba, B., Author and Digumarti Bhaskara Rao, Editor (2003). *Problems of Teaching*. New Delhi: APH Publishing Corporation. ISBN 81-7648-462-8.

Sanjeeva Rao, P.C., Author and Digumarti Bhaskara Rao, Editor (1996). *A Text Book of Geology*. New Delhi: Discovery Publishing House. ISBN 81-7141-313-7.

Satya Narayana V., Author and Digumarti Bhaskara Rao, Editor (2001). *Physical Education, Social Attitudes and Leadership Qualities*. New Delhi: Discovery Publishing House. ISBN 81-7141-593-8.

Srinivasulu Reddy, M., and K.R.S. Sambasiva Rao, Authors and Digumarti Bhaskara Rao, Editor (1999). *A Text Book of Aquaculture*. New Delhi: Discovery Publishing House. ISBN 81-7141-482-6.

Srinivasa Rao, Mandalapu, Author and Digumarti Bhaskara Rao, Editor (2004). *Achievement Motivation and Achievement in Mathematics*. New Delhi: Discovery Publishing House. ISBN 81-7141-674-8.

Vanaja, M. Author and Digumarti Bhaskara Rao, Editor (1999). *Inquiry Training Model*. New Delhi: Discovery Publishing House. ISBN 81-7141-515-6.

Vanaja. M. and N. Sneha Latha, Authors and Digumarti Bhaskara Rao, Editor (2004). *Student Shyness*. New Delhi: APH Publishing Corporation.

Valeri V. Koustiouk, Author and Digumarti Bhaskara Rao, Editor (2002). *A Text Book of Cryogenics*. New Delhi: Discovery Publishing House. ISBN 81-7141-642-X.

Valeri V. Koustiouk, Author and Digumarti Bhaskara Rao, Editor (2004). *Refrigeration and Environment*. New Delhi: APH Publishing Corporation.

Veena Kumari, Balusu and Digumarti Bhaskara Rao (1996). *Operation Black Board*. New Delhi: Ashish Publishing Corporation. ISBN 81-7024-711-X.

Veena Kumari, Balusu, Author and Digumarti Bhaskara Rao, Editor (2000). *Psycho-Social Correlates of Achievement*, New Delhi: Discovery Publishing House. ISBN 81-7141-547-4.

Vanaja, M., Author and Digumarti Bhaskara Rao, Editor (1999). *Inquiry Training Model*. New Delhi: Discovery Publishing House. ISBN 81-7141-515-6.

Venkata Rao, P. and Digumarti Bhaskara Rao (1989). *A Text Book of Zoology—Junior Intermediate*. Guntur: Vignan Publishers.

Venkata Rao, P. and Digumarti Bhaskara Rao (1989). *A Text Book of Zoology—Senior Intermediate*. Guntur: Vignan Publishers.

Venugopala Rao, K., Author and Digumarti Bhaskara Rao, Editor (2000). *Teacher Morale in Secondary Schools*. New Delhi: Discovery Publishing House. ISBN 81-7141-551-2.

Vidya, C., Author and Digumarti Bhaskara Rao. Editor (1996). *A Text Book of Nutrition*. New Delhi: Discovery Publishing House. ISBN 81-7141-309-9.

Vidya Bharathi, D., Author and Digumarti Bhaskara Rao, Editor (2000). *Educational Philosophies of Swami Vivekananda and John Dewey*. New Delhi: APH Publishing Corporation. ISBN 81-7648-309-9.

Books in Telugu Language

Bhaskara Rao, Digumarti (1986). *Dhrushya Sravana Bodhanapakaranalu* (Audio Visual Teaching Aids). Guntur: Nagarjuna Publishers.

Bhaskara Rao, Digumarti (1993). *Jeevasashtra Bodhana* (Teaching of Biology). Guntur: Nagarjuna Publishers.

Bhaskara Rao, Digumarti (1995). *Vignanasasthra Bodhana* (Teaching of Science) Guntur: Nagarjuna Publishers.

Bhaskara Rao, Digumarti (1997). *Vidya Manovignana Seshtram* (Educational Psychology). Guntur: Creative Press.

Bhaskara Rao, Digumarti (1998). *DSC Study Material*. Guntur: Nagarjuna Publishers.

Bhaskara Rao, Digumarti (1998). *Upadhyayudu Vidya*. (Teacher and Education). Guntur: Nagarjuna Publishers.

Bhaskara Rao, Digumarti (1998). *Vidya Drukpadalu* (Prespectives of Education). Guntur: Nagarjuna Publishers.

Bhaskara Rao, Digumarti (1999). *EdCET Teaching Aptitude*. Guntur: Nagarjuna Publishers.

Bhaskara Rao, Digumarti (2001). *Bharata Samajamulo Upadyayudu Vidya* (Teacher and Education in Emerging Indian Society). Guntur: Nagarjuna Publishers.

Bhaskara Rao, Digumarti (2001). *Bhoutika Sastra Bodhana Paddathulu* (Methods of Teaching Physical Science). Guntur: Nagarjuna Publishers.

Bhaskara Rao, Digumarti (2001). *Jeeva Sastra Bodhana Padhathulu* (Methods of Teaching Biology). Guntur: Nagarjuna Publishers.

Bhaskara Rao, Digumarti (2001). *Vidya Manovignana Sastram* (Educational Psychology). Guntur: Nagarjuna Publishers.

Bhaskara Rao, Digumarti (2003). *Patsala Yajamanyam/Paripalana* (School Management and Administration). Guntur: Nagarjuna Publishers.

Bhaskara Rao, Digumarti (2004). *Vidya Sanketika Sastram mariyu Computer Vidya* (Educational Technology and Computer Education). Guntur: Nagarjuna Publishers.